About a Girl: A Reader's Guide
to Eimear McBride's *A Girl Is a Half-formed Thing*

David Collard is a regular contributor to the *Times Literary Supplement*, the *Literary Review* and many other publications.

About a Girl

A Reader's Guide
to Eimear McBride's *A Girl Is a Half-formed Thing*

DAVID COLLARD

For Laura, and Frank and Edwin

Page numbers following quotations from *A Girl Is a Half-formed Thing*
refer to the Galley Beggar Press and Faber & Faber editions.

First published in 2016
by CB editions
146 Percy Road London W12 9QL
www.cbeditions.com

David Collard has asserted his right
under the Copyright, Designs and Patents Act 1988
to be identified as author of this work

Cover painting by Philip Maltman

Printed in England by Imprint Digital, Exeter EX5 5HY

ISBN 978–1–909585–06–5

Contents

Introduction

> Every now and again you read a book by an unknown author and you know immediately that you are in the company of greatness. That is a rare and precious feeling.

This comes from Gabriel Josipovici's introduction to Agota Kristof's *The Illiterate* and he's referring to her novel *The Notebook*. Eimear McBride's own enthusiasm for Kristof prompted me to begin this book with the quote from Josopovici because my feelings on first reading *A Girl Is a Half-formed Thing* were similar to his on first reading Kristof. I knew after a dozen pages that I was in the company of a great writer. That doesn't happen very often and is indeed a rare and precious feeling.

What strikes the receptive reader of Eimear McBride's debut novel as great? What is it that commands such lavish praise and critical acclaim? In a word, style. The author has created a new form of prose which employs a deceptively simple lexicon in fragmentary vernacular syncopations to represent thought at the point before it becomes articulate speech. That is an extraordinary achievement in itself, but having forged a prose style capable of doing this she then does much more, placing the anonymous narrator within a series of vividly realised scenes set at different points in her childhood and adolescence, many of which are intensely sad or harrowing, or both. Her prose combines the beautiful, the outrageous, the distressing, the farcical and the heartbreaking in courageously original, uncompromisingly experimental form. Her lexical intensity has no equivalent in contemporary writing.

Reading *A Girl Is a Half-formed Thing* restored my faith in the power of great writing, and proved to me and many other readers that it was still possible, in the 21st century, for an author to produce a great novel that built on the achievements of Joyce and Beckett and the other modernists. Even as I type this I realise that the phrase 'great writing' appears both condescendingly patrician and elitist, suggesting an established literary citadel populated (mostly) by dead white men and defended by critical gatekeepers such as myself, into which a few latecomers may grudgingly be admitted. I don't see things like that but there are those who do and whose views I respect. Nevertheless, I want to restore to any debate surrounding Eimear McBride's novel the long-unfashionable notion of greatness. Not that this amounts to a swooning abdication of the critic's role in these matters, far from it. I want to be among those no doubt reactionary commentators who claim that *A Girl Is a Half-formed Thing* is great not simply because it is by any worthwhile measure superior to almost all contemporary fiction in its aesthetic ambitions and technical achievement, but because it also represents something new and important in the development of the novel: the repurposing of modernism by (and for) a female sensibility. Eimear McBride has proved that the modernist tradition, all but abandoned by the end of the 1930s, still has a long way to go in the hands of writers who did not, in the past, have much impact on the tradition.

All novelists, in the end, write about themselves. So, in a minor way, do critics and reviewers. Some novels have a particular purchase on the reader's imagination and admiration because they speak directly to his or her own experience. This was true in my case. I was raised in a strenuously fundamentalist evangelical Christian household, one in which books and other cultural consolations were forbidden, being too much part of 'the world'. Whatever wasn't forbidden was compulsory – meetings, prayer, Bible study, evangelising, more prayer, more meetings. Thousands of hours a year were spent preaching and being preached at, on the street and in an unheated, uncarpeted hall with bright strip lighting. My formative years passed slowly in a state of boredom and fear, caught between being swallowed whole and spat out. I was eventually, fortunately, spat out.

When I read *A Girl Is a Half-formed Thing* I was especially struck by the well-meaning and ridiculous evangelical Christians, members of 'the ministry missionary fellowship' who arrive with prayers and songs as her brother lies dying in a downstairs room the girl has arranged for him. These 'holy joes' were immediately recognisable to me because they were the kind of people that surrounded me as a child. When they are present the girl whispers urgently to her brother: 'I'm here as well as fecking eejits. Don't forget that I am here.' I yelped when I read that, and may even have punched the air, because this unprepossessing series of words appeared to me a perfect expression of the redemptive power of love and the triumph of profane intelligence over polite conviction. Something cracked inside me that had been waiting to break since I was an adolescent oppressed by the religious conviction of those around me. I knew I'd found a writer who would remain part of my life, and would be there for me when the fecking eejits closed in.

The girl's alternating states of yearning and abjection, with their religious origin, were also excruciatingly familiar and rendered with an authenticity that was immediately convincing. I recovered something of my own past when reading this novel – not only in the particular detail but in the general texture. Here was a book that, my own personal identification and admiration aside, worked with equal power on two levels: as an ambitious attempt to represent human consciousness and as a virtuoso display of what can be done with the English language. The fact that my own peculiar background gave me a personal purchase on the subject, or on an aspect of the subject, was of interest to nobody else. But it gave me an immediate way in.

The early episode in which the brother and his sister make a humble and propitiatory meal of tomato soup and white bread for their mother after she has beaten the brother savagely made me cry, and for a long time. I was, for a while, inconsolable because the episode unlocked something in my own past that I'd long forgotten, or suppressed, or which may not even have happened. I'm not saying that novels should merely be some kind of homeopathic treatment, simply that I experienced an immediate and profound understanding of the author's priorities, her methods, her literary values. For the first time in very many years a book found a space in my heart as well as in my mind, and (I realised with another jolt) my mind and my heart badly needed what the book offered. So I wanted to spend my time thinking and writing about the book, and finding out more about its author and her long struggle for recognition.

I happened to write the first review of *A Girl Is a Half-formed Thing* to appear in print and later got to know the author, who has co-operated with characteristic patience and generosity to make this modest monograph the first full-length introduction to her work. I'm a literary journalist who is expected to have, is sometimes *paid* to have, what's called 'an informed opinion' based on my knowledge and experience or my *taste*. I tend to have strong opinions about stuff, or no opinions at all, and am fierce in my affections and loathings. Nothing in my writing life to date has thrilled me more or given me more satisfaction than bringing *A Girl* to the attention of readers.

1   About a girl

I'll begin by stating the blindingly obvious, which needs stating nevertheless: Eimear McBride is a novelist and *A Girl Is a Half-formed Thing* is a novel, a work of fiction. The author is not the girl in the title any more than Gustave Flaubert was Emma Bovary (and I know he said he was, but let's not quibble). In one important respect, however, the novel *is* prompted by a particular fact in her life. *A Girl Is a Half-formed Thing* is dedicated to the author's brother Donagh McBride, who died young from brain cancer in 1999, and his death was a source of emotional and intellectual malaise that would in time find its expression in a great novel.

The girl's violently transgressive sexual encounters and the elective self-harm which is her desperate way of taking control of her life are the novel's central concerns, but I'd argue that a subject of equal importance is the bleak terrain of pain and loss. Few other novels have depicted in such intimate, unflinching and heartbreaking detail the process of dying, the passage into death, and the emotional effect it has on those left behind to mourn. Few if any other novels are so driven by rage and grief, and fewer still express those raw emotions through such exquisitely judged language.

This will make *A Girl Is a Half-formed Thing* appear unremittingly serious. It *is* a harsh and harrowing book, but McBride is also a sensationally gifted comic writer. The pitch-black pitch-perfect lament of 'I sometimes wish your father hadn't died' is part Beckett and part *Father Ted* in its dry-eyed heartlessness; the grandfather's wake and the girl's thoughts as she speculates over the contents of the dead man's pockets are both farcically hilarious episodes:

> So Granda. I don't talk to the dead. So now. That's strange to see him
> here. Dead. I could give him a kick if I liked. But it's not worth the
> hassle now. I could undo his flies for shame. I know he wouldn't have
> wanted me to. Or kiss. Poke him. Squeeze out an eye. I'd lift it but.
> Maybe. No. Better not touch. I haven't seen him that to this. He's
> looking so unrumpled now. Just not that angry. (p.101)

That 'unrumpled' is marvellous. She next fumbles in the pockets of his suit and finds a sweet, a toffee chew, which she un-
wraps and eats (and what film-maker wouldn't want to shoot
that moment?). The passage culminates with the hauntingly
simple sentence 'Last night he didn't know he'd be dead', beg-
ging the question – *does he know he's dead now?*

If the book is ultimately tragic and offers the reader little or
nothing at all in the way of consolation, there are at least some
fierce laughs to be had along the way. As to that lack of consolation, of uplift and moral improvement – who says novels have
to be palliative?

I

Eimear McBride was born in Liverpool to Northern Irish parents, John and Gerardine, on 6 October 1976. She was one of
four children and the only girl. In 1979 the family moved from
England to the small town of Tubbercurry, County Sligo, in
the Republic of Ireland, where John McBride was employed as
a psychiatric nurse.

Her father died of pancreatic cancer when she was eight years
old, on 11 September 1985. McBride's younger brother, Fergal,
was just two years old and her elder brothers, Donagh and
Cillian, were 15 and 16 respectively.

She has fond memories of her father reading to her, and
particularly Russell Hoban's *The Mouse and His Child*. The title
characters are a pair of clockwork toy mice, joined by the hands,
who begin their life in a toy shop, are bought, briefly cher-
ished, then abandoned and later chased by a malignant rat as

they embark on a search to become 'self-winding'. The inter-dependency and literal attachment of the mouse and his child has a structural link to the girl and her brother in McBride's novel, although it wouldn't do to overstate the other intriguing similarities. But childhood stories settle into adult memory and, however obliquely, inform their creative development. (Many English writers, including Graham Greene, Christopher Isherwood and Evelyn Waugh, have claimed that their first influence was Beatrix Potter.) I read *The Mouse and His Child* for the first time only after hearing from the author that it was a childhood favourite. The mouse and his child are evicted from the comfort of their home and spend the rest of the story in the open air, exiled from comfort, constantly vulnerable and and prey to assaults from wild creatures.

McBride sees her father's death as a turning point in her intellectual and emotional development, and the origins of her atheism. There's a piercing sentence that appears in the earliest drafts of *A Girl Is a Half-formed Thing* and was retained: 'Our empty spaces where fathers should be.' This refers not only to the father in the novel, who walks out on his wife and their two children, but surely also to a pervasive sense of loss and estrangement that suggests the God-shaped gap in the lives of all who lose their faith.

McBride's mother Gerardine was left to raise four children alone and in 1991 she moved the family to the larger market town of Castlebar in County Mayo, around 30 miles south-west of Tubbercurry. Eimear at 14 must surely have found the transition difficult – although episodes in the novel are drawn from the school she left behind, Banada Abbey, where she had been unhappy. Eimear's brother Fergal recalls the early days in the new town:

> I wouldn't be surprised if Eimear felt a bit of an outsider in Castlebar. She would have started at Davitt College halfway through the 2nd year (what would be called year 10 in Britain), so she would

have been the 'new girl'. Plus 4th year (what was called transition year) was optional and Eimear chose not to do it so she would have skipped a school year shortly after arriving at Davitt and been in class with kids who would have been the year above her during her first year.

Fergal, six years younger than his sister, felt closer to her than to his two much older brothers. By the time he was seven Cillian and Donagh were both in their twenties, and she was the only sibling at home in Castlebar when he was growing up.

As well as reading voraciously and enjoying combative discussions with teachers and classmates, the teenage Eimear McBride had developed from an early age a keen interest in theatre, an interest which began back in Tubbercurry. Fergal had been an involuntary spectator at his sister's earliest public appearances:

> When I was very young she would sit me on a wall that I couldn't climb down off and I would literally be a captive audience for whatever performance she had dreamt up.

Performing soon became an important part of her life. Every Saturday, rather than hanging around the town centre chip shops like many of her schoolmates, she would make the journey from Tubbercurry (and later from Castlebar) to attend drama classes in Sligo. Fergal remembers his sister's participation in poetry recitals, at which she excelled:

> Every year there'd be a *feis* [feast or festival] of music and theatre that she would compete in at the Hawk's Well Theatre. It felt like the Oscars to me at the time, though she would still have been in her teens. She won medals or trophies more often than not and it was always something to look forward to for me.

At 15 or 16 Eimear took part in the annual Sligo *Feis Ceoil* and won the Yeats Cup for her recitation of 'The White Birds'. Her assertion that she has no interest in poetry today does not bear close examination, and the poetry of Yeats in general and 'The

Stolen Child' and 'The White Birds' in particular inform the structure and content of *A Girl Is a Half-formed Thing*.

The recital of poetry in a public arena isn't really acting. When Peter O'Toole described his profession as 'farting about in disguises' (my favourite definition of the craft) he hit on two important truths: that actors wear wigs and make-up and costumes when they play a character and — more significantly — that most characters portrayed by actors are required at some point to dissemble. So whoever plays Hamlet has to inhabit the role of the Prince of Denmark and, having got that right, behave for much of the play 'out of character'. Reciting poetry onstage removes the need or even the possibility for such double dissembling — the reader mustn't come between the words and the auditors (which is why so few actors are much good at reading poetry). In fact reciting poetry properly is the opposite of acting. In her later writing the author would be radically self-effacing, letting the language, as it were, speak for itself.

Fergal enjoyed watching his big sister putting the world to rights:

> By the time I finished primary school, they were all basically adults (in my mind at least) so relationships seemed to adjust accordingly; bickering about the remote control turned into debating about religion (mainly) and politics. Eimear liked to debate with anyone, friends or family, and it was always entertaining to get to listen in on her and my mother or her and her friends having a heated argument about something or another.

On one occasion Gerardine McBride noticed that through the open window of their living room in Castlebar she could hear her daughter and friends arguing at full throttle from around the corner and up the hill, far from the house where they lived.

Fergal is the only member of the McBride family to have been born and raised in the Republic of Ireland and his upbringing was settled and tranquil. He went on to attend Davitt College, the same school his sister had left three years earlier.

The teachers in Davitt remembered her, and for the most part spoke very highly of her, though it's unlikely they'd speak ill of her in front of her younger brother, I suppose. The father of one of her close friends in secondary school was my history teacher and I always thought he went a bit easier on me because he was fond of Eimear.

Before leaving to study in London McBride was writing conscientiously and engaging with all that Castlebar could offer culturally, mostly at the Linenhall Arts Centre in Linenhall Street, which offered a year-round programme of theatre, music, cinema, opera, dance, visual arts and workshops. Fergal recalls:

> She was a great older sister to have growing up because she was so restlessly creative and as a result I was exposed to lots of things like ballet and theatre and foreign cinema that I probably would never have taken any interest in as a child.

Castlebar's clubs and bars and discos at that time favoured a narrow range of music – either hard house or grunge – and the town's teenagers divided roughly along those lines. Eimear made tapes of Leonard Cohen for her younger brother when he was still in primary school, which, he says made him 'feel pretty cool as a kid'. Her aspirational allegiances were already to the moody outsider, the bohemian, the foreign. At home reading was always encouraged, sometimes in a rough and ready way as Fergal recalls:

> I remember as a very young child being sat down with a book (about Spot the dog or some such) and a clock and being told I couldn't get off the chair until I finished the book or the big hand went around the clock. I never knew that having lots of books around the house was out of the ordinary until school friends would come to visit and comment on how many books we had. When I was still a young teen Eimear always seemed to be reading something European and literary, whereas I'd be reading fantasy novels.

There were always plenty of books in the house, either borrowed from the local library or purchased at the Castlebar bookshop, or at Keohane's in Sligo or on trips to Galway. Like that of all bright teenagers, McBride's reading was part precocious, part pretentious – voracious, adventurous, unsystematic but increasingly discriminating. Edna O'Brien was a discovery. In March 2015 McBride delivered a brief and generous tribute to O'Brien as her contribution to an *Irish Times* series in which authors, academics and critics were invited to celebrate their favourite Irish writers. Placing O'Brien 'at the forefront of our literature' – thereby aligning herself for the first time with an Irish literary community – she remembered covertly reading *The Country Girls* at the Gaeltacht (a kind of Gaelic summer camp) in the summer of 1990, when she was 14, then spending a year reading 'everything from the hugely undervalued *Night* up to the wonderful stories in *Lantern Slides*'. She especially admired 'the deep, beautiful humanity of her prose and the incautious honesty of her portrayal of the Irish female experience'.

It was only years later that she came to appreciate the extent to which O'Brien had, at considerable personal cost, blazed a trail that others could follow when writing about Ireland. *The Country Girls* (1960), O'Brien's first novel, shocked contemporary Irish society with its frank depiction of sexual matters and was banned by the state censors. The O'Briens' family priest organised a public book burning. As a sign of how far things had changed in the half-century since, nuns were lining up to buy signed copies of *A Girl Is a Half-formed Thing* at the Castlebar launch.

McBride gave her younger brother, for his 14th or 15th birthday, Milan Kundera's *The Unbearable Lightness of Being*. She had by now developed a taste for novels in translation and was committed to a European, modernist school of writing and performing, a commitment that would later see her engage with European drama at Drama Centre. Fergal also had literary leanings, but it seemed certain that his sister was heading for the stage:

> I wasn't aware of her writing at all. I wrote a lot myself (poetry about dead people mostly) and when I was in primary school I thought I'd

be a writer when I grew up, but Eimear always seemed destined to be a famous actress so I probably just never noticed she had other things going on. I wouldn't be surprised if it was something very private for her though.

Now an accomplished musician, Fergal is engagingly modest about his achievements. His elder brother, Cillian, is Senior Lecturer in Political Theory at Queen's University, Belfast.

Gerardine McBride was energetically dedicated to her children's cultural development, paying for art classes, ballet classes, membership of a local chess club, keyboard lessons and much else, including her daughter's fortnightly drama classes in Sligo. This involved a 40-mile round trip twice a month and Eimear would sometimes take her younger brother along for the day.

Davitt College in Castlebar, one of three secondary schools in the town, was the only one catering for girls and boys. This is where Eimear first met Jarlath Killeen, who appears in her novel's acknowledgements with thanks for 'being a friend indeed'. Today Dr Killeen is Lecturer in Victorian Literature at Trinity College Dublin and has published on Oscar Wilde and on Gothic literature. He has a particular interest in popular writing, including Victorian Gothic and Victorian children's literature. Eimear made a great and abiding impression on him, as he later recalled:

> I have a lot of memories of my friendship with her. I can honestly say that, from the first few weeks of knowing her, I knew that she was the most creative person I had ever met, or was likely to meet, and that she was going to do something important with her life. She was reading writers I had never even heard of (such as Christa Wolf), and had already worked her way through Thomas Mann and Flaubert, while I was sticking to Dickens and Hardy. Our conversations and arguments are probably some of the best memories I have of my teenage years, and she deserves a lot of credit (or blame!) for the person I turned out to be.

On reading this tribute the author commented: 'This is generous of him, and untrue. He was always a mile ahead of everyone else and still is.'

The East German writer Christa Wolf (1929–2011) was certainly not on the average teenager's reading list. Thomas Mann was another early influence and *Death in Venice* made such a strong impression that she attempted her own version, while glumly recognising that that her home town lacked the necessary pestilential backdrop. She would go on to study German for her Leaving Certificate, and as the school had no German teacher she took private lessons in town with a tutor called Cornelia Lengyel. The two became good friends, as McBride recalls:

> She and I are still close. Her son and I share an exact birthday, which I find oddly interesting. She was very important to me as a teenager for a number of reasons. She was very well travelled, well read, something of a polyglot. She was interested in art and culture and loaned me books I would never had read otherwise.

Cornelia Lengyel encouraged her to write to pen pals in Germany and this, recalls the author, 'added considerable colour to an otherwise arid schoolday landscape'. Growing up in a small rural community in those pre-internet days, the only way to engage with the wider world was through reading and writing and this type of correspondence.

Jarlath attended History and English classes with Eimear and the two began to spend more time together as part of a group in which he was the only boy. Eimear had skipped the fourth year at school – known in Ireland as 'Transition', and not compulsory – and, at 15, was almost a year younger than Jarlath.

> The History class was very small, so everyone in that class got to know each other very well. It was also quite a contentious class, and for some reason we often ended up discussing current affairs, religion, politics rather than history. I think it fair to say that we disagreed with each other a lot, but still got on very well, and by the time we did our Leaving Certificate, we were close, and would have considered each other very good friends.

Ireland in the 1980s was, Killeen recalls, a claustrophobic, navel-gazing society with little interest in the outside world apart from the stream of American and Australian soap operas beaming melodrama into Irish homes. These, he reflects, were matched only by the religious melodrama offered by a succession of scandals in the Catholic Church. It was a time when the brightest and best migrated, often to England.

> The novel is certainly evocative of what Ireland in the 1980s was like for a lot of people. The 1980s was, in my own view, a very dark time in Ireland. Emigration was very high and was causing an extraordinary psychological strain on families. No one had any money, and, as is often the case in times of extreme economic distress, diversions were sought in the form of public theatre, where politics and social debate functioned as ways we could all distract ourselves from boredom and penury. To say that public debate was carried on in a hysterical manner would be, in my own view, to understate the case. And this public hysteria often leached into domestic relations. Behind many of the conflicts between the mother and her family in the novel I can hear those public debates and feel that tension again. Conor Cruise O'Brien famously referred to Ireland in this period as 'GUBU' (grotesque, unbelievable, bizarre, unprecedented).

Killeen stresses that the novel probably has a more acute relationship to the time when it was written and to the circumstances of its composition than to the 1980s. But it is certainly about the 1980s, not because of any contemporary details (which are hardly super-abundant) but because it arises from the author's memories of the time. He would be wary about describing any work of fiction, however realist, as an 'accurate' portrait of the era because there were and are many different versions of 1980s Ireland which, he says, it is the historian's job to analyse and reconcile.

Killeen left Castlebar to work in England the summer after their final exams, and he and McBride began writing to each other, a correspondence that continued for many years. They also met back in Ireland at Christmas and during the summer, so an important and enduring friendship was maintained.

2

In September 1994 at the age of 17 Eimear McBride left Ireland for London to spend the next three years studying at Drama Centre. She found digs in Finsbury Park, renting a room in the home of an Irish landlady who proudly displayed her absent daughters' Irish dancing medals on the wall. Escaping from this outpost of the old country, she soon found herself living independently in various parts of north London. This was her first extended experience of living in a large city – materially and culturally more advanced, more tolerant and anonymous than Castlebar.

Drama Centre was founded in 1963 and today operates as a school within Central Saint Martins College of Arts and Design in King's Cross, running degree programmes in acting, directing and screenwriting, although degree status was only granted the year after Eimear graduated. Unlike the more establishment institutions – RADA (the Royal Academy of Dramatic Arts), LAMDA (the London Academy of Music and Dramatic Art) and the Central School of Speech and Drama – Drama Centre has an international and modernist outlook. It's known by some as 'Trauma Centre' (a reference to the extreme rigour of the training), and there is a particular emphasis on 'the Method', the technique pioneered by the Russian theatre director Konstantin Stanislavski. Largely misunderstood by non-initiates, the Stanislavski approach makes great demands on the actor's dedication and discipline in a process that involves rigorous self-analysis and intense personal reflection. A Method training involves entering emotionally and physically into the interior life of the character as the crucial element in creating a role, employing an intense identification with a character's inner world and deepest motivations. Drama Centre also bases its approach on the movement work of Rudolf Laban and the character typology of Carl Jung to produce a 'movement psychology' when analysing and developing character.

McBride has on several occasions referred to her literary approach as 'method writing'. There is a clear link between Stanislavski and the intense engagement with character that makes the unnamed protagonist in *A Girl Is a Half-formed Thing* so immediately convincing. I'm unaware of any novelist who has explicitly applied the celebrated Method to writing, so this may well be a first. She emphasises the direct and important influence of her Drama Centre training on the composition of *A Girl*:

> There's also something about the physicalisation of language and the slight irreverence that breeds which was influential too, as in 'You might be Antigone, love, but I still have to put feet on you.'

Drama Centre training also drew on an English tradition beginning with Joan Littlewood, whose left-wing Theatre Workshop was formed in 1945 with her husband, the folk singer Ewan MacColl. This hugely influential group performed the first British production of Brecht's *Mother Courage and Her Children*, as well as now-legendary hits including the musicals *Fings Ain't Wot They Used T'Be*, *Oh, What a Lovely War!* and plays by Brendan Behan. The populist undertow is also reflected in McBride's attitude towards her readers – her desire to communicate to a wide audience, her aversion to the bloodlessly intellectual and theoretical.

Alongside European modernism the Drama Centre covered the entire Western theatrical tradition from the Greeks onwards. For the young Eimear McBride the three years of immersive study were a time of new freedoms and new opportunities, living and working in a cosmopolitan city and spending days and nights with kindred spirits. It was in her third year at Drama Centre that she first met William Galinsky, her future husband.

Following her graduation in the summer of 1997, Eimear and William moved to 87 Beaconsfield Road, Tottenham, an unglamorous suburb in the north London Borough of Haringey. They would continue to live in the area for the next ten years.

Her first acting job shortly after graduation was (as she puts it) 'third warm prop from the left sort of thing' in a touring production of *Il turco in Italia*, the two-act opera by Rossini, directed by Drama Centre alumnus Simon Callow. But acting jobs were few and she and William were both employed for a time in telesales alongside other Drama Centre alumni, including William's former classmate Michael Fassbender, selling Cable and Wireless products over the phone. The offices were in Greater London House, formerly the Carreras Cigarette Factory in Camden, a colossal 1920s Egyptian Revival-style building opposite Mornington Crescent underground station.

Six months after McBride's graduation from Drama Centre her brother Donagh became terminally ill with a brain tumour. She spent most of the following year travelling between London and Ireland, remaining in Castlebar for the final four months of his life while William worked in Newcastle as Assistant Director at Northern Stage. Donagh died on 26 February 1999. (The novel is certainly not an accurate portrayal of her brother's life, as he spent several years training for the priesthood before becoming a care worker, unlike the girl's friendless brother whose life is severely circumscribed and is employed stacking shelves in a supermarket.) McBride spent a further month in Castlebar after her brother's funeral, returning to London in April in a state of despair. Donagh's death had come at the point when she was about to set out in life, but now acting seemed to have no value or purpose.

> I stopped wanting to be an actress. I felt as though the bad thing that would happen in my life had happened previously, and when my brother died I realised that anything can happen at any time, and there was nothing you could do about it.

She continued working as an office temp, with occasional trips abroad, usually with William and mostly in Eastern Europe. She recalled that her 'best job' in May that year was for Cancer Research and involved drafting handwritten 'thank you' notes to families who had asked people to send donations to the charity rather than funeral flowers, a task she later described with pitch-black irony as 'cheery'. She temped for a variety of firms until, in November 1999, she started work at the Wellcome Trust on Euston Road, where she was employed in the Registry department, scanning grant applications. Here she stayed until May the following year, when she travelled alone to Russia, where she would remain until September.

It was in St Petersburg, far from friends and family, that she began to write seriously. This was a vital stage in her development as a writer and marked a symbolic severance of any link to the theatre. No writing survives from the period, but those months spent largely alone helped her to negotiate the sorrow and anguish that followed the death of her brother. Living in a distant country where she could barely speak the language was an act of self-effacement, and spending months in a place where she had no friends or relations meant she was forced to rely on her own mental and emotional resources.

Returning from Russia to Tottenham, she resumed temping at Kohn Pendersen Fox Associates for a few months, then Asra Housing Association. A data entry job for the railway company EWS involved a long hike to a crowded prefab building at Stonebridge Park where, surrounded by friendly colleagues, she worked her way through all of Proust in six weeks. Between these contracts were 'lots of days here and there at various places'. Later in 2001 she switched to a library/archive agency and found work in the Marks & Spencer archive in Wood Green, walking distance from home. In 2002 she worked on an English Heritage project for some months, then returned to the Wellcome for a while. She continued to write with fierce and single-minded dedication, rising before dawn to do so:

> I was temping. We were very poor. I got up at 5 a.m. to write before going to work. I sat at a desk in our sitting room in Tottenham. I can't remember what I wrote but some of it exists. I think it was called *The Annunciation Doc.*

3

In mid-2002 Eimear and William moved a short distance from Beaconsfield Road to 94 Campbell Road, N17, a 'part-buy part-rent' property which would become their home for the next five years. It was here that *A Girl* would be written.

In September she got a job in the records department of Deutsche Bank and began to commute daily on the overground line from Bruce Grove station to Liverpool Street. One morning on the crowded train to work she started reading *Ulysses* for the first time. She had not read anything else by Joyce and had, up to this point, largely avoided most Irish literature. Discovering his masterpiece at the age of 25 had a profound impact and might be described, appropriately, as an epiphany:

> Joyce really set my universe on its end. Reading *Ulysses* changed everything I thought about language, and everything I understood about what a book could do [. . .] I don't think it is an exaggeration to say the entire course of my life had changed.

She worked her way through what Joyce called his 'Blue Book of Eccles' on the daily commute and during her lunch hours. When the weather was fine she would take her copy to the park in nearby Finsbury Circus, a few minutes' walk from her workplace in Great Winchester Street. Joyce soon became, and remains, her major influence. I can't help thinking that this first encounter came at the right age – too many of us read (or attempt to read) the greatest of all novels when we are too young, too inexperienced, to do so properly. What Harold Bloom called 'the anxiety of influence' also figures here. In his groundbreaking 1973 book of that name, he considered the way poets may be hampered in their creative development by the necessary but ambiguous relationship they have with earlier poets. Eimear McBride, far from being daunted by her encounter with Joyce as a literary precursor, found in his prose a way to develop her own authorial voice.

Eimear and William were married in April 2003 in a ceremony held at Bruce Castle, a 16th-century manor house and
local history museum licensed for marriage ceremonies a short
distance from their Tottenham home. Their honeymoon in
Beijing was poorly timed as the city was in the grip of a SARS
epidemic and the newlyweds spent much of the time wearing
medical face masks.

Eimear was usually the more regular breadwinner while
William worked sporadically as a director, but temping was
poorly paid. In the summer of 2003 William accepted a contract to direct Shakespeare in Japan and suggested that on their
return Eimear could devote six uninterrupted months to writing without having to temp as his fee, frugally managed, would
be enough to keep them afloat. She leapt at the chance, but a
few days before they were due to fly to Japan disaster struck.
Their house was burgled and her handbag was stolen, along with
two years' worth of handwritten notes, the basis for the novel
she planned to complete in the six months now available to her.
She spent the next three days distractedly searching the bins and
hedges of Tottenham, to no avail. This setback was, she later reflected, a good thing – it forced her to start afresh, from scratch.

They arrived in Tokyo in July and stayed for six weeks.
William later self-mockingly described the trip as a real-life
version of the movie *Lost in Translation*, with his wife in the
Scarlett Johansson role. Eimear, severely jet-lagged, worked her
way slowly through *Finnegans Wake*. From Japan they travelled
on to Russia, Romania and Paris and, arriving back in London,
Eimear threw herself into six months' uninterrupted and inten-
sive work on an as-yet untitled novel. She would be working
to a real deadline – they could afford to maintain this arrange-
ment only until late the following spring, after which it would
be back to temping. As yet she had no clear idea what book she
would be writing.

A blurred snapshot of McBride's work desk in Campbell
Road in around 2004 shows a long vertical road map – a leaf out

of Joyce, who referred constantly to maps and trade directories when recreating Dublin in Zurich. Before starting work on what would become *A Girl Is a Half-formed Thing* she had been working on a novel (set, like *Ulysses*, on a single day) based on a walk from her north London home south to the City's financial district. There are photographs of places on that route, including Liverpool Street station. To the right there's an A4 'to do' list and below the photographs she has copied out some lines from Joyce's letter to Harriet Shaw Weaver. There's the corner of a computer screen with an oriental knickknack balanced on top and, on the wall to the left, three pink flying pigs. This is where she worked, for six months, in a routine she later described in an interview with the American writer JoAnna Novak in 2014:

> It was very intense. I felt like I was having some sort of break-down. Like sticking your head in a beehive for six months. It was all heat and pain [. . .] I knew that I had a very short amount of time to write the book in and I didn't know if I could write a book, I mean all the writing I'd been doing beforehand was sort of building around the idea of writing a book, but not actually writing a book and then a couple of months before I sat down, my house was burgled and my notes were stolen.

She wrote every day throughout the day, wasting no time, finding new ways in, digging deeper:

> I just had to sit down and start from the beginning . . . with this kind of tremendous sense of urgency, and so I just decided that I would write a thousand words a day and that was the way to just get the words on the page. And you know, some days that was just writing the same word over and over again to get it down. But every day I would write it and then the next day I would get up and I would read it and then I would cut and usually cut 900 words, 800 words, and just start again from the most interesting sentence and just keep going. And so that was just how I got it out onto the page and I had no plot.

These are not the words a reader sees on the first page of the published novel, but the author had finally discovered a way to approach her material, a style, a voice. I once asked her whether the local environment of Tottenham had any influence on her writing, and wondered whether the proximity of the vast reservoirs supplying London households with fresh water might in some way have suggested the lake that features in the novel, and the more general imagery of water that saturates the text. Could it be, I asked her, that Tottenham's saturated psychogeography had somehow worked its way into the drenched prose of *A Girl Is a Half-formed Thing*? The answer was no:

> I don't think Tottenham particularly informed it but its complete otherness from the world of the book was what allowed me to get there.

She completed *A Girl Is a Half-formed Thing* in summer 2004 and started temping again – first for Camden Libraries, then a return to the Wellcome Trust, where she worked in the library for almost three years. Money remained scarce. Sometimes supper was chicken soup from one of the many Turkish places along Tottenham High Road. On match days, when the local team, Tottenham Hotspur, played at home, they could hear the roar of the crowd from the White Hart Lane stadium and – depending on the weather – smell the supporters' piss for days afterwards. There was a menacing urban backdrop of stabbing, burglary, vandalism, gang-related crime and constant sexist abuse. Eimear McBride's feelings about the Tottenham years may be mixed, but she says they were happy times and retains a deep love of London.

William recalls their long perambulations together, a favourite being the Ermin Street Walk from Tottenham Hale station south along the River Lee, through a terrain of marshlands and reservoirs, pylons and railway lines, warehouses and tower blocks, down to the Thames at Bow in the East End. Whenever funds permitted, they travelled abroad – by rail from Budapest to Bratislava, Cracow, Warsaw and back, staying in cheap hostels; to Khartoum in 2005 and to Egypt in 2006, where William was a judge on a theatre festival panel. There were trips to Berlin, Paris, Barcelona, Prague, as well as tours of Italy and the United States.

Eimear describes William as 'my first reader', although he tends to play down any such role, simply saying: 'She asks me to read things and to give an opinion.' It was William who read the earliest drafts of the still-untitled novel, finding them brilliant and unlike anything he'd ever read before. He describes the process of its composition as 'like a cat coughing up a furball – it just came out, just *emerged*'. It was William who, on hearing the phrase 'a girl is a half-formed thing' when it came up during a conversation, suggested that it should be the title. Eimear later confirmed that she wanted to use the word 'thing' in the title because much of the book is about the objectification of women and how women learn to objectify themselves.

4

Throughout the Tottenham years Eimear McBride's only direct link to the literary world was through her friend Elizabeth McCracken, the American novelist whose husband, the writer and illustrator Edward Carey, had attended the National Youth Theatre at the same time as William.

McCracken is a wildly inventive, funny, unpredictable and wholly original writer. I think of her as V. S. Pritchett crossed with Dorothy Parker, and a better writer than either. I first became aware of her work in 1996 when *Granta* magazine published an extract from *The Giant's House* in their collection *Best of Young American Novelists*. *Niagara Falls All Over Again* (2001) was a melancholy, lovingly observed account of a failing vaudeville act. In 2014 she published *Thunderstruck and Other Stories*, a mesmerising, brilliantly accomplished collection.

When Elizabeth and her future husband, Edward, came to London to meet his parents for the first time they borrowed the Tottenham house from William and Eimear, which was unoccupied on their arrival apart from a cat named Poshif, as Elizabeth recalled:

> My memory is that there was a bottle of vodka in the freezer waiting for us. Later – when? What trip? – we came back to the house when William and Eimear were there, and I loved them instantly. As you get older (Eimear was in her twenties, but I was ten years older) you sometimes worry that you'll never make fast friends the way you did when you were younger, but I don't remember any getting-to-know-her time with Eimear. One of my favorite memories was one night when she and I stayed up drinking, the husbands gone to bed, and we just kept turning over the same record – was it Vera Lynn or Loretta Lynn? Whoever it was, we'd confused her with the other – until we decided we needed more wine so we walked to the off-license, which was closed: Eimear talked her way in and we got our bottle.

Authors are generally reluctant to talk about their own writing, especially to other authors. Fortunately Elizabeth and Eimear had many other things to discuss:

> What I remember are long and wonderful conversations about people – family and friends, our own histories, the peculiarities of human beings. But those are in the end, I think, the most literary sorts of conversations, really. That is, I remember being tremendously excited talking about *stories* with her, if not fiction. We spoke about *Girl* fairly often, but I think it was just her wondering about what would happen to it, and me being certain that it would find a place.

It would find a place – but not for many years. After two more drafts Eimear started sending the manuscript to agents, and after a year it was taken on by David Grossman. Eimear later described what she calls 'the long journey of failure' in her interview with JoAnna Novak:

> I just put it in the drawer, and decided I would get on with the second book and that was a very hard decision to make because I didn't know if I was just going to be writing another book for the drawer. It's very hard to take the weight of failure off. You know, it's hard enough to write as it is, without that kind of 'oh my god, is this

going to be another one of these' [. . .] and you know, every sort of year, something would pop up and someone would be interested for a while and then there'd be a flurry of excitement and then it would all just go away again.

What was particularly exasperating was the often positive quality of the negative responses. In one case somebody scrawled across a standard rejection letter, 'I suppose this is some kind of masterpiece.' Nothing happened, repeatedly, and as the years passed all prospect of publication began to fade.

In 2006 William was appointed director of the Cork Midsummer Festival and the following year they moved to Ireland's third largest city, on the south-west coast 170 miles from Castlebar. Eimear didn't much enjoy life in Cork, but was pleased to have a writing room at the top of a dilapidated Victorian four-storey house on a hill overlooking the Murphy's brewery. It was so small there was only room for her, a writing desk, a chair and a few boxes. When the wind blew the whole room felt like it might collapse.

That desk, a dilapidated Georgian-style affair, was purchased in a house clearance sale in Tottenham, travelled with them to Cork from London and is now installed in their Norwich home. It looks much the same as it did during the writing of *A Girl Is a Half-formed Thing*, with a little shelf of books, a letter rack, a miniature set of drawers for paperclips and foreign coins and an old draft of *Girl* as scribble paper. (When I told her that Ian McEwan had sold his archive to the Harry Ransom Center in Texas for two million dollars she was deeply unimpressed.)

During their time in Cork an application for an Arts Bursary was turned down, but despite anxiety and uncertainty McBride still managed to spend six or seven hours each day writing. Much of her effort went into what would eventually be her second novel, *The Lesser Bohemians*. Four years passed uneventfully, punctuated by further foreign travel and visits to Castlebar and London. At the end of 2010 William was appointed director of the Norfolk and Norwich Festival and in early 2011 they moved back to England, to Norwich, where their daughter Éadaoin was born in 2012.

The author's close friends knew little about her novel during these years, as Jarlath Killeen confirms:

> I knew she was writing (and then had written) a novel, but I hadn't read it, and I didn't ask. Writing is so personal, and this is especially the case when someone has written their first novel. I hope I was supportive, and did encourage her to keep sending it to agents/publishers when she had been rejected. I also knew it was an experimental novel, but I can't remember when she told me. I think I always assumed it would be something different in any case.

Throughout this period Elizabeth McCracken offered constant support and advice and encouragement, as well as practical help. She was tireless in her efforts to bring the book to the attention of American publishers:

> I knew she'd been working on a book – she called it her beast – and when she was finished she'd asked me to read it. I took it nervously, because I wanted to love it and yet I knew there is no guarantee you will feel the same way about someone's fiction that you do about the person. I knew nothing at all about it. And for the first page and a half I thought, Oh dear, no, too self-conscious, what a shame. Then about halfway down the second page my brain figured it out and the book had me, and I realized that the prose was the opposite of self-conscious: it just took my self-conscious brain that long to give itself over to the language.
>
> Only recently have I thought, *thank god I had that experience*. I mean, a lot of serious literary people read the book early on and somehow they missed it? failed? What a chump I'd feel like, if a dear friend had given me that book and I'd said, 'Well, maybe you'll get there with the next book.'
>
> I tried to help her get it published, and so did Edward. I gave it to people I was sure would love it. This is something I nearly never do – I teach and have a lot of current students and former students and meet a lot of writers, & if I started sending around books I would

never stop. When someone asks for an introduction to an editor or agent, I usually demur. Eimear didn't ask, I offered. It shocked me – not that she might have a bit of a hard time, since the book has its (entirely rewarded) difficulties but that (it seemed then) she couldn't find an editor who would have the same experience as I did.

2 About a book

I'd say that's what you did.

> For you. You'll soon. You'll give her name. In the stitches of her skin she'll wear your say. Mammy me? Yes you. Bounce the bed, I'd say. I'd say that's what you did. Then lay you down. They cut you round. Wait and hour and day.

Forty-six short words, all but two of them ('stitches', 'Mammy') monosyllables. The vocabulary could hardly be simpler, but simple isn't the same thing as easy. While all these words can be correctly read and spelled out by an average eight-year-old child, they appear here in combinations that actually unsettle or intimidate the unwary. Here's a representative disgruntled reader – let's call her Rebecca – on the Goodreads website:

> so so so awful. i hated almost every minute. pretty sure all the awards are a result of the emperor's new clothes syndrome, as if you rewrote it in English you'd find neither the plot nor the characters interesting. as it is though it's written in pathetic fragments which, painful enough the first time, you are forced to reread far too often as (surprise surprise) the meaning is often lost when you dispense with grammar and half the words you need to say something.

Why should such simple words arranged in a slightly unconventional way, in a way that avoids 'proper grammatical sentences', actually *anger* some readers, and make them want to express their anger online? Why, come to that, does Rebecca avoid using capital letters when criticising an author who uses them correctly? I don't want to mock Rebecca, who is entitled to her opinion, but I choose her to stand for all those readers who, presented with something new and original and unusual, react with fear and derision and rage, a contemporary variant of Aristophanes' 'Don't make your house in my mind', which might be expressed as 'Don't hog my Kindle', because most of the negative online comments are clearly based on the free sample pages available on an e-reader.

I don't expect I'll ever be able to persuade Rebecca that Eimear McBride's use of language is a dazzling quality and not a disabling flaw. She's made her choice – but there may be others who are open-minded enough to be curious, to want to know more about the book's genesis and the way the author achieves certain effects. *About a Girl* is for them.

The first-time reader isn't expected to know straight away, on the first page, that these oddly arranged but very simple words represent the thoughts, or unuttered speech, of an unborn child, still a foetus in the womb. Of course, this is not something you expect on the first page of any novel. Novels begin, traditionally, like this:

> Hale knew, before he had been in Brighton three hours, that they meant to murder him.

That's Graham Greene's buttonholing opener to *Brighton Rock*. Who wouldn't read on? Or this:

> A man called Berg, who changed his name to Greb, came to a seaside town intending to kill his father . . .

On the face of it a similar first line, but something a bit trickier is going on, as the self-conscious and artificial reversal of Berg to Greb suggests. This is the opening sentence of *Berg*, a novel written by Ann Quin (1936–73) and published in 1964. Quin, an undervalued author of experimental fiction, wrote three more novels (*Three*, *Passages* and *Tripticks*) before walking into the sea near her home town, Brighton. The first time I spoke to Eimear McBride I asked her whether she'd heard of Ann Quin. She hadn't, but then hardly anybody has. Yet Quin is among the small cohort of experimental women writers, and one not to be valued simply because she's rare but because she's a thrilling and original writer.

The opening lines of *A Girl Is a Half-formed Thing* are nothing like the opening lines of *Brighton Rock* or *Berg*. Graham Greene is an A-writer, and we read on to find out who it is who wants to murder Hale, and why, and whether they succeed. The plot and characters allow the author to smuggle in lots of other material, much of it to do with Catholic guilt and redemption. Ann Quin's interest as a writer lies not so much in plot and character as in the mechanics of the novel, and different ways of telling stories – her prose isn't particularly radical or challenging but her use of the novel form is new and strange. This makes her an exemplary B-writer.

It was Anthony Burgess who first proposed that novelists could be divided into these two classes: A-writers and B-writers. The A-writer, he said, is a storyteller – concerned above all with plot and character and psychological motivation. Most novelists fall into this category. Think of *Robinson Crusoe*, *Gulliver's Travels*, *Pride and Prejudice*, *Middlemarch* and *To Kill a Mockingbird*. Think also of Toni Morrison's *Beloved* and E. L. James's *Fifty Shades of Grey* (the categories have nothing to do with quality or longevity). A-writers are part of a long tradition and add to that tradition without much changing it. They are part of the literary mainstream and tend to work within popular forms, or genres – the crime novel, the horror story, romantic fiction, science fiction and so on. Not all A-writers are great writers, or even good ones, but some certainly are. B-writers, on the other hand, often employ plot and character and so on to a high degree of sophistication, but their real interest lies elsewhere. They are interested in language and form and structure, and the potential of the novel to say new things in a new way. They are explorers, and they are never popular in the way that some A-writers are popular. Burgess saw himself as a B-writer but often managed to be both.

The greatest of all B-writers is James Joyce and his masterpiece is *Ulysses*, the greatest of all B-novels. Eimear McBride would insist that it's the greatest novel full stop, and to hell with categories. You may never have read *Ulysses,* or you may have tried and given up. It's not easy. Or rather, it's not simple. But it's certainly worth the effort and if you admire *A Girl Is a Half-formed Thing* you might give *Ulysses* a go. If you're a reader who admires *Ulysses* then *A Girl Is a Half-formed Thing* is likely to knock your socks off.

In the category of B-writer novels we can include Russell Hoban's *Riddley Walker,* Thomas Pynchon's *Gravity's Rainbow* and Samuel Beckett's *How it Is.* Joyce's *Finnegans Wake* is the most extreme example of B-writing and of it Beckett admiringly said: 'His writing is not about something; it is that something itself.' This is a line that seems to me to sum up the challenge of modernist writing and can easily be extended to include all forms of modernism: films and books and theatre and art, everything. It's a line I tend to quote whenever I'm confronted with something I don't understand, which is often.

Not all B-writers are great writers, or even good ones, but many certainly are. Anyone aware of the Burgess categories who comes across *A Girl Is a Half-formed Thing* for the first time will immediately see that the author is primarily a B-writer. Her use of language is unique and her heavily punctuated 'ungrammatical' prose may alarm some readers but, as many more readers have been quick to discover, the eye and mind soon adjust to the rhythmic syncopations of the words on the page and something quite extraordinary happens, something uncanny and practically alchemical. I can only put it like this: *the book begins to read us.* What happens to the anonymous girl is never described *to* the reader but directly experienced *by* the reader. This is unsettling, often distressing, and also startlingly original – nobody has ever written quite like this. Caitlin Moran, one of the 2014 Bailey's Prize judges, muddled her metaphors but spoke for many when she said, 'Ten pages in and all the bells start ringing. It explodes into your chest.'

McBride's opening alerts us to the fact that this is not an A-writer's novel, although it doesn't appear to have much in common with *Berg* either. But both *Berg* and *A Girl Is a Half-formed Thing* set out in different ways to explore the potential and the limitations of language to express human experience. They don't offer the usual pleasures and consolations of a conventional novel, or even the off-trail pleasures of other experimental fiction. Many readers regard experimental fiction as heartless, highbrow and unfeeling, and in some cases they are right. We need to proceed with caution but also with an open mind and (why not?) with high expectations.

So. 'For you.' Who is speaking, or thinking? Is it the author, addressing us? Is what we are about to read a sort of gift, or offering? Who is he – or she – speaking to, or thinking about? We don't know, yet. So, curious, we read on.

> You'll soon. You'll give her name. In the stitches of her skin she'll wear your say.

You? Her? Who *are* these people?

> Mammy me? Yes you. Bounce the bed, I'd say. I'd say that's what you did.

On my first reading I assumed the speaker was a small child (a careless error I perpetuated in my review and which has been repeated ever since by other writers). I suppose at the back of my mind were the opening lines of *A Portrait of the Artist as a Young Man*:

> Once upon a time and a very good time it was there was a moocow coming down along the road and this moocow that was coming down along the road met a nicens little boy named baby tuckoo . . .

The speaker is not a child but the language is appropriately childish.

> His father told him that story: his father looked at him through a glass: he had a hairy face.

The voice in this case is the author's – it's Joyce's voice, and we are aware of that. For a first-person pre-natal voice we might consider the poem by the Belfast-born Louis MacNeice, 'Prayer Before Birth', written at the height of the Second World War: 'I am not yet born; O hear me. / Let not the bloodsucking bat or the rat or the stoat or the / club-footed ghoul come near me.' No foetus could be so eloquent – the words, the conceit (in the poetic sense) are again those of the author.

Eimear McBride insists that she is no poet, but her writing certainly has a poetic quality in its pace and rhythm, in its linguistic virtuosity and capacity to astonish, in the way it yields a deeper meaning on closer reading, and in its memorability She briskly denies any poetic tendency: 'No poetry. Occasionally I try to sally forth on it but have neither the pith nor the wit, sadly.' She's wrong about that, I think. Poetry isn't about sallying forth but burrowing in, and it isn't just a question of wit and pith (although she has both in abundance) but of insight and organisation. Prose is currently what she does, and does supremely well, but she has a poet's ear for the potential of language, and any poet would kill for 'My thud cheeks up'; 'we lilt our chamber'; 'consumed with all my dreams and shames'; and even the bleakly supplicating sound of a telephone ('Bring bring'). E. E. Cummings hovers behind a line such as 'I lie on beds I stare and watch island by in clouds of up', a line that reflects a McBridean tendency to end sentences with a preposition, in mid-air as it were. But for most of the time it's a rhythmic pulse that gives her prose the throb of life, as when the ailing brother is momentarily angry at his sister's apparent condescension:

The temper slugged with drugs looked out again at me like old.

There are countless moments like this that seem to appropriate the metric concerns of poetry, moments that are even more vividly realised in the author's audio recording of her book. Not only the beat of metre but also a recurring concentration on images of birds and water, mucus and tears and blood, skin and flesh, and a highly selective lexical palette of red and white and black. Her prose is, to borrow Nabokov's elegant formulation, *mnemogenic*. Memorability is, like originality, hard to quantify – but in McBride's case the two combine seamlessly.

Let's return to that opening passage. It isn't clear immediately what 'in the stitches of your skin she'll wear your say' means. It makes sense, however, if we assume it's the mother speaking to her son about her unborn daughter – she is making a promise to the boy, that he can name his sister. When and where is this happening? Annie Ryan (director of the stage production of the novel), prompted by discussions with the author, says that it occurs at a point when the brother is about to undergo the surgery for the brain tumour that will later kill him. There is an implicit pact between mother, son and unborn daughter – that if the boy survives the operation he will get to name his sister. His early illness and partial recovery inform the relationship between the girl and brother and are at the heart of the book.

In plain language she (the unborn girl) will bear the name given to her by her brother, she will 'wear his say'. The use of 'say' as a noun is uncommon, apart from in phrases like 'to have one's say', but its reappearance as a conventional verb in the next line ('I'd say that's what you did') is proof of the author's sensitive handling of simple language.

Try reading this opening paragraph aloud. It's not only the words that are simple. The sounds fall within a narrow range also, between short vowels (give/in/stitches/skin/did) and long vowels (name/say/say/say/lay/wait/day). Other vowel sounds – diphthongs – pulse in the background (bounce/down/round/hour), while the most important word, central to the novel's structural relationship between the girl and her brother ('you' throughout), is insistently repeated with minor variations: 'you . . . You'll . . . you'll . . . your . . . you . . . you . . . you . . . you'. The sounds are layered, an aural palimpsest. I'm reminded of the diastolic/systolic thump of the human heart.

Finally we twice hear the first-person pronoun, both with the modal auxiliary 'would' – 'I'd' and 'I'd'. This offers the reader a traditional way into a text through the narrator (who may or may not turn out to be reliable). Throughout this first paragraph the tenses are untethered – past, present and future blend, the temporal fluidity expressing the pre-natal state of the girl in her mother's womb, a time before time. So much is achieved with so little – a few commonplace words tightly bound by a narrow phonetic range, dense yet airy.

Back to the two first words: 'For you'. Who is being addressed? I'd suggest it is the brother, addressed by his mother. The gift or tribute is the naming of his sister and, by implication, his 'ownership' of her.

Such close scrutiny of the first four lines could be applied to almost any other passage in the book. McBride's prose deserves and rewards such an intense focus yet is best read quickly, as she has said she prefers her readers to do. Astonishing effects are achieved through great concentration and effort, yet she makes it seem as natural as breathing.

There is an intimate complicity between the unborn girl and her brother, an undertow of whispered conspiracy. This is, we shall soon discover, a love story, and an especially powerful and distressing one. It's about the deep love between a brother and sister that begins even before the younger sibling is born ('I loved swimming to your touch. Your strokes'). It's also a novel about other kinds of love, and about sex, and different kinds of sex, sometimes degrading and violent sex. All that comes later.

Before the end of the first page we learn that something is terribly wrong with the brother. This information is introduced impressionistically – the second paragraph, with its corridors, stairs, 'dettol', mops and 'diamond floor tiles' gives us a hospital setting without using the word 'hospital', an early instance of how the author pares back information to the minimum, leaving the reader to do much of the work, or at least to meet the author halfway. Almost nothing in this book is ever *described*.

'She saw it first when you couldn't open your eye'. It's yet another simple sentence rich in implication. The mother 'sees' the illness and becomes aware that something is wrong with her son when the boy has trouble seeing. Eyes, looks, glances – the text is dense with the act of looking, and in the girl's case with being the object of the male gaze. The male gaze extends beyond the human to the metaphysical: 'Where God is looking in he isn't if he was.' Birth, when it comes, is a fall from grace, a loss of insight: 'I saw less with these flesh eyes.' We cannot ignore the homophonic link of 'I' and 'eye', because seeing and being seen are a constant preoccupation. The girl is constantly seeing, and reacting to what she sees. The idea that 'to be is to perceive' (and to be perceived) was expressed by Bishop Berkeley in the 18th century in the brisk Latin formula *esse est percipi*. (At this point I picture the author rolling *her* eyes, but I expect she will know that the same Latin phrase was used by Samuel Beckett at the beginning of *Film*, the script for his short film starring Buster Keaton.)

Analysing the text for word frequency reveals that by far the most frequently occurring word in the novel is the first-person pronoun 'I' (3,742 times), followed by 'the' and 'you' (2,400). The use of this pronoun produces the direct experience that so impresses and destabilises the reader. To use the third-person pronoun (he/she) is to impose a distance between the reader and the character. This is what almost all conventional novelists do. Emma Woodhouse is a 'she', not an 'I'. Things happen to *her*, not to *us*.

The ten most frequently occurring words in *A Girl Is a Half-formed Thing* are: *I, the, you, and, it, that, to, my, in* and *me*. Apart from pronouns, conjunctions, prepositions and all the other 'form' words, the most frequently occurring verb (ignoring the various forms of 'to be') is *know*, followed by *say*, *like* (in its various meanings), *see*, *go* (in various forms, including the last line of the novel, 'My name is gone.'

The opening and closing sentences of the novel contain the word 'name', although we never find out what that name is and, by the end, whatever it was is gone, is no more. The girl, never fully formed, is finally *unformed*, as if she had never really been born. Her name, whatever it may be, is not what she *is* but merely what she is called. We never for a moment see the girl from the outside – her name, whatever it is, is outside her self. A girl is (as William Empson observed in his essay on Lewis Carroll's *Alice* books) 'the least obviously sexed of human creatures' and our half-formed girl is deformed by her violation at the hands of her uncle. That she later uses sex as a means of empowerment doesn't mean she is not exploited, and horribly, by the boys and men she encounters, but it is her exploration of her own sexuality, and that of others, that gives the novel its velocity and vitality. The implication is that a woman while 'fully formed' will still be a 'thing', not a person – exploited, vulnerable and objectified.

She remains half-formed, or at least not fully formed, because she dies young, at twenty. Of course, fictional characters never *really* die because they are never really alive, and no death in fiction is ever accidental. But it is in the nature of fiction that – even when it is written in the modish present – the reader's experience is informed by a knowledge, perhaps not consciously articulated, that whatever happens in a novel *has already happened*. Not simply because the novel has already been written (and edited and typeset and printed and, by the time we get around to it, already read by numberless others) but because, and distinct from all that, the narrative is long over before we first encounter it.

We might adapt Roland Barthes' observation (in *Camera Lucida*) applied to Alexander Gardner's *Portrait of Lewis Payne* (1865), an early photographic image of a shackled man awaiting execution for murder. It is captioned by Barthes, 'He is dead and he is going to die.' This haunting image has an internal grammar of 'this-has-been' and 'this-will-be' – it's an image of an imminent catastrophe that has already occurred. If I say that the protagonist of *A Girl Is a Half-formed Thing* dies at the end it invites the question: was she ever alive? Alive in the sense that we like to think we are? Alive as other fictional characters, from Chaucer's pilgrims to Mrs Dalloway, can be said to be alive in the minds of their readers?

The girl herself is never named and the brother, equally anonymous, is referred to by his sister by the second-person pronoun 'you' throughout. There is only one 'you' that matters in this book, and that's him. The other characters also have no names, just titles – mother/mammy, father, uncle, aunt, grandfather and so on – and it comes as a slight jolt when real writers' names appear (Milton, F. Scott Fitzgerald and Zelda).

There are no fancy 'literary' words in this book, no adverbs even, or hardly any. A comparison with the early drafts of the first pages demonstrates how carefully the author has worked her material into a rhythmic pattern of carefully paced and scrupulously balanced monosyllables.

To begin before the beginning

I'd completed a first draft of this book when I met the author in a coffee shop in Norwich. She passed me an envelope which, to my surprise, contained a bundle of draft manuscripts and unpublished typescripts. I was touched by her generosity and the implied trust and daunted by the responsibility. Rather than quote selectively from these fascinating early drafts I reproduce them below in full. I have not included the later amendments (surprisingly few, and which appear in the manuscript as neat annotations in red ink).

Practically nothing of the first draft survives in the published version apart from a few phrases such as 'Our empty spaces where fathers should be' and 'We were busy with each other long before I came' and 'The heart cannot be wrung and wrung.' What is present in draft form are early versions of what would become terse, naggingly memorable fragmentations in the final draft:

No we're not for loving anymore. I understand that. Built for it. Our bodies now. Doing the housework. Paying the bills. No not a home for satisfaction. For joy. For us. We shall live in children and they shall live because of us.

This becomes, in the published version, the intense compression of 'Board me up. I'm not for loving any more.'

What these drafts reveal is the painstaking labour of composition, the meticulous elimination of the superfluous, the over-explicit and the 'writerly'. They show how much can be achieved with the barest minimum of materials. Writing of this quality may come naturally, but never easily. I'm reminded of Yeats's reflection on his own writing: 'Even when the poet seems most himself . . . he is never the bundle of accident and incoherence that sits down to breakfast; he has been reborn as an idea, something intended, complete.'

[First draft] PART I – LAMBS

Wait now. Wait now just til I say this. Wait now.

To begin before the beginning. I record that I could see. Hear the outside. Do what I should not and been aware. So I know this story of yours and mine inside out. From the inside out. And really. Not vibrated down to me in snug womb by cords and blood but sight at first then sound. So what's before that I won't mention. I'll leave that to you alone because you were there. What's said is before the beginning, at the very start of myself – conceived in disarray, now thinking back. I knew that busy outside in life something was going wrong.

That. It ran through your head I know bilious tumour. Chewing at the mountains of your brain. Busy healthy child head filled with ample things to be forgotten skills to walk and write. Things to hold your mouth up straight when you smiled make your left eye open wide as the other. Inside our mother I saw you. Nosebleed cry. Oh God. Do that. Beg for no more operations. Have you Daddy by the tie. Get pushed under the knife. Fall out of what you were. Supposed to have been. Busy healthy child bright. Precocious. Fine. That you were head wrapped white tight. Your skin hang limp to the touch. Lost all. Inside on the other side of that operating slab. Something. In the waking up bed. Some new disordered you were who now?

That our parents smacked and broke on the rock of. Your. Something. Split bow each other. Broke at the sight of you. Dying they said. Doctors saying that. All the scan said it's growing. That won't stop. No. And the knife lifted hunks and hunks away but it's still growing and it will not stop. Until you're dec and so they wishes they were. Prayed at night to stand in your stead. I saw that. Offered up their eternal salvation and all that. Offered then each other in your stead. That the critical vicious thing. And then they could not move or touch. Look each other eye to eye. What a forfeit rots there their marriage away. Cold thing but anything. For you to live. I saw. I swam in bitter waters. Swallowed bile. Her tears and rip out desperation. Murky womb. That bed for me to lie in.

And on you didn't. Puked and chemoed. Radiated little skull. Scared and bald and wet the bed but breathing still a little and then more. Moving then a little and then more. But he'll soon be dead said the doctors and the nurses. Enjoy him now and while he lasts. He's running out. He's running down. And I grew there. Circling through her fresh defeats and yet. And yet you went on moving. Kicking up your legs. Ate an egg. Expressed a yelp. A fresh desire for rally cars or the jackdaws croaking by the window. Ice cream. Getting to the outside.

They said. They said. Oh now. It had gone quiet in you. Sleeping in it's little evil nest the cunning thing. Such a small bit of death in a seed womb of your brain. Coiled modest over under matter. We'll never take it out said doctors nurses. That would make him blind deaf good as dead there is no reason. There is no cause for him to be alive and yet and yet.

You went on. On. better, Growing. Good for a breath. Teeth and hair. Alert and angry. Aware now of the times of day and of the Spring. And then of me. Growing. Lurching forward to the time when I would be alive like you. You saw me. Swirling cells. My busy atoms knitting up. Looking out at you. Gawking in.

Ah but then. Ah but then. Our father saw all that and so went away. All too much living and survival to be borne when everything like safety was dead. It was enough and he must. Leg it. To see you it was enough. To smell the success of your living expedition was enough and now too much. The experiment of me was much too much. The heart cannot be wrung and wrung. His. Place layer of fear and fear inside him. Panicky parent fear of all again falling to the wayside. Flinging his seed on barren ground. Sun come out and down we go.

You see I see the way that did not he left her. Like a calmest Virgin Mary on the edge of her very neat made bed. Twin cots they were under the hospital roof to be with you. All the time. Her hands warming the sides up of herself for me. Taking the breaths in. Really. Really going. Leaving leaving leaving me here with our children. I see one has just stopped dying one to come. I'll not stop you. Know you'll support me. Yes I know the house is mine. You'll give me all you can. It is the best thing. No we're not for loving anymore. I understand that. Built for it. Our bodies now. Doing the housework. Paying the bills. No not a home for satisfaction. For joy. For us. We shall live in children and they shall live because of us. You cannot. I know that. Cannot bear but the gas bill will always be paid on time. Food will be on the table. As much as you can and more. I know. Well. Goodbye then. Goodbye. Then he did. Leave. Her there. Sitting quiet as ages. Never even crying moving. Just sad. I think. Stroking her full and wilted heart. Thinking I think of me and you. It sounded. Our empty spaces where fathers should be. When we'd find them and what – in time – we'd do to fill them up.

So anyway on and on. Forth and forth for days and week. You and me fastened side by side with her. Inside. Out. Being life. Giving her good reason. Go on forward marching her and us. And so pleased when strength went back to your hands stroked her. Round belly of baby that's kicking was me. Hello. So busy in myself. Bustling womb. Bit of swimming to your touch. Shove against the lining. I felt the sob of her blood over and under her children's touch. Press our hands together. My swirling butterflies laughter too. For her a flutter. For her. For her. My foot for you to see. See that. My gaudy fist pressed under the skin. Your pressed face against her whisper baby in there I will call you. I will be giving you a name. Soon enough. We'll be up and out of here. We were busy with each other long before I came.

She was furtive. Blipping. Monitor the time. Waiting out. Even keeling – a breed of health for you. Now nice and slow. Say thank God for this chance. Giving her a gasp of air. A routine. Dressing and redressing you on that ward. Nurse I'll. Strip bed washing sleeping eating. Crouched. Craven. Learning you. Our Fathers art in. She taught you. I listened at the side. I became me, into that trundle of things working quietly. Tick to tock.

Then I came out. Fresh out into the world. Mucus and things up my nose and a fine bawling net of lungs for screaming with. I. Punctured – surprise – out of her on the day. Somewhat early. Ruptured into that day and night shift of you and more you that she had. Unexpectedly goring the seat on which she sat in my impatience. Holy God. Nurse look I'm very sorry about that but now I think it's time. Gripped belly sitting by your side and I pushed out into the world ripe as fruit. Her pain but delight I'd say. Breathing as a creature. Snorting. Hauling. Pressing me into the chilly air that stung. I smelled a vinegar life in that delivery room. One good thing, said the doctor, being here. No crashing taxi's just end of the ward. He whack the rear. Oh. You're safe now. Into the world with her. Little beast. But I saw less than I had with my these flesh eyes open. The outside was like night and dark. Not. She, asking, someway off, just how I am and well? And fine? She is. She is. Her hand on my head. Her hand on my back. Allocating me my body near the sweet and warmth of mother flesh that could not take me in again. I soft. I curled there learning limb from limb. Her torn up insides and my tender suck. My little girl. A little girl. I see you now. But as the lights went on for me I heard her crying. That she's alone with me and no one's here to. What can I do grey eyes bouncing with new sight. Feeling curdled under the hot lamps. Clacking nurses gone away. Doctors closed up shop and done it seemed. I smelled the world begin to drown this white room. Under us some flood [illegible] coming up. Something from her tears. Leak. Brother. And your brother and your brother. And you'll see him. It will be like. It will be. It will. It will. That new. Her sorrow lapping up at my hands and held. Erasing. Something's somewhere coming up. To swallow. To prise me off my recollection of the time when I began. All the things I know before I was. The smell of milk. Drunken baby. Struggle up to. That's knocked blank then surely enough. Brain.

It's made for just sucking teats. And making shits. Such busy work of growing going on alone it seems. No thinking there now. So. It's gone. Blinking eye. I don't know again for years you and her. Well two.

And you? Not the first time I met you after that. Do you remember just before the start? Your one? It's before the ending now. Somewhere about. It is. I think. That's different. Will you remember me? I'll whisper here. I'll tell you all the things I never. And what I can recall.

Nobody could mistake this for a final draft – there's too much slack, too many fancy words not earning their keep, too much *writing*. There's not enough pressure; as the critic and poet Michael Hofmann would say, there's bite but no chew. The prose in this first draft is more disrupted than fragmented and, although this may seem paradoxical, it's less powerful because it's more explicit. It's semi-immersive, describing a situation that we do not experience.

Now here is later version of the same opening section, which came with a note from the author:

> This is the third draft, untouched since 2004, and the one Galley Beggar first read. The beginning and end were the only disagreements. In fact, when we met up to discuss the re-write none of them noticed the loss of eight thousand words – which was a little disheartening after my manic six weeks. Sam [Jordison]'s complaint about the original opening was about it being too explicitly set in the womb which could prove an immediate turn-off to potential readers. He wanted to start at the beginning of the next section but I wouldn't. So we compromised and I made it more ambiguous. We did not compromise on the end in the end, which stayed as I wanted.

I'm swimming through. Eyes swimming through. Moving in the under water. I hear you heard you first. Shout through the water. Red milk of it. Someone saying there son there. My mother. Yours and mine saying no no don't do that don't. She says. Please no. Don't say that.

Them walking up the corridors up the stairs. Are you alright? Will you sit down, he says. No. I want she says. I want. No leave me I want to see my son. Through her skin smells of dettol to me. Mops benches diamond floor tiles all the same strong. All the burn your eyes out if you had some. I have. But I'm in the womb. I'm there safe in there. And you are out. Get your brain cut, breathing stink and green air too. I hear her heart going pat pat pat. Going dum dum dum. Racing. Mind me. Don't bother now she's going to your room. See the. Jesus. Oh Jesus Jesus. What have they done? Jesus what have they done? Bile for me. She gives. Tidals of bile coming over me. Burn my. Ssssh. What's the. All over me. Mother. Oh no no no she cries. Sit down.

I know. The thing wrong with you? It's a. It is called. Something. Where your nosebleeds, your head aches. Where your eyes go funny. Where you can't hold tight. Stuff falling mugs and dinner plates when she says help Mammy clear up please. Ah just too young he says for that, fussing woman, would you ever give the child a break.

You fall off things. Swings and roundabouts where you hold on as well you can. Can't well. Slipping off into the muck. Bang your. Poor head wrapped up white and the blood come through now. She feel the sick of that. Little head. She hold our father's hand. What they done to him? What they done to my son? He says shush.

She saw it first when you couldn't open your eye. Stop that don't be winking so long, the wind'll change and you'll stay that way. Mammy I'm not. It's got stuck down. Mammy Mammy make it open up. Make it go away. She pulled it, fall again. Hold it open. I can't it's all fall down.

I shan't use up space by including the published version of the opening pages, but just compare, if you will, the now familiar published opening to that first draft:

Wait now. Wait now just til I say this. Wait now.

To begin before the beginning. I record that I could see. Hear the outside. Do what I should not and been aware. So I know this story of yours and mine inside out. From the inside out. And really. Not vibrated down to me in snug womb by cords and blood but sight at first then sound. So what's before that I won't mention. I'll leave that to you alone because you were there. What's said is before the beginning, at the very start of myself — conceived in disarray, now thinking back. I knew that busy outside in life something was going wrong.

This became:

For you. You'll soon. You'll give her name. In the stitches of her skin she'll wear your say. Mammy me? Yes you. Bounce the bed, I'd say. I'd say that's what you did. Then lay you down. They cut you round. Wait and hour and day.

When the novel was taken by Galley Beggar, much discussion revolved around the beginning and end of the novel, the author resisting her publisher Sam Jordison's wish to change both. She rewrote the opening passage — only the words, not the sense — while the end remained as it was. Jordison originally wanted the book to end with the line 'Go out where the water's fine', which is more upbeat but less powerfully dramatic and moving. The morning after that rewrite meeting the author woke up at around six, uncertain what to do about the opening. She went downstairs, picked up a shopping-list pad and wrote, 'For you. You'll soon . . .'

Take me backwards into that dark room

The novel is in five unequal parts, each sub-divided into numbered sections apart from the last, which runs for more than 50 uninterrupted pages. This reflects and embodies the acceleration of the brother's illness and the increasing harshness of the girl's situation. The seamless temporal continuity is at odds with the fragmentation of the language and the violence to which the girl is subjected. The structure can be summarised thus:

I LAMBS – 5 numbered sections, 29 pages
II A GIRL IS A HALF-FORMED THING – 4 numbered sections, 45 pages
III LAND UNDER THE WAVE – 3 numbered sections, 35 pages
IV EXTREME UNCTION – 5 numbered sections, 42 pages
V THE STOLEN CHILD – 1 unnumbered section, 49 pages

Any consideration of the plot will overlook what makes the novel so remarkable, because the plot is subordinate to the prose. Invited to give her view of plots in the previously cited interview with JoAnna Novak, McBride said:

> I'm not interested in it. I know what kind of writer I am, and that's not where my talent lies, and I enjoy that when other people do it well, so you know, for me as a reader, I can enjoy it, but as a writer it doesn't interest me. But story does interest me, and that is something that is quite different. And people interest me, and their lives, and what happens to them in their lives, and that is often not enhanced by intricate plots.

In that same interview, however, she was at pains to distinguish between 'plot' and 'story':

> I think for me story is a much more organic thing. It is something that emerges like life. Plot is a series of ideas that you impose upon your characters, whereas for me the writing process is about discovering who those characters are.

McBride's use of language was developed in isolation and from scratch (with a nod to her literary forebears and especially Joyce) during an intensively creative six months when she was 27 years old. The effect on the reader who trusts the writer and engages with the novel fully is intense, profound and long-lasting.

When I asked the author about particular passages in the novel that struck me in some way as exceptional, or that best exemplified her approach, she invariably replied that whatever it was that had particularly snagged my attention and admiration was a first draft, never revised. What about those virtuoso flourishes, those moments when she makes phrases such as 'Chew it lurks me' or 'My thud cheeks up' or 'We lilt our chamber'? Each of these goes off like a firework, each is strange and wholly original yet immediately comprehended. One doesn't, after a few pages, feel any need or inclination to – as it were – *translate* these into straight un-McBridean English as, respectively, 'I'm still anxious', 'I blush suddenly' and 'We love our room'. This confirms the author's genius at managing language on our behalf. She does not work standard English up into something more original but (as I see it) starts at a naturally high pitch and works *down* – she takes out, rather than puts in. She is more a Beckettian minimalist than a Joycean maximalist, and what she does is hard won but seemingly unforced.

Part of the achievement is that the author has removed herself from the book entirely. In creating a language that expresses thought prior to the point of its articulation in speech, she renders the girl's experience with a directness that we share without any of the sense of distance that an authorial presence or voice introduces. What happens in *A Girl* to the girl happens to the reader, and with extreme vividness and intensity. We share her pain and it becomes our pain. *A Girl Is a Half-formed Thing* is a book about a girl, and the girl is all of us.

PART I LAMBS

A girl is born. We will never learn her name. Her older brother – also unnamed – has not fully recovered, and will never fully recover, from a childhood operation for a brain tumour that has left him with scars both physical and mental. He has what are now referred to as 'special learning needs'. He is slow, has a limp and is poorly coordinated. But the book, as we know, begins before the girl is born and the opening pages – among the strangest and most haunting in modern fiction – express her pre-natal, pre-rational thoughts (rather than speech) as she communes with her brother from within the womb ('And I loved swimming to your touch').

Their mother (capitalised as 'Mammy' or 'Mam') is fiercely defensive of her son and, as a form of malign compensation, treats her daughter coldly. Her husband, the father, has walked out on his wife, his poorly son and newborn daughter, leaving them to fend for themselves.

The 'where' and the 'when' are suggested, but not explicitly. It's Ireland in the 1980s, although you have to pay close attention as the author doesn't rely on any shorthand to suggest a place and a period. McBride once said in an interview that the book is 'set in Mayo' but her approach, she says, is to avoid including 'stuff' because she has no interest in writing any kind of social history of the period and, above all, wants to avoid nostalgia or sentimentality.

There are very few suggestive details such as brand nouns, consumer language or topical references and those few that do appear have a fleeting, muted resonance: they include octons (a children's game), star wars (not the film but, in this context, the spin-off figurines), Miss Piggy (of *The Muppet Show*) and a range of unglamorous household products in lower case – dettol, j-cloth, ribena, biactol, cotton buds, walls and carte d'or ice cream, impulse (a perfume spray) and coke (the fizzy drink). These are used sparingly and unemphatically. At one point hair gel is mentioned, and the marvellous phrase 'all your walkmans fizz in tune', and both imply the 1980s, but slantingly. The *Encyclopaedia Britannica* makes an appearance; there are jaguar and volvo cars (also lower-cased) and the washing-up fluid Fairy Liquid (capitalised, presumably to avoid any ambiguity). There's a challenge for the book's translators in the reference to 'funky gibbon', a 1975 novelty song recorded by The Goodies, a popular comedy trio. The setting, then, is clearly Ireland at some unspecified, unverifiable point in the 1980s. It's a given, and we are aware of the location, if not the era, by the time we reach the bottom of the first page. How is that?

It's a combination of vocabulary and cadence. 'Mammy' is suggestive, and the doctor's 'Will you sit'; then the mother's repeated cries of 'Jesus' and the Holy Family reference followed by 'Gethsemene dear Lord hear our prayer our. Please. Intercession.' We're in a Catholic culture, clearly. Just as the hospital is evoked and experienced rather than merely described ('smell from dettol through her skin. Mops. Diamond floor tiles all as strong'), the setting is implied but never explicit.

The years pass quickly and as the girl develops the language becomes more complex while remaining fragmented, sporadic and impressionistic. She matures, or at least grows older, in a series of temporal lurches, like crudely edited flashbacks (although these are too immediate and unmediated by memory to qualify as such). But these are not really like flashbacks at all because they are always happening now. By 'now' in this case I mean the *reader's* now, the moment at which the reader is reading the text. This is part of the novel's power – we are not kept at a distance from what happens by any mediating technique, by any conventional third-person approach.

The mother's father visits from Northern Ireland, staunchly and overbearingly Catholic. Aghast that his grandson cannot repeat the catechism, he leaves in a fury. A violent scene follows as the mother assaults the brother verbally and then physically in the first of the novel's many harrowing episodes. Reviewing the novel, Anne Enright said that the reader can hear, and almost feel, the blows that rain down on the children.

One can feel this writing, physically. One can feel it also emotionally. The two children make their mother a simple meal of tomato soup and bread to win her love, or at least to persuade her not to send the brother to 'handicap school'. This short passage beginning 'Tomato soup we made . . .' can only be read in a whisper. There's an almost Dickensian undertow to the scene and it is intensely moving. The two children become fearful supplicants to their own mother, preparing the simplest of meals (red soup, white bread), folding the kitchen roll as a gesture to gentility, using a wooden spoon so as not to make a noise.

PART II A GIRL IS A HALF-FORMED THING

The beginning of teens us. Thirteen me fifteen sixteen you. (p.33)

That's the opening line of the second section of the novel, and harks back to earlier and similar phrasing – 'Two me. Four you five or so' / 'Now when you are seven eight, me five'. (p.7)

We learn that the absent father has died and the family is provided for, with money to move to a better house. The girl and her brother attend their new school together, and the ride on the bus is vividly evoked. In a symbolic scene the girl smashes a plaster statue of the virgin Mary from Lourdes while travelling in her mother's car. This is an explicit act of iconoclasm, equivalent to Stephen Dedalus and his cocksure *non serviam*, but also anticipates a later car scene between the girl and her uncle. He makes his first appearance in the third and longest section of 'Lambs', introduced with typical immediacy and the minimum of detail ('Say hello to your aunt and uncle. You haven't seen them before.').

There is a flurry of impressions when the aunt and uncle arrive (a sexual charge anticipated in the makes of car – a 'jaguar', a 'volvo'). The encounter between the girl and her uncle is quietly momentous:

> I look at him. I look him back from looking right at me. His eyes
> flick a switch. (p.45)

The tension here is meticulously calibrated, and it's not just a
sexual tension. It's partly a playground game, like a who-blinks-
loses staring contest, although that doesn't conceal an implicit,
underlying violence. His eyes 'flick a switch' and it's unclear
what's activated. His lust? Her sudden awareness of her own sexuality? Something, in either case, is turned on. That 'flick' im-
plies a knife, and while 'switch' suggests an electric light there's
also, in the background, the archaic word for a disciplinary cane
with its onomatopoeic 'swish'. With a string of monosyllables
hinged around the central bi-syllable 'looking', the encounter is
fully realised without being described.

The succession of unvoiced velar 'k' sounds in that terrific
line tick away in the background – look / look / back / looking
/ flick – and the I / I / eyes sequence takes us back to the *esse
est percipi* theme that runs through the novel. The uncle's 'eyes'
flick back at the double 'I' of the girl, suggesting that she is both
divided *and* doubled – a half-formed thing, objectified by her
uncle's predatory gaze and aware of herself for the first time as an
object of desire. Adam Mars-Jones pinned it down in his review
for the *London Review of Books* (which appears in full in Chapter 3): 'She opens up space where there shouldn't really be any,
by bruising the cadence and roughening up the grammar. The
charged inconclusiveness of "I look him back from looking right
at me", for instance, reproduces those aspects of the encounter.'

'Charged inconclusiveness' is right. We are in the hands of a
writer who knows exactly what effects she sets out to achieve.
She is particularly adept at capturing the girl's constant state of
equivocation and self-contradiction, a state of being described
by Joyce in *Finnegans Wake* as 'twosome twiminds'. The girl's
probing intelligence and questioning insights never falter and
never settle into a predictable pattern – she is constantly experiencing the world and developing as she does so. One is reminded

of Simone de Beauvoir's view that 'one is not born, but rather becomes, a woman'.

What is about to happen is predictable enough in plot terms but incendiary in style. First we have to negotiate a slightly laboured scene of social embarrassment as the shallow, snobbish *nouveau riche* aunt lords it over her sister. This is the only episode in the book that fails to convince me, simply because the snooty distinction between ice-cream brands (walls, carte d'or) is thin material in any context, and the tone seems forced.

The girl loses her temper and is sent to her room. The two women and the brother go out and through her sobs she hears her uncle's footfall on the stairs. He seems to want to make peace and to cheer her up. He also seems to offer his support ('Shouldn't we be friends? I am your uncle after all.') but this soon becomes a clumsy one-sided flirtation:

> You're a funny girl. Why's that then? Cheeky madam. Maybe I am. Oh you are. Well that's me. Good for you can I ask you. What? Do you climb out that window to meet your boyfriends at night?

The night before the visitors are due to return to England the girl finds herself alone in the house with her uncle.

> Sit down here. They're gone to the shops and someone's mother who gets messages in photographs. (p.52)

His jocular tone disguises his predatory intent. The girl's feelings are compressed into the very McBridean 'My thud cheeks up', four words embodying the pulse of the blood rushing to the head, of the face reddening, of the heart pounding, an immediately comprehensible way of expressing a particular physical and emotional state. She has become the object of her uncle's scrutiny – the repetition of 'see' echoing that first exchange of looks but this time the point of view is wholly male, and threatening.

> I think you're too shy of me for comfort's sake. Sorry I. He says I see you. What? I see you very clear. I see you. I do. So come here. And I can't help wondering if you see me? You see, I think you do. (p.53)

Their first physical encounter is experienced by the girl, and therefore by the reader, in a powerfully sensory passage:

> The burn of it. That smell. That deep in his neck like warm and rich and far away. Like memory I might have had.

Although the girl's senses of touch and taste and smell are heightened there is, significantly, no visual aspect to the encounter. When she tentatively places her hand on his trousers he recoils: 'No! Not for me he says. I stop that. I am not. I go red. I'm not that man.' They part and the girl spends a restless night – confused, angry and aroused. What her uncle is doing, of course, is grooming her, while at the same time pretending to himself that he's not doing what he's doing. His apparent horror at her touching her crotch is part of that strategy. The following day she leaves the house at dawn and walks to the nearby lake and pages 54 to 56 are a tour de force of lyrical writing. The girl wades into the icy water where her immersion is a foretaste of oblivion ('I fear not. Hear not. See not. Feel the rap on my knuckles of the water going in.'). This is the same spot where, at the end of the novel, she will drown herself, but for now the lake is a place of cleansing, baptism and communion with nature. The passage is densely populated with birds – geese, curlews, swans, a duck, a heron – which have, as we shall see, an important mythical resonance. She floats in the water, fully clothed, and emerges with what seems to be a new sense of purpose:

> I don't think I will be clean now. Think instead I'll have revenge for lots of all kinds of things. The start is. That is love.

She returns to the house. It is still very early in the morning but her uncle is awake and comes downstairs to find her in the kitchen. What follows is among the most disturbing episodes in the novel.

> I think I'm filled with blood. I'm wet and wet the whole way through. I'm sogging. I'm. Viscous lake. I. Sway. My eyes back.

This is intensely felt and intensely rendered. It is also entirely distinctive: the Irish idiom 'sogging' (i.e. 'sodden'), the pervasive sense of saturation (water, blood and later sperm and snot and phlegm), the repeated first-person pronoun, the alliterative nursery rhythms ('wet and wet the whole way through'), the importance of eyes and seeing.

'I am pure white,' says the girl when the uncle pulls out of her, though when she goes to the bathroom to wash she feels that the space between her legs might look like a butcher's block. 'Whiteness' in this novel stands for everything and nothing (like Melville's whale). In this instance it suggests an anaemic pallor rather than purity, a sense that the girl has – literally – lost all her blood. White and red hark back to the meal of tomato soup and bread the girl and her brother prepared for their mother, another example of the novel's austere palette.

A problem is the extent to which the girl seems on a first reading somehow complicit in her sexual abuse ('I'll drink I'll not'), and this ambivalence has been grotesquely misinterpreted as compliance, as if the girl meets her violator half way. This is to misread such finely balanced phrases as 'the busy silent want of me', which can equally describe the uncle's desire for the girl and the girl's own needs. It is also the case that we are simply unused to reading such a depiction of child rape in fiction – it thwarts our expectations. Some reviewers have described the girl's violation as a 'seduction' and what happens between her and the uncle as a 'relationship' – it's nothing of the kind, but reflects the lack of ease with which we write about sex, or write about writing about sex. Literary critics of my generation are likely to be more at ease with innovative syntax than transgressive sexuality. The author has noted that in Australia the sexual content of the novel was more freely discussed than in Britain, and I expect the same applies to parts of the United States.

After the rape the uncle prepares breakfast: 'cornflakes toast and jam for me and tea and anything I would want', echoing again the bleak propitiatory meal the children prepared for the

mother. Further sexual violations will follow, graphic and upsetting, powerfully immediate and harsh. The girl may be a precocious teenager but is a child still, is vulnerable and confused
and unsure of herself. What happens to her at the hands of her
uncle is simply and unambiguously a criminal assault without
nuance or mitigation, and what happens to the girl after that is
a direct consequence of her violation. She does not become, despite what some male critics have said, a slag, or 'the town bike'.
Damaged, she invites further damage, seeking through pain and
abasement to find a place beyond either. There is a terrible exploitation at the heart of this novel, and a correspondingly terrible exploitation at the heart of our society.

The grooming and violation of vulnerable children, usually
young and troubled girls, by predatory adult males is happening
all the time, everywhere; this is condemned by a press which at
the same time contributes to the sexualisation of minors through
salacious advertising and chortling insinuation. Our public discourse has yet to find a way to engage with this horror, but
there's a lot of noise. Nowhere in all that noise is the space or
clarity or time for a moment such as this:

> There is an extreme concentration at. It was so quiet all around that I
> could hear him open me. (p.57)

I held my breath when I first read that, and still do. We feel
implicated and complicit as readers and we are naturally shocked.
In a book that's light on circumstantial detail this is a detail of
particular potency. The uncle 'opens' her and this confirms her
objectification in his eyes – her body like so much disposable
packaging. She hears rather than feels him opening her, bringing a neurasthenic sense of detachment and incomprehension
to what's happening. That commonplace verb 'open' is made to
work hard here. It's her own body that she hears, but that body
is being appropriated.

The aunt and uncle leave for England and the girl and her
brother go back to school – but they are drifting apart.

> We were moving off now. From each other. As cannot be. [. . .] Who
> are you? You and me were never this. This boy and girl that do not
> speak. But somehow I've left you behind and you're just looking on.
> (p.61)

The next section opens three years later – 'Fifteen sixteen'
(the brother's age, poignantly, is no longer noted). The girl's
language has become more sophisticated, sometimes self-
consciously so. Of her school friend she is able to say, or think:
'She is sufficiently hated by all at home to make the escapade
worthwhile.' That's not language at the point immediately
before it becomes conscious thought; that's the language of a
brightly precocious teenager with literary leanings: 'I'm up for
Art and nothing else.'

In what may be a concession to autobiography the girl fa-
vours modernism in the form of Scott Fitzgerald while her
friend dies her hair orange in a commitment to Rossetti and the
Pre-Raphaelites. They spend time together by the lake where
the truanting local boys hang out, gauche and slightly older.
The friend seems to enjoy their attention and the girl goes off
for a walk to get away from them. One of the boys follows her
and is crudely disparaging about her brother. She takes him
to a thicket and challenges him to fuck her. He nervously at-
tempts to do just that and the girl feels a sense of power and
self-realisation:

> He was the first off. Worst off. I begin. Now I know full well what I
> can do. For me and for you. (p.70)

She becomes conscientiously promiscuous as a means of taking back control of her life and distracting the attention of her
brother's tormentors. Her indiscriminate sexual choices – if they
really are choices – will later involve masochistic self-abasement.
For now she takes on any boy in the school and finds – or tells
herself that she finds – a source of power in her sexuality, even
a philosophic certainty: 'The answer to everything is fuck.' But
if that's the answer what are the questions? And of course 'fuck'

can be both a term for copulation and a nihilistic profanity. Fuck isn't love. Fucking, however, is a power.

Two bad things happen. First the brother discovers that his sister 'did the it the thing with one of the lads from my year' and they have a violent tussle, although there's a dark comic moment when the mother intervenes ('That's no way to talk my boy as though you're on TV'). The second bad thing is the the brother's disastrous examination results arrive: 'It's the start of the end of this life.' His plan to join the Irish Defence Forces is also dashed on the grounds of height and weight and IQ and eyesight. He gets a job stacking shelves for 60 pounds a week, and this now looks likely to be his only working future. Life is closing down for him as it opens up for his sister.

PART III LAND UNDER THE WAVE

The girl's examination results are good enough for her to win a place at university and her departure is an exhilarating moment of independence and potential: 'Right now. Next now. What I'll be?' She leaves home to study at a college in an unidentified city. There is a fleeting reference to America across the Atlantic so we can, if we feel a need to, assume that it's not Dublin or Belfast. It's also unclear exactly what she studies. English Literature? Probably, but does it matter? College for the girl is about drinking and sex.

The events experienced by the girl – and therefore by the reader – unfold in abstract locations with the minimal necessary information to let us know where she is (and therefore where *we* are): on a bus, in a pub, at home, by a lake and so on. These are humble examples of what the anthropologist Marc Augé has called 'non-places' – airports, railway stations, superstores, motorways and international hotel chains, all of which have a Ballardian glamour in their anodyne and anonymous solitude and offer the transitory occupant the illusion of being part of some grand global scheme: a fugitive glimpse of a utopian city-world. The McBridean non-space, on the other hand, is without machine-age slickness and smoothness, is rougher and closer to nature and offers no comfort or consolation beyond its own solitude. But Augé also considers what he calls traditional 'anthropological spaces' – in particular the symbol-laden site of an altar – and we find in McBride's pared-down world many instances of what might be called non-anthropological space: the statue of the Virgin Mary is displaced, transported in a car and deliberately smashed; the late exchange between the doctor and dying brother is rendered in a quietly liturgical manner and is free of any destabilising fragmentation – all McBride's techniques are suspended, which in itself is breathtaking.

But all this comes much later. At college, the usual undergraduate depravities are much in evidence but hers are complicated by what seems a commitment to self-destruction, although the girl's range of references is expanding. Section 2 of 'Land Under the Wave' concludes with what is surely a homage to Joyce as the girl decides not to kick a pebble under her toe. The passage brings to mind Stephen Dedalus on the beach in 'Telemachus', the opening episode of *Ulysses*. It concludes with a jokily self-conscious use of the Joycean term 'epiphany'.

Reflecting on her new freedoms the girl says: 'In the new world I am do this every single time I can', and we may sense in this a combination of Miranda and Caliban. She returns to the family home for Christmas, where her mother's bitter disappointment in her brother is expressed in a seriocomic monologue – 'He's got this job and he won't drive but won't get a lift with yer one and he won't give me his pay now', and so on, and on. This is both funny and sad – a parent's doting horror at the way their children develop as teenagers. It's complicated by the brother's medical condition, and the extent to which this is a cause of his behaviour. The brother is absorbed by computer games, eats junk food and stays in his room. There's no mention of sex, as if this could somehow taint his essential innocence, his blamelessness. It's as if the girl is accumulating sexual experience on his behalf.

Broke on her birthday, the girl checks her bank account and discovers a hundred pounds in credit, a gift (she assumes) from her brother. There follows the bravura passage beginning 'I met a man. I met a man. I let him throw me round the bed' (p. 196). As a list of sexual encounters it's sometimes unclear if we are hearing of many meetings with one man, or a few different men, or many different encounters with many different men – the last, probably. It's a litany by turns grim and bleakly farcical, as the girl is approached by, and sometimes accommodates the needs of, a priest and a farmer and a man with condoms in his pockets. They all, in one way or another, exploit the girl who, in turn, seems to seek out her exploiters.

The girl's maternal grandfather dies and the family drive to the North. What follows captures a fading rural tradition, that of the washing and laying out of the dead and the ensuing wake. In the crowded kitchen of her grandfather's house she sees her uncle again and kisses him on the cheek. The girl is confused:

> They laugh. Approve of saying. And I can't tell what's the. Join up. What does. Makes me uneasy. (p.104)

She leaves the house, stepping out into the cold, and reflects that her rape at thirteen was 'a thing that happened on my route to here'. Her thoughts are eloquent and coolly self-examining as she speculates on whether her aunt might know of her husband's behaviour:

> And that would be something worse again but no she doesn't. I would tell. I'd see it on her. Who cares forget.

'Who cares forget' has a Beckettian compression and precision in its manifold meanings, and we might compare Beckett's own translation of the line 'tout ce qui précède oublier' as 'all that goes before forget' in his short prose piece *Enough* (1965), originally written in French.

Her uncle appears and they go into town to buy whiskey and candles. 'Awkward', used twice within a few lines, sets the tone. The girl makes the purchases and gets back into the car. Small talk. They arrive back at her grandfather's house but the uncle explains to his wife that he wants to show the girl where they first met, so they drive on to 'a beautiful spot'. When they begin to talk (and the repetition of a rhetorical 'look' continues the theme of observing and being observed), the exchanges are fraught and inconclusive, the language in this paragraph sliding into more nursery rhymes (that/chat; okay/say):

> Why did you do it if knew it was so wrong? Squirm him. I couldn't somehow not. You were like. You were like. It doesn't matter he sighs there is no good thing to say. Well then. That's that. And that concludes this little chat. Your conscience is clear and I won't be calling the guards. I'm A-okay as the Yankees say. (p.107)

She then surprises herself (and the reader) by asking him to kiss her. The uncle becomes immediately aroused and she pushes him away, assuming control of the situation. They return to the wake and the girl runs to the bathroom to puke. She takes her uncle's place by the coffin and observes, sardonically, the hypocrisy of those in attendance ('The biddies are having their sup'). The funeral is the following day ('As we cared. We did not.') and the uncle and aunt leave straight afterwards. But before they do her uncle joins her on the nearby beach and, after some internal struggle, she gives him her number (and a rare succession of commas serve to emphasise her equivocal feelings:

> I don't think, I say I don't think I don't know what is I don't what is if this is we should, or, you know. So many things things things curling up in my head. Jesus. Jesus. (p.110)

She gives him her number ('Because I have no idea what is right') and he touches her and says he will see her again - both a promise and a threat. Travelling home in the car with her mother and brother, the three 'offer up a few prayers for the Holy Souls'. As elsewhere, the liturgical language offers stability, continuity and reassurance:

Oh clement oh loving oh sweet Virgin Mary. Pray for us sinners.
Now and at the hour of our death. Amen. (p.111)

PART IV EXTREME UNCTION

The title of this section refers to the anointing of the sick. Extreme Unction (not to be confused with Last Rites) is the sacrament that serves to give health and strength to the soul – and
perhaps the body – of those facing death. The term means 'final
anointing' and links us to the many liquid continuities of the
novel. The priest uses olive oil to anoint the forehead of the
penitent, saying: 'Through this holy anointing, may the Lord in
his love and mercy help you with the grace of the Holy Spirit.'

The girl is back at university and more sex with anonymous
men, starting with a drunken night in a pub. Her mother's frequent calls complaining of her brother's unravelling behaviour
bring her back home again, although she is reluctant to tear
herself away from 'fucks and books'. She visits her brother and
finds a fraught situation, her mother tearfully depressed and her
brother withdrawn into a world of computer games and sweets.
The girl wants no part of this:

> I make off from it. I make my escape. Leave you cough it up fight
> it out amongst yourselves. Get away from it oh god. And don't. No.
> Answer the calls. Fill my ear up. Fill my mouth instead. Man drink
> do what you like to me. I am safe. I am free. In my own way I am
> but it weighs me, beats me when I'm not doing the rounds. Split and
> splatter my heart head. So I get cold in the mouth on answering her
> bring bring. (p.119)

That needy telephone is a fine touch. When she hears that
her brother has not gone to work one day she has a terrible
premonitory fear, almost immediately dismissed, in a paragraph
that could itself stand for what McBridean English is capable of
doing:

> I do not want. I do not want to hear this. But suddenly it's clawing all

over me. Like flesh. Terror. Vast and alive. I think I know it. Some-
thing terrible is. The world's about to. The world's about to. Tip.
No it isn't. Ha. Don't be silly. Stupid. Fine. Fine. Everything will be.
Fine. Chew it lurks me. See and smell. In the corner of my eye. What.
Something not so good. (p.120)

Another call follows soon after. Her mother says she thinks
her brother is going to die. We cut almost immediately to the
hospital. The girl visits her brother, who has cracked his head in
a fall and is undergoing tests. There appears to be a shadow on his
scan. Mother and daughter pray together in the hospital chapel:

> In the chapel. Down on my knees. Oh god Jesus. I beg you. I am
> pleading. See. I plead. But stones in my mouth. Lead on my tongue.
> You are not the praying person. But I. Not you. Not you. After all
> you have done. Good people do the praying and sinners go to. Hell.
> Thank you Jesus. Amen. (p.125)

The prognosis, when it comes, is not good – 'Perhaps a year'.
The girl leaves her mother praying and telephones her uncle
from the hospital foyer, turning to him for – what, exactly?
Salvation? Consolation? Refuge? An escape from the reality of
her brother's condition? The uncle is an ambiguous figure. His
violation of her as a child is the trauma that drives her into self-
harm and makes her seek oblivion through drink and sex. That
she seeks in some way to locate and sunder a continuity with that
trauma by maintaining contact with her violator is (if we want
to be literal about it) a form of Stockholm syndrome, in which
victims identify with their captors and abusers, often mistaking
the lack of abuse as a form of kindness. But kindness does not
inform the girl's decision to begin a relationship with her violator – rather it gives her some sense of control of her life.

In the third section of 'Extreme Unction' the girl is back in
her shared flat and the uncle arrives on a visit. They have sex:

> I say Don't leave me alone. There is something going on in my. Please
> don't stop I say and again. Til I am hurt or I am sick. Keep going until
> I. Then you can let me die. (p.132)

She seeks a place beyond pain, beyond thought – an unconscious place. Her flatmate realises there's something happening between the girl and her 'Uncle-in law' and the two girls go out together, on the pull.

The girl visits her brother and they spend a brief idyllic time together, remembering their childhood (with references to the underlying Children of Lir legend in the lyrical description of birds). The uncle remains a presence in the girl's life and members of 'the ministry missionary fellowship' turn up at the brother's home. The girl listens to their pious cant and sends them packing:

> Get out. You need to get off this step. I don't want your sort round here. Poisoned. Well God forgive you. And he can shove it. And damn you. He will. You too. Bastards. Showers of shite attend your every waking shitting prayer. So there so there so there so there. Bang the door on them that hard I'd shatter glass. Christians go and shite. (p.138)

There's a faint echo of *Hamlet* in 'Showers of shite attend your every waking shitting prayer' ('And flights of angels sing thee to thy rest'), and this tragic resonance adds to the scatological force of the girl's furious imprecations. Shitting and religion are linked throughout the novel – as when the girl runs out of a prayer meeting that takes place in her home and squats to produce a white turd, the result of her habit of licking and eating chalk.

The brother is becoming progressively sicker. The girl nurses him through an early crisis and puts him to bed while her mother is away praying at church. When her mother returns the girl leaves the house for 'a little breather' and heads to the place among the trees nearby where a group of local men gather. She has rough anonymous sex with a stranger that leaves her feeling 'sore and used up', which is how she says she wants to feel. She is brutalised, and in a state of post-traumatic stress caused by her rape at thirteen:

> I went home. On the stones. In the pale moonlight. Nothing in or

by my side. Full my mouth swelled. His guck between my legs. His. Horrible. Even better if it run down. Skanky. Laughs. This is the way I'd like to be. If I had a chance. To start again. I wouldn't. I'd do this. I would. But every day. Every day. (pp.141–2)

This is part bravado, part denial. But it also impresses as an act of self-possession – the girl embraces and finds a source of power and fulfilment in her apparent abjection and exploitation. There's a kind of malign homeopathy at work here – using sex to resist and overcome the brute demands of sex. The girl (troublingly, because she seems to suffer unrelievedly) objectifies and debases herself. This may be, as she seems to think, on her own terms, but of course they are the very terms on which each subsequent sexual partner (and 'partner' is an anaesthetic term) further exploits her for his own pleasure – see the grim yet intermittently hilarious 'I met a man' sequence.

In the final section the girl moves between her mother's house, where her brother is slowly dying, and increasingly violent bouts of sex with her uncle. In an attempt to control her life she trades thought for feeling, for pain. She insists that her uncle hit her in the face:

So he hits til I fall over. Crushing under. Hits again. He hits til something's click and the blood begins to run. Jesus he says. I feel sick. But I'm rush with feeling. Wide and. He thinks he's bad when he fucks me now. And so he is. I'm better though. In fact I am almost best.

A few lines later she says: 'This is the closest thing to love.' Given the coldness of her mother and the abuse by her uncle, this is a devastating revelation. But she is wrong. Love is what we find when, answering a telephone call from the doctor confirming that her brother has perhaps two or three months left to live, she explains how she and her mother will care for her dying brother:

We'll keep him. Me my mother. We. Will. Take care of him. Here. He won't. Let him be somewhere on his own. In the dark. He's a little boy. (p.146)

There are painful exchanges between the girl and her mother, whose belief in the power of prayer offends the girl's pragmatism ('Something awful's going to. You can't believe it away'). She believes that her brother has at least the right to know that he is going to die, something her mother cannot countenance. The girl leaves the house and walks the streets; she sees a man looking at her and considers momentarily

> Who's him there having a looking at me he. look at my. Tits. Sss. Fuck word. No don't. Fuck that. No. Will. Not that. Not. That. But. If I want to then I can do. And it would fill me up fine. And I. I do. Dot it. Take him back with me. Give him. The word. I want that. Hurt me. Until I am beyond pain. (p.148)

The last seven words could be a coda for the novel. The girl's commitment to self-harming herself as a malign kind of homeopathy takes many forms. On the train home from university she sees an unprepossessing passenger ('Dip biscuit mild and not prepared for anything like that I cough'); her coughing becomes a fit, deliberately, and he comes to her aid, slapping her back. She feels in control ('I reel it and reel him') and they head for the toilet together. Following their rough congress she feels 'sedated'.

She arrives home to find her brother alone in the dark kitchen, making pasta. He is so helpless, so sweetly kind and gentle, so innocent and troubled. He drops a sieve and scalds his hand and is confused. The mother briefly absent, their tender understanding and allegiance are immediately reconfirmed, and their original childhood love returns in a wave of memory:

> And you start. To cry. Like my little boy I knew. I knew. When I was younger than you. So many years ago when. You sit. You say. I'm just so tired. I'm just so ill. (p.151)

The last three pages of this section are a tour de force. In what appears to be a dream monologue of particular eloquence and intensity, the girl addresses her brother. This virtuoso passage culminates on page 153, from 'For I won't let go' onwards. This combines the author's virtuosity with the diverse elements that make up the novel's unique language - the Biblical and liturgical cadences, the reference to the Children of Lir myth ('Once thousand years I'd press their sap on you'), the simple unliterary and largely monosyllabic vocabulary, the emphasis on seeing and being seen, the references to the natural world and to childhood. Throughout there is an urgency, a prevailing gentleness, and emotional tug and drag, the assurance of a writer we have learned to trust entirely:

> Answer me this. Do you think you're going home? For a walk or for the night? Will it be good there? Any chance you'll let me know? No. How would that be just a bad idea. Just a thing wrong. You. Us. For the meantime. In the meantime. I'll say. Hold my hand. I'll do. My. For you. My best for you. For what we should be. If you can show me all the parts that are working. And the not. Hurting or sleeping. Show me this in secret code. To fix. I'll purge it. Kill it out. I'd kill anything for you.

PART V THE STOLEN CHILD

The final section of the novel is the most gruelling, both in its depiction of the brother's final illness and the girl's response to it. The brother gets progressively sicker; spends time in hospital and is then sent home to die, in a downstairs room prepared by his sister. We are close to the heart of the book, the still centre. The flurry of practical domestic arrangements, of new routines, acts as a counterpoint to the sense of imminent loss.

A great calm prevails throughout the searing exchange between a visiting hospice doctor and the dying brother, beginning: 'Tell me how you feeling? You say. I'm so tired now.' All of the author's authority and virtuosity is on display here, but none of her dazzling technique. It's as if the girl's frenetic and fragmented consciousness is briefly suspended and for a few intense moments we are able to experience something true and pure and real:

> When am I going to get well?
> She says.
> You're not. I'm sorry to.
> Am I
> this silent moment you say,
> Am I going to die?
> You are.

This exchange is indented, a typographical choice that isolates the passage from the main body of the text (p.173). This contrasts starkly with all that has gone before, and all that will follow. The piercing moment when the brother asks whether he might have children who might inherit his condition takes the reader by surprise – the shock and recognition and pity are overwhelming. This exquisitely delicate exchange ends with the mother's tearful abdication: 'There's no reason in the wide wide world.' The brother has weeks, not months to live.

Inconsolable, her mother embraces her:

> She puts her hands on me. She puts her arms around me. Oh my little. My boy my boy. My mother. Feel the. Strange and I am comfort there. I am the. Right. I am the right thing. In this time. (p.175)

But 'comfort' is unstable here, or ambiguous – is the girl a source of comfort to her mother, or does she find comfort in her mother's arms? There are very few moments of such familial warmth beyond the girl's love for her brother, and it is all the more touching for that. The doctor leaves and the aunt (who has come to stay with her husband) prepares chicken soup. 'This is her best thing' says the girl, who elsewhere expresses disgust at the sight and sound of people eating: 'Spoon the peas the carrots in and dry spud choke me make sick I like'; 'There's the kitchen air stink like fat. Mounging their breakfasts. Globle it up eat that eat that.' We might recall the 'Lestrygonians' episode in *Ulysses* in which the fastidious Leopold Bloom is revolted by the slobbering lunchtime customers 'wolfing gobfuls of sloppy food' in the Burton Hotel: 'Scoffing up stewgravy with sopping sippets of bread. Lick it off the plate, man! Get out of this.'

The girl's fleeting approval of her aunt's soup is another rare instance of simple contentment. The only other consolation comes in a dream of being with her brother underground, snug and secure ('We sing. We lilt our chamber'), in communion with nature.

She escapes the claustrophobic family home and the gaze of her uncle and makes her way alone to the lake, but is intercepted by her uncle who has followed in his car. He drives her to the lake and she leaves him in the car, although his interest is aroused. She makes her way through the trees, aware of the presence of others ('That smell of stink cigs smell of stink of shit and cloy. Stink I want.'). In the darkness two men are implied (in the brilliant, almost off-hand compression that is typical of this writer: 'I hear them laughs'). One of the two ('fish shit man') knows the girl from an earlier anonymous coupling by the lake. They fuck very roughly and the girl is then courteously invited to share some beers. The uncle (who may have been watching) attacks the man and beats him up, despite the girl's pleas. He then assaults her and bundles her into the car and drives her home. A paragraph consisting of thirteen consecutive sentences beginning 'And' or 'And he said' relates their return, and the uncle's heroic status in the eye of the girl's mother and aunt.

There follows a routine of vigils and doctors' visits as the brother slips away, amid small acts of kindness and prayer. McBride is unflinching in her portrayal of his care and the love that underlies it over the following few days. The pages are saturated with intimacy and clear-eyed truthfulness. The girl even attends communion, but on leaving church sees again the man beaten up by her uncle by the lake. He makes an implied threat (and calling her 'girleen' again strikes a sinister note) but she ignores him and returns home. Arrangements for the funeral are made, a priest delivers a sacrament for the sick (dispassionately, meticulously described). The days pass, the girl dreams, until the day on which she knows her brother is sure to die arrives. Movingly she washes and dresses with care in jumper and skirt and puts on lipstick and perfume.

To her horror the evangelical 'holy joes' arrive, her mother's friends, and troop into the house, violating the private communion with her brother as he dies. They surround the bed and the girl manages to hold her brother's hand as the uncle and aunt join the crowd in the room. What follows defies summary and must be read.

The brother's eyes are on the girl as he dies: there is a flurry of 'eye' references, a final exchange of looks, and death comes with quiet finality:

> My. lllllllllllllllll. Love my. Brother no.
> Silent.
> He's gone. He's gone. Goodbye.
> No. Oh please. My.
> Done. And. Quiet.
> And.
> Gone.

This passage is indented on the page, as was the earlier exchange between the brother and his doctor, and is a further demonstration that less can be much more. The author's diligent use of a spartan lexicon will later be re-used to great effect - that final 'gone' is premonitory.

By now the reader is wholly aligned with the girl's experience, her consciousness, and there is no sense of an intermediary, no authorial intervention or direction. We endure this moment of loss with the girl and, in effect, *as* the girl, and we are bereft. She is alone, and so are we:

> Who am I talking to? Who am I talking to now?

Summarising the final section of *A Girl Is a Half-formed Thing* is particularly difficult. How the author must have navigated the emotional and intellectual terrain that can produce writing of such power is hard to imagine. The section dealing with the brother's final illness and passing, however many times it is re-read, never loses its power to move, never allows the reader the freedom to approach the prose with detachment. The hooks go in, and stay in. What is strange, given the straightforward chronological chain of events, is the way these become rearranged in the reader's memory. I had repeatedly to check, and double-check, the order of certain central events in 'The Stolen Child', to disentangle my feelings and memories from those of the girl.

The undertaker arrives to take the body away and the girl seems to lapse into a trance-like, affectless state. There are prayers, and more prayers, and the family home becomes a place of mourning ('Bursting house with all the sorry ever heard'). There is a flurry of comings and goings, and the girl seems detached, even from herself ('I think I'm sleeping now'). Her brother's body is returned to the house and she gazes at it in an echo of the earlier scene at the grandfather's wake, but in a very different register.

At the lake she encounters for a third time the man who calls her 'girleen' and a brutal assault takes place. Rich in incident rather than plot, the novel is carefully stuctured around such re-encounters and repetitions (which may even be said to 'rhyme'), using such mundane situations as meals and car journeys, or more momentous episodes.

There seems to be a self-destructive impulse that drives the girl back to the lake, some urge for self-mutilation and destruction.

> Scream. Kracks. Done fuk me open he dine done on me. Done done Til he hye happy fucky shoves upo comes ui. Kom shitting ut h mith fking kmg I'm fking cmin up you. Retch I. Retch I. (p.193)

The homophonic retch/wretch combines physical debasement and literal sickness as the girl is beaten and kicked and abandoned. The typography is unstable - upper case suddenly erupts within words ('Here. mY nose my mOuth I. VOMit. Clear. CleaR. He stopS up gETs. Stands uP. Look.') and there are extended spaces between words in which it seems the girl is holding her breath as her attacker's footsteps crunch away.

If I have slight reservations about these distortions it's because what happens to the girl in the woods is so terrible that mere typographical oddness seems somehow inadequate to the task, and given the author's unbroken success in evoking the girl's experience at every stage of her life this seems almost a gimmick. As Adam Mars-Jones said in his *LRB* review, if your prose is up to the challenge of incarnating a pre-natal foetus it can manage anything. But it would be wrong to consider these verbal and typographical effects in isolation – they are a culmination of a fully-realised whole and the assured continuation of a modernist, avant-garde tradition. What McBride's writing represents is a startling tension between method and subject, something new and challenging; that she arrived at this form of writing independently is significant. I'm reminded of the Swiss writer Robert Walser, who said: 'Anything great and bold must be brought about in secrecy and silence, or it perishes and falls away, and the fire that was awakened dies.'

The girl staggers back to the house, bleeding and vomit-stained where she is ferociously berated by her mother ('Making a show of yourself on today of all days'). In the bathroom she looks in the mirror at 'that fuck purge of my face'. Then she is fucked by her uncle, at which point the earlier erratic and unstable upper/lower case typography becomes a rushing torrent of unspaced, harsh and quasi-Joycean phrases:

> Stick it ionthe don'tinside wwherhtewaterisswimming
> htroughmynoseandmouth throughmysense myorgands
> sthroughmythrough. That. A. My brain. He. Like. Now. (p.197)

Even after several readings I misunderstood what happens in the bathroom.

Now. Ithink i smell of woodwherethe river hits the lakebrownwash-
foamy up the bank side Isee allcreaturesthere fish ducklings inthe-
spring spring water going throughmyveins sinktheocean seeoutfar
my salt my. Sea firsttime. Ahhhh pisses. Up me. Is the love that. No
the other. Finisch lovely. He is done. Drop to earth. Tender. Can't
smell this room.

I had the impression that the uncle doesn't only ejaculate but
also urinates ('Ah pisses. Up me. Is the love that. No the other'),
which might explain why the girl fleetingly asks herself whether
this is 'the love that dare not speak its name' from the poem
'Two Loves' by Lord Alfred Douglas, aware of a transgressive
act. The author told me that this is not the case, and that the language changes at this point because the girl is wearing out and
giving up, and her sense of helpless debasement and humiliation
prompts the thought.

If the earlier scene between the hospice doctor and the brother involved a suppression or suspension of technique, then this
passage is an explosion of technique and may risk at times becoming technique at the expense of feeling or meaning. Of
course the girl – and the text – are by now so traumatised that
it is silly of me to cavil over issues of grammar and style. In any
case part of me wants to abdicate any critical approach when
considering 'The Stolen Child' because it is (and I know I speak
for many) simply the most shatteringly sad piece of writing I
have ever read. Each time I tackle the final section of *A Girl Is a
Half-formed Thing* I cease being a critic and become, gratefully, a
reader. I am moved to tears, real tears.

After a quiet dreamless night the girl wakes and makes her
way downstairs for a final exchange with her embittered and
unloving mother. The priest is due in an hour and the mother is
concerned about keeping up appearances ('The priest is coming
and you be here for the prayers.').

The girl visits her brother's room briefly then makes her way
from the house and returns to the lake for the last time, where
she drowns herself.

Turn. Look up. Bubble from my mouth drift high. Blue tinge lips. Floating hair. Air famished eyes. Brown water turning into light. There now. There now. That just was life. And now.

What?

My name is gone.

'My name. My name for me. My I.' Oblivion. The girl has lost a name we never knew and with it her purchase on life. What does a reader feel at the end of this uniquely gruelling experience? A sense of release and relief perhaps but also, surely, of exhilaration, and admiration. There has never been writing quite like this, and it seems to me to be a perfect culmination, a perfect match of form and content, of tone, with variations on verbs of arrival and departure – going and coming – and references to the whiteness that features elsewhere in the text. It is a magnificent coda, and links to the opening pages with the mention of 'cold hard tile' that we first encountered in the hospital on the first page. It is a recapitulation, and echo, of all that has gone before. There is a Biblical echo in 'Oh my brother where have you gone?' and a Beckettian precision and richness (if that's not a paradox) in:

Over the stones. Close out the cold door. On me. My love. Close out those old stones.

Authentic unscripted human utterance is full of repetition, redundancy and hesitation – 'to "er" is human', as the poet Michael Rosen says. These features are usually removed from otherwise 'naturalistic' dialogue and from (say) transcribed interviews for the simple reason that they would drive the reader nuts. A few recent innovations aside (Paul Kingsnorth's *The Wake*, rendered in an Old English 'shadow tongue', springs to mind), contemporary novelists tend to avoid engaging with the potential of human speech beyond declarative utterances, and the kind of eloquent exchanges in which the interlocutors are all but indistinguishable.

But I saw less with these flesh eyes

McBride has on several occasions mentioned that throughout the writing of the book she had, pinned above her desk, a quotation from a letter that Joyce wrote in 1926 to his patron Harriet Shaw Weaver, in which he defended the language of *Finnegans Wake* by stating:

> One great part of every human existence is passed in a state which cannot be rendered sensible by the use of wideawake language, cut-and-dry grammar and go-ahead plot.

Joyce was here referring to the unconsciousness of sleep and the dream state. McBride fruitfully repurposes the Joycean approach, applying comparably radical innovation to express the waking state – because *all* of human existence, not just 'one great part', is passed in a way that cannot be rendered sensible by conventional language. Or rather, our lives (awake or asleep) are not neatly structured linear fictions, are not plotted. It is in her repurposing of the Joycean approach that McBride has made her mark on literary history, realising that Joyce missed an opportunity by not applying the *Wake*'s lexical ingenuity to the waking state.

A Girl Is a Half-formed Thing might be described as a supercharged soliloquy. The critic James Wood has described the Shakespearean soliloquy as 'uttered privacy' (with its roots in prayer) and contrasts it with the fictional stream of consciousness which is, or at least aims to resemble, *unvoiced soliloquy*, observing that the latter 'seems to meet our own unfinished thoughts, with the request that together we – the reader and the fictional character – complete, voice, a new ensemble. Their failed privacies become our more successful privacies.' The McBridean stream of pre-consciousness might be described as *unvoiced privacy* – sourced in the consciousness of the fictive girl (and nowhere else), pre-verbal (though relentlessly verbal) and without an authorial presence.

There's no presence because we are never aware of McBride

as a mediator, as a storyteller. She offers no commentary, no prompts, no direction. She shows but does not tell. In this she is radically self-effacing yet wholly in command because while the language throughout is the girl's, or reported by the girl, it is also – of course – entirely McBride's. This proximity between character and form is what makes the girl's experiences inextricably part of the reader's own experience.

There are moments – surprisingly many – when language becomes conventional, or less radically original. Consider the babbling hubbub overheard at a gathering of 'polyester tight-packed womanhood', which opens with the girl explicitly observing the women and their flurry of gossip:

> Ah she'll not sit down for years. Apparently the smell of it is something wicked but god knows it's not her fault. Their brother's second wife – ach the first died leaving five behind. Tell me where's the sense? (p.23)

The girl is both repelled and mesmerised by these grotesques and has a keen satirical eye and ear for their absurdity, their combined weakness and indomitability. This is equally the author's eye and ear, but it's the girl who gets to see and hear. This is McBride at her most Joycean, and having fun.

There are snatches of Catholic liturgy which, with their relatively grammatical coherence and 'completeness', seem to offer a sort of textual stability, a calm in the maelstrom of thoughts and feelings. There is some cold comfort to be found in the ritual, and consolation, although the girl's personal experience of religion is entirely oppressive. McBride has said that she finds the language of church ritual beautiful and moving, and would have included more hymns but was unable to do so because some were subject to copyright.

McBride is often described as an Irish writer. In early interviews she preferred to align herself to the European modernist tradition, and, though not allied to the social realist tradition, *A Girl Is a Half-formed Thing* is a novel set in rural Ireland and populated with Irish characters. Particular idioms aside, the 'Irishness' of the language – 'There now a girleen isn't she great' – comes from the underlying presence of Gaelic, as the author confirmed in an interview with Noah Charney:

> We all learn it at school. Some of us speak it better than others. But it informs, absolutely, the way we construct sentences. How we arrange the words. There's a pleasure in constantly making a play between the two languages. That's why Irish writers are devils for prose. Sometimes they're slightly incomprehensible to people who don't have any Irish, because they are playing between the two languages as well. Irish writers have a lot of fun with that.

I don't have any Irish, and I soon learned not to email the author about a particular word or phrase that baffled me, because the response was a regular, politely emphatic 'No glossary'. Which is fair enough, because there's nothing in *A Girl Is a Half-formed Thing* that cannot be looked up in a dictionary or online. The meaning of a few Gaelic words and phrases is immediately clear in the context (such as the countdown to a drinking game: 'A huan, a dó, a huan do tre' (standing for the Irish Gaelic 'aon, dó, trí'), as is that of Irish idioms ('Mucus stogging up my nose') and pronunciations ('troat' for 'throat').

There are some odd examples of onomatopoeia ('Pthoo too' when spitting out loose strands of rolling tobacco) as well as many lovely portmanteau words – perhaps my favourite is 'glitching', a combination of glancing and twitching. A deliberately impoverished vocabulary is often enriched by some extraordinary coinages; James Wood in his review for *The New Yorker* singled out 'plomp' ('a plomp load of books'), 'harlotting', 'forlorning', 'wilter' and 'miracling'.

There's also a technique that relies on omission, or inclusion by implication, as in an early passage in which the mother's breast is entirely present but never mentioned: 'I struggle up to. I struggle from. The smell of milk now. Going dim. Going blank. Going white.' There are constant repetitions, redundancies, non sequiturs and all the other clutter that surrounds and supports language and enables speech to happen. McBridean language churns and boils or trickles and laps, it can be fast or slow, loud and harsh or soft and soothing. There are passages of serene calm and of terrible ferocity. There are polyvocal sequences where speech is unallocated, as in the kitchen at the wake; there are monologues by (among others) the Mother and the grandfather (both tragicomic set pieces which capture emotional tides of frustration, anger and reproach). Verbs routinely become nouns ('wiping off all my begins') and nouns take verbal form ('Can he see all about me patients miracling well?'). Verbs also tend to take their uninflected base form, a neat way of suggesting 'natural' unconscious or preconscious thought before 'cultural' grammar is imposed on articulate utterance.

All of which confirms the fears of the timid reader – that this is not a book to skim idly on the beach, not a book that offers the conventional satisfactions. The academic and author John Sutherland wrote in a *Guardian* piece: 'This is not "narrative". It's a bunch of clues at the scene of the novel.' We might extend Sutherland's analogy and say that many episodes in this novel resemble the chalk outline of a murder victim, from which we must build up an image of what happened, and how. The novel is not in any sense cryptic because it reveals far more than it conceals, but what it reveals is always partial, limited to the girl's own perspective. It's notable how little of what happens in the book is imaginary or conditional or speculative (apart from odd moments when, for instance, the girl imagines living in the 1920s as Zelda Fitgerald).

There isn't a single word or phrase that will confuse any reader prepared to make the effort. It's the combination of words that may present a challenge, but it's always a worthwhile challenge because the act of understanding brings (and this may seem odd given the harshness of the subject matter) tremendous and continuing satisfaction and pleasure. I can only urge you to read the novel several times (with a good break in between) and experience for yourself a uniquely kaleidoscopic experience as the parts seem to reconfigure and an entirely different book emerges, with different emphases, different patterns and feelings.

The most challenging manipulations of the text are during the violent assault and rape at the end – when language becomes contorted and the fonts go slightly wild. This is the book at its most self-consciously literary and a reminder that the girl is thing of words, a modernist construct. She is made of truth, not facts. Readers such as Rebecca who object to the 'ungrammatical' form of McBridean English are blinding themselves to what is known as the 'propositional content' of her prose, what it *means*. They are rejecting truth because it doesn't respect whatever grammatical conventions they were taught at school. But language is natural and grammar is cultural, a set of arbitrary rules to which there are countless exceptions. McBridean prose, in its high artistry, gives primacy to the natural.

I'll do. My. For you. My best for you.

McBride's idiosyncratic punctuation is the most easily misunderstood aspect of her prose. There are, first of all, a lot of full stops (or periods, if you prefer). Full stops (and the subsequent capital letter) make any page of her writing instantly recognisable. This is no small thing in itself – McBride's prose on the page has a distinctive appearance that makes an immediate impact before we even begin reading. She does use commas too, if sparingly, although there's never anything as exotic as a semicolon.

Theodor Adorno wrote in a playful 1956 essay that punctuation marks were traffic signals – 'Exclamation points are red, colons green, dashes call a halt' – and insisted that they were marks of oral delivery. For most of us punctuation is a prompt to pause, or to slow down – it shows us where to breathe, literally (if we're reading aloud) and mentally. The author has said that she would prefer her readers to read quickly, ignoring the traffic lights as it were, and the pace of her audio recording of the book, while not rushed, is certainly headlong.

A troubling example of McBride's rhythmic rhymes (in a text which is an almost unlimited source of troubling examples) is a passage already cited, in which the girl delivers a list of barely differentiated sexual encounters connected by the phrase 'I met a man'. The man could be the same man in each case, of course, but we are left in no doubt that this is all part of her dense sexual history: 'I met a man. I met a man. I let him throw me round the bed. And smoked, me, spliffs and choked my neck until I said I was dead.'

The violence is all the more troubling for its sing-song rhyme:

I met a man
I met a man
I let him throw me round the bed
And smoked, me, spliffs
And choked my neck
Until I said
I was dead.

This could be a hand-clapping playground game, or a sexualised version of baby tuckoo's moocow coming down the road. Much earlier in the novel, the compressed paragraph in which the father leaves the family – 'He left her with a fifty pound note. Take care! Stroke combing full, untidied hair. Thinking I think of you and me. Our empty spaces where fathers should be.' – can be teased out into another nursery rhyme:

He left her with a fifty pound note.
Take care!
Stroke combing full, untidied hair.
Thinking I think of you and me.
Our empty spaces where fathers should be.

The anguish is all the greater for its jaunty expression, and the reader's feeling that this is how a child would call on simple resources, the only resources they have, to make sense of traumatic change. This nursery prose is touching and effective, and the following passage, almost a coda, featured on the cover of the original Galley Beggar Press edition:

> I think your face the very best. When we were we were we were young. When you were little and I was girl. Once upon a time.

Here in concentrated form are many McBridean tropes – the simple language, the short phrases with their headlong progression, the incantatory, almost onomatopoeic repetition, the balanced pairs of prompt words, the destabilising omission of the article, the fairy-tale collocation ('Once upon a time') that here serves to close down a memory rather than open up a story. There is the seamless elision between present and past, a gentle wistfulness and underlying sense of loss and sadness.

A McBridean 'sentence' (if by that we mean whatever happens after one full stop and before the next) can be a single word, and that word is often, simply and complicatedly, 'I'. This annoys some readers, as if nobody in real life would ever utter the first-person pronoun and leave it at that. In fact, prompted by reading the novel, I did a little unsystematic research and found that it's actually commonplace (and especially at the start of utterances which begin 'I, er', or I, um'. We do not, generally, speak in grammatically impeccable sentences (unless reading from a polished script, or reciting from memory) because the mind doesn't organise language into neat subject/verb/object combinations. There are of course some public speakers gifted with rhetorical skills that allow for almost supernatural levels of grammatical accuracy, but they are exceptions; and, let's not forget, our culture is one in which incoherent sincerity (at one extreme) and shallow loquacity (at the other) count for far more than eloquence, which is often viewed with suspicion.

For eloquence see the novel's closing lines:

> There now. There now. That just was life. And now.

What?
My name is gone.

The moment of oblivion ends as simply as the moment of consciousness that began with 'For you' on page 1. A diminuendo of monosyllables, with a faint ambiguity in the comforting maternal connotations of 'There now. There now.' On a narrative level the girl is drowning, has drowned. The catastrophe has happened. Her name ('My I') is gone and with her name her being. With the loss of her name the girl relinquishes any purchase on life, on consciousness. The book doesn't so much end as stop dead.

McBride has discovered and occupied a space on the spectrum between Joyce and Beckett – the former a maximalist, putting the world into a book and claiming, famously, that if the real city of Dublin ever disappeared it could be recreated by consulting the pages of *Ulysses*; the latter a spartan yet tirelessly productive minimalist, paring away, working more and more with less and less. Feast and famine, flood and drought. She employs a Beckettian approach to achieve a Joycean effect – the throb and pulse of life in all its messiness and contingency. In common with both authors she has a virtuosic command of language, a feel for how words rub up against one another, how fragments can build a whole greater than their parts. Her virtuosity is deep-rooted, not only in the modernist tradition that dates back a century or so, but in older traditions, in poetry and myth.

'The Stolen Child' and the Lir legend

A Girl Is a Half-formed Thing contains (although the author refuses to give away much detail) many literary references to favourite books and authors. Two of these are of central importance in any understanding of the novel.

The title of the final section of the novel owes a debt to W. B. Yeats, among the greatest of Irish poets, whose influence can be felt throughout the novel. His poem 'The Stolen Child' was published in 1889 in *The Wanderings of Oisin and Other Poems*, Yeats's first regularly published book, of which only 500 copies were printed. It is widely regarded as one of his finest early poems.

Where dips the rocky highland
Of Sleuth Wood in the lake,
There lies a leafy island
Where flapping herons wake
The drowsy water rats;
There we've hid our faery vats,
Full of berries
And of reddest stolen cherries.
Come away, O human child!
To the waters and the wild
With a faery, hand in hand,
For the world's more full of weeping than you can understand.

Where the wave of moonlight glosses
The dim gray sands with light,
Far off by furthest Rosses
We foot it all the night,
Weaving olden dances
Mingling hands and mingling glances
Till the moon has taken flight;
To and fro we leap
And chase the frothy bubbles,
While the world is full of troubles
And anxious in its sleep.
Come away, O human child!
To the waters and the wild
With a faery, hand in hand,
For the world's more full of weeping than you can understand.

Where the wandering water gushes
From the hills above Glen-Car,
In pools among the rushes

That scarce could bathe a star,
We seek for slumbering trout
And whispering in their ears
Give them unquiet dreams;
Leaning softly out
From ferns that drop their tears
Over the young streams.
Come away, O human child!
To the waters and the wild
With a faery, hand in hand,
For the world's more full of weeping than you can understand.

Away with us he's going,
The solemn-eyed:
He'll hear no more the lowing
Of the calves on the warm hillside
Or the kettle on the hob
Sing peace into his breast,
Or see the brown mice bob
Round and round the oatmeal chest.
For he comes, the human child,
To the waters and the wild
With a faery, hand in hand,
For the world's more full of weeping than he can understand.

The author read this poem to an audience in Vancouver during her North American promotional tour in 2014, followed by what she calls her 'paltry bastardisation' of it in the novel. This she did, she said, 'in order to make clear the difference between what I was attempting and what poetry does'.

I have an aversion to the more esoteric side of Yeats, but that repeated heptametric line is magnificent: 'For the world's more full of weeping than you can understand.' It has a beguiling, hypnotic quality – and we are beguiled as the boy is beguiled, as the fairies lure him away. The 'solemn-eyed' boy is escorted to the leafy island where the faeries live. It's a poem about sundering and loss in which childhood is equated with innocence, and innocence is a good thing. The title is misleading as the boy is neither 'stolen' nor 'abducted' but rather lured, or charmed, into following his faery escorts.

McBride achieves equally impressive if less existential effects with a fourteen-syllable heptametric line: 'Swish swish all the hospital doors in the world sound the same.' This may be no more than a coincidence, but the structure of the line and the presence of 'world' is surely an echo of Yeats. McBride was aware of Yeats from an early age and learned some of his poetry by heart, so it should come as no surprise if elements of the poet's prosody run deep beneath her prose. Her novel shares with Yeats's poem a deep engagement with the natural world, the local topography of lakes and woods, 'the waters and the wilds' and – most significantly – the central figure of the boy-child.

Another underlying myth, far older than anything in Yeats, is central to an understanding of the novel. *The Children of Lir* is an Irish legend (*Clann Lir* and *Leanaí Lir* are the variant original titles) which forms part of the Irish Mythological Cycle made up of prose and poems derived from medieval manuscripts.

Bodb Derg was elected the king of the Tuath(a) Dé Danann (usually translated as 'people of the goddess Danu'), a supernatural race representing the gods of Gaelic Ireland in the pre-Christian era, a kind of Olympian cohort. His election angered Lir, a sea god, and to appease him Bodb gave one of his daughters, Aoibh, in marriage. She bore Lir four children: one girl, Fionnuala, and three sons – Aodh and the twins Fiachra and Conn. When Aoibh died, much mourned by her children, Bodb sent another of his daughters, Aoife, to marry Lir and care for his children.

Aoife, jealous of her stepchildren's love for one another, ordered her servant to kill them, but the servant refused. In a rage she then tried to kill them herself, but, lacking the courage to do so, used her magic powers to turn the four children into swans, chanting this song:

> Out with you upon the wild waves, Children of the King!
> Henceforth your cries shall be with the flocks of birds.

Hearing of this Bodb transformed Aoife into an air demon for the rest of eternity. The children had to spend 900 hundred years in the grip of Aoife's magic spell; the first 300 years as swans on a lake near their father's castle, called Lough Derravaragh; the next 300 years in the Sea of Moyle; and then 300 years on the waters of Irrus Domnann Erris, near Inishglora Island. Only the blessing of a monk – the arrival of St Patrick to convert Ireland to Christianity – could break the spell.

During their nine centuries of cygnine enchantment the four children were manacled to one another with silver chains. But Deoch, daughter of the King of Munster and wife of the King of Leinster, wanted the four swans for her own, so she instructed her husband Lairgean to attack the monastery and seize the swans. He did so, but the attack broke the silver chains and the four swans were transformed – not into children but into withered old people.

There are other versions of the legend, in one of which the four children are released from the spell by the tolling of a church bell and, before they die soon after, are baptised and then buried together in a shared grave. In another ending, the four live miserably on the three lakes for 900 years before hearing the bell and returning to the land, where a priest finds them. The swans ask the priest to turn them back into humans, which he does, but again they return not as children but as aged relics.

There are explicit references in *A Girl* to the Lir myth in the passage that begins:

> I dream of underground where the warm earth is where the fire goes. Where we're sleep creep you and me in holes. In burrows rabbits safe from rain. Roots growing caverns round our heads. And blind as mice popped out and new and cling and soft our bright pink skin. Who's there? There's no one. You and only me. We sing. We lilt our chamber. No one coming. And we lie. A thousand years of sleep. And get beards wrinkle old and small and we. Troubleless in our deep. (p.176

Performed by the author on the audiobook recording, this

passage is memorable and moving – the invocation and repetition of 'roots' takes us back to the doctor's words on the first page ('It's all through his brain like the roots of trees'), providing a complex convergence of metaphor and allegory, and the language of illness, dreams and mythology. The phrase 'We lilt our chamber' captures the delicate intimacy, innocent trust and mutual dependency of the brother and sister, their safe enclosure away from the wild world.

The most explicit reference to the myth comes on the penultimate page:

> You say. You tell. You tell me your name and tell me the truth this time. Ssssh. We'll live there for a thousand Lir years. There now. There now. Take my hand.

'There now. There now' is repeated three lines before the end of the novel, and combines the conventional expression of comfort and consolation with a sweeping and elegant topographical and temporal gesture – there, then; here now – which suggests the continuity of the myth in time and the ambitious reach of this novel.

I asked Jarlath Killeen for his views on the way McBride employs the myth as a kind of substructure, as Joyce used the *Odyssey* as an organising principle of *Ulysses*:

> I think the connection of the novel to the Children of Lir relates to the sacrifice of childhood (and children) in that myth, and the central place of the lake in both stories. They are also both stories of transformation and (perhaps) transfiguration. The link to 'The Stolen Child' is interesting, and Yeats has always been important to Eimear.

Killeen also suggested looking at Yeats's 'The White Birds', written in 1892 for Maud Gonne the day after the poet had unsuccessfully proposed marriage as the pair took a walk along the cliffs of Howth, south of Dublin. Gonne later recalled that that she had told Yeats that she would rather be a seagull than any other bird, and Yeats posted her the poem three days later.

Would that we were, my beloved, white birds on the foam of the sea!
We tire of the flame of the meteor, before it can fade and flee;
And the flame of the blue star of twilight, hung low on the rim of
    the sky,
Has awakened in our hearts, my beloved, a sadness that may not die.

A weariness comes from those dreamers, dew-dabbled, the lily and
    rose;
Ah, dream not of them, my beloved, the flame of the meteor that
    goes,
Or the flame of the blue star that lingers hung low in the fall of the
    dew:
For I would we were changed to white birds on the wandering foam:
    I and you!

I am haunted by numberless islands, and many a Danaan shore,
Where Time would surely forget us, and Sorrow come near us no
    more;
Soon far from the rose and the lily, and fret of the flames would we
    be,
Were we only white birds, my beloved, buoyed out on the foam of
    the sea!

The 'Danaan shore' refers to the imaginary realm of Tir na nOg. Gonne's wish to be a seagull (which links to the Lir legend and the bird imagery in A *Girl Is a Half-formed Thing*) was interpreted by Yeats as a desire for freedom, and a wish to escape from sorrow and the passage of time. His wish was for an escape from the circumstances – social and political – that kept them apart.

Yeats contrasted a mythic Ireland as a repository of ancient wisdom with his view of modern urban England, constrained by bourgeois conventions, and Killeen suggests there is a corresponding contrast between the unspecified west coast city where the girl attends university and the small country town where she and her brother are raised. He emphasises that the Yeatsian child embodies a link between the ancient and the modern, and that the child's innocence, upon which such a link depends, will be lost on growing up and becoming involved in the world.

The figure of the child in Yeats often stands for the link between the contemporary and the ancient, though the threat is that the child will be ruined by growing up and involvement in the dirty business of money-making. In 'The Stolen Child' the fairies come to rescue the child from potentially being destroyed by maturity, and while Yeats valorises the world of faery, he is also clear that they are frightening figures.

A Girl Is a Half-formed Thing taps into these faery myths and also, Killeen notes, the Irish Gothic tradition:

> Ireland in these kinds of narratives is a dislocated space, a kind of distorted mirror image of the 'Ireland of the Welcomes' associated with popular culture more generally – we could call it the Mr Hyde version of the tourist's Dr Jekyll Ireland. These narratives are often motivated by a savage love of the country.

Killeen cites Patrick McCabe's *The Butcher Boy* (1992), a first-person account of Irish small-town life with a teenage narrator, and Edna O'Brien's *Night* (1972), a novel praised by McBride in an *Irish Times* article (7 March 2015) and which, in its darkly subtle use of myth and legend, can also be seen as an influence.

Most writers have equivocal feelings about their home country, their culture, their family. There's certainly a fierce love – what Killeen and others have called 'the attraction of repulsion' – in McBride's descriptions of the family gathering at the grandfather's wake, or the drunken nights in the pub following the girl's return to university. John Sutherland provoked some hostile online responses when he asked the rhetorical question, in his *Guardian* piece on McBride: 'Why does Irish fiction so hate Ireland?' He quoted Joyce's line about Ireland being 'the old sow that eats its farrow', although we should remember the speaker is not Joyce himself but the character Stephen Dedalus. One might turn Sutherland's question around and ask: why does Ireland so hate its writers? If Ireland is a complacent, narrow-minded and inward-looking society (it's hard to name any country that isn't), it's worth noting that writers and artists often thrive in such societies, kicking against the pricks – or, as Joyce put it, speaking on behalf of all writers: 'Squeeze us, we are olives.'

The last words of *A Girl*, the last words of the girl, are serene and conclusive: 'My name is gone.' Her name will remain unknown to us, and unknowable, and in any case was never wholly hers. It was bestowed by her brother in the first lines of the book and known only, we infer, to the pair of them, as co-conspirators.

3 Galley Beggars

The Book Hive

Norwich, the county town of Norfolk, boasts a magnificent cathedral and (since the RAF firebombed Dresden in 1945) the largest number of pre-Reformation churches in Europe. It can paradoxically lay claim to being the least religious city in England, with the largest proportion of census respondents with no reported faith. It is also the city where, in the 14th century, the very first book in English by a woman was published: *The Revelations of Divine Love,* a collection of Christian mystical devotions was written by Julian of Norwich (1342–*c.*1416). The real name of the author is unknown and 'Julian' derives from the fact that her anchoress's cell was built onto the wall of the Norman Church of St Julian in Kilderkin Way.

Her saintliness was strikingly masochistic – she prayed when young to be afflicted with a mortal illness that would bring her close to death, the better to experience the sufferings of Christ and the fate of all humanity. Revelations followed and she recovered, miraculously. It was from Julian of Norwich that T. S. Eliot adopted the resonant lines of 'Little Gidding', the fourth of his *Four Quartets*:

> And all shall be well and
> All manner of thing shall be well

A Girl Is a Half-formed Thing was first published by the Norwich-based Galley Beggar Press, co-founded by Henry Layte, Sam Jordison and Eloise Millar. Without their belief in the book, it would quite possibly remain unpublished to this day.

Henry Layte studied drama at Hull University and then

worked for eight years as an actor, running a small theatre company called Rank Taxi, the name coming from the old red London cab which was the company vehicle. He'd started writing plays as an undergraduate and that, along with directing, soon became his main interest. After meeting his future wife, Sian, he decided to stay in London while doing a part-time MA in Creative Writing at Oxford, later working in the National Theatre bookshop and living in Brixton. In early 2006 they moved to Norwich, where Henry had previously lived with his parents.

Henry's mother Caroline died of cancer in October 2008, aged 55, and her early death forced Henry to take stock of his life. She had left him some money and he had a choice: either to use it as a deposit on a house or to invest in something that could provide him with an income and some free time in which to write. He also wanted to be his own boss and it was his brother Sam, who had also recently moved back to Norwich, who suggested opening a bookshop. The city at that time could boast two branches of the Waterstones chain and one of the now-defunct Borders, but there was no independent bookshop.

He had set his heart on a distinctive 19th-century building in a pedestrianised thoroughfare running parallel to Castle Meadow. Number 53 London Street is built on a slight slope which gives the structure a slightly off-balance, top-heavy look, as if it's staggering as it rounds the corner to the narrow St Andrew's Hill. Contracts were exchanged and the Layte brothers together spent six weeks renovating the dilapidated interior, retaining the old 'Interflora' sign from the days when the place was run by a florist. With the paint still wet on the walls the Book Hive opened in October 2009, a year to the day since the death of Caroline Layte, whose legacy had made it possible. Two years later the Book Hive was voted by readers of a national broadsheet as 'Best Independent Bookshop in Britain'.

Looking back more than five years later, Henry seems bemused at how things turned out: 'I had no idea how to run a business, no idea how to run a shop, really, although I'd seen it done before a lot, and Sian found out she was pregnant a few days before we opened. It was a challenging time.'

There was no plan to become a publisher. He simply wanted to create a particular kind of place:

> My ethos for the shop was always to create a place which felt like you were walking into someone's house who had an amazing collection of books over various subjects, laid out easily so you could pick them up and have a read, the difference being they were all for sale. I had no interest in celebrity writers, the bestseller lists, anything like that, just interesting well-made and well-written books.

During the first eighteen months of trading that Henry Layte got to know Sam Jordison and Eloise ('Elly') Millar, a Norwich couple who were, as Henry puts it, 'in the literary world'. Sam and Elly originally met in Cambridge, where they studied Classics and English Literature respectively, but only got to know one another after graduating in 1999. For three years from 2000 they were both employed as night-shift subeditors on the *Guardian*. Sam, while completing an MA in Journalism at Goldsmiths College in south London, was diverted into the production of what he calls 'toilet books' as the co-author, with Dan Kieran, of the bestselling series called *Crap Towns*. Sam talked his way back into journalism and started working for the *Guardian* in 2006, writing regularly about books and hosting an online reading group. He is energetic, plain-speaking, non-establishment, and has a well-informed love of good writing coupled with an eloquent loathing for Jeff Bezos, the founder and CEO of the Amazon organisation.

In the same week in late 2002 Sam and Elly landed separate book deals (Sam with Macmillan for *Crap Towns*, Elly for her novel *Wednesday's Child*, published by Virago in 2005), and they decided to live on the advances for as long as they could by moving to somewhere cheaper. They went first to Somerset, then a friend's aunt's house in Oxford and finally spent a few months in North Carolina. They eventually moved to Norwich, where they married in 2008, and became regular visitors to the Book Hive. Sam recalls:

> We would chat in the shop about books and bemoan the fact that so many are published and so much of it is utter crap, and a shop like the Hive, which sought to sell only the better stuff, was a good place to be able to make a really good example of what publishers could do if they wanted to, if they were braver and taking more risks – there are shops that will sell it and people who will buy it.

Then the White Goddess intervened, in the shape of a family friend. Simon Gough owned an antiquarian bookshop in north Norfolk attached to Henry Layte's father's antique business. The Laytes and the Goughs were unrelated but formed a loose kind of extended family, spending holidays in Majorca together. Gough was a great-nephew of the poet Robert Graves and in 1960, at the age of 17, spent a summer in Majorca with Graves and his second wife, Beryl, at their house in the village of Deia. Nearby lived Margot Callas, the latest in a succession of the poet's beautiful young muses, through whom the White Goddess herself communicated directly to the poet. Gough became besotted with Callas and, when she suddenly left for Madrid, Graves asked his great-nephew to follow her and report back to him. What happened next would form the basis for his book.

Following a diagnosis of lymphoma in 1988, Gough took early retirement to dedicate himself to writing the story of his time with Graves and his circle. Henry recalls:

> He would come to our house for dinner at least once a week and my parents would go there another day in the week and he would read aloud new drafts – there were always piles of drafts of it lying around – it was just something that everyone lived with (with, it has to be said, less and less patience as the years rolled by, but nonetheless everyone, especially his wife, stuck by him and it). In late 2010 Simon was told that his cancer – which he had had for many years and in fact had been the spur to write his story in the first place – was back, and

it was angry. In a final fling of desperation he told me one night that fuck it, he'd had enough, he was going to self-publish his manuscript at great expense, which he had whittled down to 1,000 pages (and it was only the first volume!) and was going to give it to family and friends. He'd had enough of no one being interested but wanted to see it in print. I stopped him, seeing that maybe this could be our jumping-off point for publishing.

Galley Beggar Press was funded by Henry's friends and family – the music producer Rollo Armstrong, an old friend whose father was a publisher, lent £5,000 and Henry's godfather Charles Carey made a generous donation. Other backers rallied round. The three founders – Layte, Jordison and Millar – were looking for authors with completed books who had been turned down by mainstream publishers rather than bright young talents at the start of their careers. Gough's manuscript, despite its great length, seemed to fit the bill perfectly. Henry read a copy, telling his co-founders that this might just be the book with which to launch the new venture. In March 2011 he wrote to Gough who, after some thought, was happy to offer the book to the new firm. The two men then began work on reducing the manuscript to a manageable length.

The designer Niki Medlik happened to be visiting her sister in Norwich and came with her one day to the Book Hive. They fell into conversation with the proprietor. Niki recalls:

> It was great for me, as head of jacket design at Thames and Hudson, to walk round the shop with a bookseller who was such a nice man, who obviously had a good eye for design, and to hear about what sold well, what he thought worked, etc etc. He told me he had started his own publishers, and they were just producing their first book. He wasn't sure about the cover design, so I said I would be happy to look at it. I gave him my card when I left, and he sent me the cover for *The White Goddess*, a title I was to know and love.

She suggested to Henry that she should make three designs on spec and that if he liked any of them she would be paid.

This was the beginning of hours of very pleasurable research in independent bookshops round London. It was an opportunity to style a publishing imprint, as I realised that if this was their first cover, then they also needed their whole identity to be resolved, and their branding set before it could be done. They had what I thought was a brilliant logo already, which Henry had got one of his mates to design, but I spent many hours and there were many variations using British and American themes on the branding itself before I came to the final solution.

The mate of Henry's who designed the Galley Beggar Press logo was a fellow drama graduate from Hull. Philip Bosworth – known as 'Boz' – is an actor and an artist and illustrator. Elly recalls the thinking behind the logo:

> We wanted something impish – that had some sort of nod to the idea of a mischief-maker (which is essentially what we wanted/want to be). So Puck had an outing, as did Robin Goodfellow, as did plain-old Lucifer . . . In the end I pulled Katharine Brigg's *Encyclopedia of Fairies* off my bookshelves. From this I drew up a list of around twenty names. Hinkypunk was one of the contenders – but I think for everyone, immediately, Galley Beggar stood out. Partly because of the 'galley' thing, partly because they – galley beggars – are properly annoying little sods . . . it was perfect.

Niki designed around fifty covers before returning to Norwich, where she met the three Galley Beggars in a coffee shop. The four squeezed into a corner around her laptop and she showed them around twenty ideas. There was, happily, complete agreement between them and the final design was chosen without any fuss.

> It was the best jacket meeting I had ever had – not the fraught argumentative occasion I was used to. The black book was born. As we walked along the street, I rather nervously asked if they wanted me to do the job. 'Of course!' they replied.

Niki had designed the cover to be the first of many, a brand that would work for all future titles and give Galley Beggar

Press a strong, recognisable identity on the bookshop shelf. She chose sunshine yellow as the obvious second colour for *The White Goddess* and made sure that the printer got the lettering to match the splash of the endpapers. She was amazed at how easy the Galley Beggars made it seem to produce a high-quality book on a tiny budget:

> I think lots of professionals in the business worked for them for free or for very little just because we believed in what they were doing and because Henry is so likeable and has contacts everywhere. Also, they didn't know what could go wrong/what mistakes could be made, so there was no fear of screwing up like there is in a big publishing house (where much larger sums of money are at risk too). I would say things like, 'Do you have a barcode for me?' and they would say, 'Oh! Where do we get one of those?' Then within the hour one would drop into my inbox.

The White Goddess: An Encounter was launched in August 2012 at the Voewood Festival in north Norfolk, and early reviews were positive. Throughout the process of publishing Gough's memoir the three Galley Beggar co-founders had also been looking for other things to publish. Eloise had a manuscript from an author called Andrew Lovett – *Everlasting Lane* – and the three agreed that it would be their next title, although the manuscript needed some work. The process was very simple – the three co-founders had to agree and if any one of them didn't the other two wouldn't pursue the matter. As things turned out they did not publish *Everlasting Lane* until after their second title, the first book by an unknown author who had recently moved to Norwich from Ireland.

An encounter

Henry first met William Galinsky in May 2011, soon after Galinsky and his wife had moved from Cork to Norwich. Layte told William about setting up Galley Beggar and his excitement at their first title. William mentioned casually that his wife had written a book and Henry said, with a publisher's non-committal courtesy, that he would be pleased to have a look at a manuscript. Nothing happened.

On 1 June Henry emailed William to say that a book he had ordered was now available. The reply would have momentous consequences:

> Thanks for that Henry. Will be in to pick it up. My wife's name is Eimear McBride. [. . .] If you want to meet her I can put you in touch. She is currently working on beast number 2.

To which Henry replied:

> I would be very interested in having a chat with Eimear. I wonder if you might be able to give me an email address for her. This would just be for a chat of course. I understand that to be approached by a new, small publisher might seem like a bit of a backwards move after having been in talks with the big boys, but our first author – and the next in the pipeline – were both in exactly the same situation. And whatever – a chat can't hurt anyone!

Following this flurry of exchanges nothing happened again. Then on 30 August William emailed again, with an apology:

> Henry – apologies, looking back through the email string yesterday I told you that Eimear would contact you and Eimear that you would contact her which probably explains why you haven't hooked up. Sorry about that. I will make an introduction between you both.

After three months of what Eimear McBride would later describe as 'Feydeau farce' an email finally arrived from the author herself on 1 September:

> I am the Eimear in question. Apparently William told you that I'd be in touch while telling me that you'd be in touch. So to avoid any further Scooby Doo mysteries I thought I'd say hello and that I have a book and if you're interested in reading it, I'd be very pleased to drop a copy in to you. Alternatively, if you'd prefer to check I'm not mad

before making the effort, we could have a cup of coffee first. Let me know what suits you.

Henry told her told her he would like to take the manuscript away on holiday in a week's time, to which she replied: 'That's no problem. I'll drop one in to you. I should warn you though, it's probably not holiday reading for the faint-hearted . . .' A manuscript was dropped off at the Book Hive and Henry took it away to France on a late September break. Apart from the author's vague warning he had no idea at all of what to expect. When he arrived back in Norwich he immediately emailed the author:

> I think your book is absolutely stunning. I read it over a few days when I first went away and was captivated by it. There is so much to say about it − its subject, the writing − (of course) − why it works, HOW it works . . . It really was an inspiring experience reading it . . . Perhaps we might arrange to meet, then, at some point. If nothing comes of it, I am grateful to have read it, but if we can now have a chance to show you what/who WE are, then, well . . . who knows? I for one am excited at the possibilities, and trying not to be, yet!

The author had finally found a publisher willing to commit to her 'difficult', uncommercial novel, a publisher who loved the book and didn't have to persuade a marketing team to back his judgement. That the publisher was on her doorstep in Norwich was an unexpected bonus.

Eimear and Henry met again at the Book Hive a few days later, on 6 October. They talked through the situation, with Henry gently explaining that since Galley Beggar hadn't yet published their first book and since so much depended on *that*, and since there was no money coming in and the future was so uncertain that they couldn't commit, yet, to her book, but would like to when the time came, if it came. It wasn't a great start, as Henry admits: 'It wasn't a hugely inspiring meeting for her and I don't think she was very happy when she left.'

Henry continues:

The first hurdle was getting the others on board, only because, for any of us bringing something to the table, that was the first hurdle. Eloise was clearly in favour and it only remained for Sam to like it. The next contact I had was Eimear was six months later in May 2012, telling her that we would love to publish it and we should start trying to meet up (she had never met Sam and Eloise before) to talk about how and when and all that.

Meanwhile Elly was working hard to put a case together for Arts Council funding, but no application was made as the three Galley Beggars were all too busy with editing *The White Goddess* and running the bookshop. The Gough book was a reasonably safe bet, Henry felt, given its link to Robert Graves, but the real risk was that if Galley Beggar now took on the publication of *A Girl Is a Half-formed Thing* and it bombed then the company would plunge straight back into debt. Given the costs incurred in setting up the Book Hive and the parlous state of the economy both national and local, Henry was anxious:

> I was terrified the risk might not work – after all, money men at bigger places had said it wouldn't, had they not? I was also buying a house and we were expecting another child, so the stakes seemed horribly high.

In September 2012 the Book Hive hosted an event at which Pete Ayrton, the legendary Serpent's Tail publisher, gave a talk about how small publishers were the people picking up the mess left behind by the marketing men at bigger houses. This prompted Henry to talk with Sam and Eloise, restating his commitment to Galley Beggar's founding principles and quelling any fears about the risks inherent in what they were taking on. The three were agreed, and their commitment to their second book was reaffirmed.

Henry and Sian had a new baby and were moving house. He was exhausted from working with Simon Gough on the *White Goddess* manuscript, from which 400 pages had to be painstakingly excised, then organising the publicity for the book's launch.

It was Elly who now became more closely involved with the author, and she remembers the early days of their association:

> We lived around the corner from each other (and what luck to have a genius living round the corner when you're setting up a publishing company) so got to know her as a new mother as well as a supremely talented writer. Our first big discussion was over editorial, when she was tremendously impressive. But initially we also got a sense of huge relief from her – and happiness. That at last some people believed in her art and were going to take a risk on her book . . .

Sam had overcome his earlier misgivings and was now completely convinced that the book should be published. One Sunday late in October 2012 Henry and Sian and Eimear and William met for lunch at Sam and Elly's tiny terraced house for what Elly remembers as

> a very jolly, squashed occasion: three children under five, six adults, a table full of food – and a quick half hour beforehand where we asked Eimear if we could publish her, she said yes, and Henry rushed down to the local Co-op to buy a bottle of champagne. In the days after that I put in our offer, complete with our tiny advance (£1,000 originally, but we had to drop this down to £600, as we needed all the money we could save for production/publicity) – and the rest is history.

Even that much-reduced advance wasn't forthcoming, as Henry admits:

> We didn't in fact pay her her £600 for ages as we couldn't afford it and it was a bit of a sore point for Eimear after a while. She was very generous in saying just give it when you get it, but it took a while . . .

The Galley Beggars met their author for editing meetings at the Mulberry Tree pub in Unthank Road, close to their respective homes. Here over cups of coffee (it's that kind of pub) much painstaking editorial work was carried out. Sam recalls:

> Essentially the book was all there and one of the most complete and finished manuscripts any publisher is likely to see. There were a few tiny suggestions and changes within the main body of the text. But

essentially, what can you say, other than that's bloody good? I think what I said, in fact, was 'Don't worry, you're going to win a shitload of prizes'. At the time Eimear looked at me like I wasn't serious . . .

But he had concerns about the manuscript and suggested substantial alterations, which led to plenty of what the author calls 'head-loggering'. The opening section was changed, and unquestionably for the better, for which Sam must take much credit. As a commercially minded publisher he saw the need for an opening page that would not frighten off prospective readers.

> It was a question of timing and of introducing the reader to that in-credible pre-conscious prose. It was to do with the way you get inside the narrator's head. I thought the original opening caused conceptual difficulties. Explaining that wasn't easy! Eimear is quite rightly de-fensive of her work – but she was also a very good listener, and I did manage to persuade her. I count it as one of my greatest contributions to literature. But editorial is only ever as good as the writer. The reason I count my suggestion at the beginning as successful is that Eimear went off and wrote those incredible opening lines and sud-denly, everything slotted into place.

Sam was also worried about the end of the novel, and in this case lost the argument:

> I had an issue with the way the book ended. Here, luckily, Eimear won the argument, because I was essentially wrong. I've read in a few articles that we wanted a happy ending – which is hilarious and won-derful, but sadly not true. Imagine asking for a happy ending on *Girl*! But I did have a problem with the finality of the resolution and also was confused about the timing of things. Eimear convinced me – in the same way as I had convinced her about the beginning – that the ending had to be as it was, and oh boy was she right. But there was a question of timing, and the stage at which the girl dies. It was that sticking point that we managed to clear up which had – I think – led to my initial doubts. So that discussion was fruitful too.

Once the final version of the manuscript was complete the exacting business of copy-editing could begin. Eimear and Elly each had a marked-up manuscript copy of the book and the laborious process involved comparing the two copies and marking any final changes the author wished to make to the text. There were many tiny but significant recalibrations which Elly dutifully noted. As the two women worked through the manuscript Elly was deeply impressed:

> I think it was that night that I realised that Eimear was more than just an excellent writer: that she was the real thing, someone who was going to make it to the history books. Because each of the changes that she made – tiny adjustments of phrase, a small shift in the syntax – were so absolutely *right*, and so absolutely measured. It was an astonishing few hours, and I'll always be so glad that I bore witness to that.

They started at around seven in the evening and continued until two in the morning of the following day, by which time several bottles of wine had been polished off.

The version of the manuscript shows hundreds of changes, with at least one or two on almost every page. Most are minor alterations to spacing or punctuation, the odd hyphen added, a proper noun put into lower case (such as 'volvo'), numerals replaced by words and so on. Lexical changes are (as one might expect) all for the better and generally involve a simple cut, and in some cases a tweak to improve the rhythm or cadence of a line. For instance on page 125, 'I dither looking dither at your dither eyes thinking they don't know at all' is subtly improved by the fifth word becoming 'in', a more euphonious preposition, linking to the same vowel sound in 'thinking'; it also avoids the repetition of 'at'.

There are few noteworthy deletions. On page 61 the first new paragraph originally began 'Something sad not sure what', and a few lines later 'That's quite an impression young lady you made' has been cut down from 'That's quite an impression young lady you made on him. Tells everyone about his beautiful niece.' The earlier version opens up the narrative too much, and beyond the girl's perspective. The single most substantial cut is to some lines from a popular hymn that were to appear on page 196, sung by the visiting 'holy joes'. The author's choice was 'Be Not Afraid' ('You shall cross the barren desert but you shall not die of thirst'). Composed by the Jesuit priest Fr Robert J. Dufford (born 1943), it dated back to 1975 and therefore remained in copyright, so it was replaced with lines from Isaiah 43: 'Do not be afraid – I will save you. I have called you by name – you are mine.' It's no loss and, if anything, the 'recycling' of the lines from Isaiah, which appear in more fragmented form on the previous page, adds to the intensity of the episode.

Finally, and significantly, on the very last page of the novel the first-person pronoun is twice deleted. 'I turn. I look up' becomes 'Turn. Look up', appropriately enough, as the girl is about to cease to be. In fact the first-person pronoun is used for the last time, climactically, in the line 'What's left behind? What's it? It is. My name for me. My I.' This takes us back to the homophonic I/eye first encountered at the start of the book.

The copy-editing process now complete and with the publication date fast approaching, the book could be made up into advance copies and circulated to reviewers. How I came to receive my copy is another of the many happy coincidences surrounding the book's long-delayed appearance in print. Henry was stripping paint off the windows of the shop one morning when the writer Paul Willetts, who lives nearby, stopped for a chat. I'd first met Paul in 2003, when he published *Fear and Loathing in Fitzrovia*, his acclaimed biography of the Soho bohemian Julian Maclaren-Ross, a terrible role model for all writers. During their conversation Paul suggested that Henry should send a copy of Simon Gough's book to an old friend of mine called David Holzer, who has lived in Majorca for years and has many friends in the Deia community. Later that day Paul forwarded Holzer's email address to Henry and, as a serendipitous afterthought added mine, recommending me as a potential reviewer of forthcoming Galley Beggar Press publications.

First responses

My advance copy duly arrived in the post on 7 May with a note from Henry Layte:

> This is a Marmite book. Nothing about it elicits – or deserves – a mediocre reaction. It is for that reason that I urge you to have a read, because it was the discovery of what this book achieves that made it one of the most startling manuscripts I have come across.
>
> It is not always an easy read. But it is always rewarding. And that is why it deserves to be read by so many.

I'm regularly sent novels to review, but this was a first: a publisher telling me that I was unlikely to enjoy his book. I'm indifferent to Marmite, the yeast-based sandwich spread that has entered the language as a symbol of polarised taste, but I liked the suggestion that a mediocre reaction wasn't an option.

The advance copy had the usual featureless white wrappers and no identifying marks at all. There was nothing at all to go on – no blurbs, no brouhaha. I read the first few pages, was pleasantly baffled, and flicked to the back to check whether or not this was just a virtuoso opening. I was was impressed (a little daunted is closer to the truth) to see that whatever the author was doing on page 1 she was still doing 200 pages later. This was a book that would demand and, I hoped, repay close attention. It was special, in some yet-to-be apprehended way. It was something new.

About a week later I picked it up late one afternoon and started to read properly, with occasional breaks for fresh air and heaving, gulping sobs, finishing the book in the early hours of the following morning and having a restless night's sleep. It had made a deep impression on me. The following day I sent the acting fiction editor at the *TLS*, Toby Lichtig, a longish piece on Stan Barstow's collected short stories and added the following cover note:

> Have just finished reading *A Girl Is a Half-formed Thing* by Eimer [*sic*]

McBride and I have to say (all hyperbole aside) that it's an absolutely astonishing debut and I'd love to review it – she joins the vanishingly small roster of female experimental writers from Woolf to Duras and is every bit as good as the best of them. I envy and admire her and have never read anything like it. She's the real deal – a fully-formed and immediately essential modern writer. Hope that snags your attention!

It did. Toby contacted Galley Beggar Press for a copy, read it and a few days later emailed me back:

I've had a chance to look at the Eimear [he has editorial skills and research capabilities denied to lesser mortals] McBride book and I do think it looks very interesting, formally innovative, annoyingly unignorable. I'm very tight for space but if you think you could do justice to it in, say, 600 words, then it's all yours. I presume you don't need a copy? Why don't you aim to deliver for the end of the month?

I didn't need a copy – although I wish I now had a cache of first editions in lieu of a pension – and I have never since missed any opportunity to remind Toby of that 'annoyingly unignorable'. The Barstow review was put on hold and I dashed off 600 words, sent them in and thought no more about it. But as it turned out this was to be the first ever review of a book that would soon become an international literary sensation. It appeared in the *TLS* issue dated 17 June 2013 (auspiciously appearing in newsagents the previous day, Bloomsday) under the embarrassing headline 'Gob impressive'. Here it is in full, complete with my gaffe in the second paragraph:

Here is the opening paragraph of Eimear McBride's debut novel, *A Girl Is a Half-formed Thing*: 'For you. You'll soon. You'll give her name. In the stitches of her skin she'll wear your say. Mammy me? Yes you. Bounce the bed, I'd say. I'd say that's what you did. Then lay you down. They cut you round. Wait and hour and day.'

The two-year-old female narrator is, we soon learn, addressing her older brother (anonymously 'you' throughout). Within a few pages the reader's eye and ear have adapted to the surface oddness of the text, seduced by the beautiful syncopations of McBride's prose as she charts her unnamed narrator's development from infancy to the age of twenty. This is set against her growing alienation from a pious mother and the harsh demands of Irish Catholicism. Joyce comes to mind, of course, and this could be Molly Bloom's great-great-great-granddaughter's soliloquy: the story of a bright young woman who is argumentative, confused, sexually adventurous, sad and angry. Here's a passage from much later in the book, in which the narrator realizes that her brother may be seriously ill:

'I do not want. I do not want to hear this. But suddenly it's clawing all over me. Like flesh. Terror. Vast and alive. I think I know it. Something terrible is. The world's about to. The world's about to. Tip. No it isn't. Ha. Don't be silly. Stupid. Fine. Fine. Everything will be. Fine. Chew it lurks me. See and smell. In the corner of my eye. What. Something not so good.'

What McBride pins down here is the headlong, ungrammatical immediacy with which the mind responds to the world. A spartan lexicon captures the redundancy, repetition and inconsequentiality of the narrator's skittering thoughts, as she flinches from the painful truth. Her responses are half-formed, tentatively refined, contradicted and negated; then comes the astonishing flourish: 'Chew it lurks me.' Elsewhere, prepositions are routinely excised and verbs take their uninflected base form ('When they've gone out we see sitting prop in the bed'). That this elective spareness does not lead to monotony is down to McBride's virtuosic phrase-making in passages that are not just memorable but often unforgettable. I was repeatedly (as the author puts it) 'gob impressed'. Writing of this quality is rare and deserves a wide readership.

Apart from Joyce, other major influences seem to be Henry Green's *Living* and *Party Going* and the breathless accumulated fragments of Samuel Beckett's *How It Is*. But such models are subordinate to the author's own distinctive voice. The novel is reassuringly conventional in structure – a chronological account of school, adolescent rebellion, loss of virginity (a brilliantly rendered episode), conflicting loyalties, flight from home to college, undergraduate depravity, the death of a grandfather, a wake (also brilliantly rendered), a rejection of religion, and the psychological contortions of love and sex. Above all it explores the narrator's love for her dying brother, which underpins the most emotionally charged episodes in a very moving book.

The publisher tells us only that the author was born in Liverpool, raised in Ireland, studied in London and currently lives in Norfolk, where she is working on a second novel. This is something to anticipate with interest because Eimear McBride is a writer of remarkable power and originality.

I was quite wrong about Henry Green, as the author had not at the time read any of his modernist masterpieces. I was also quite wrong in assuming the first voice we hear is that of a child, an error that subsequent reviewers duplicated.

The previous month I had broken the critic's unwritten (and therefore unbinding) code of practice by sending Galley Beggar Press an advance copy of this review. This was to give them a chance to print stickers for the cover carrying a positive word or phrase from a literary hack which might lead to a few dozen extra sales. The review prompted the publishers to take a gamble and commission Clays of Bungay to print another 500 copies, bringing the print run up to 1,000. (Collectors should note that the true first edition is the one printed by T. J. International of Padstow. At the time of writing a Clays edition was listed on abe.com for two hundred pounds; a TJI copy would fetch much more.)

A few months later Henry took the opportunity to send me some reflections on his relationship with his author:

> I liked her from when we first met. It sounds terribly patronising to describe a woman as being feisty (Sybil Fawlty dealt with men who said that with violence), but she had, despite her obvious weariness at the length of her journey with *Girl*, a strength which was tangible. She was resilient. It must be a hugely difficult, frustrating and often demoralising experience having your work rejected, especially over a period of nearly ten years. Add to that that she seemed prepared for *Girl* to be forgotten – she was about to give up on it altogether when we met, I believe. I have such admiration for her, for believing in her work enough to keep showing it, and also to be very strong about her decisions in editing.
>
> She was absolutely determined that things wouldn't change just

because we had decided to publish it – if we wanted to do things to it that she didn't approve of she would simply walk away. That was very clear and with regard to the ending it got down to a discussion where the phrase 'deal-breaker' was used. But getting notice from you that real people thought it spectacular, and were going to tell the world, began, in the most basic way, really, to make her happy. And I saw over a period of a few months that she seemed to begin to allow herself to believe it, and then as the reviews came in – and they took their time – she ran with it.

It was such an astronomical rise, so quickly after the Goldsmiths nomination, that as well as being a game changer for Galley Beggar, one can forget that it was only a year before that prize that I had first read it and met her and despite my enthusiasm, really, all had seemed pretty gloomy for Eimear's career. Something that remains impressive, and telling I think, is that the resilience she always had simply changed its face, but never left her. She just walked right into the shoes of the extraordinarily accomplished and *well-known* writer she was always going to be, always was in a way, and remained level-headed, realistic and grateful for the appreciation – if a little taken aback as the awards really did just keep flowing in.

Sam confirms that Galley Beggar Press was caught off guard by the early success:

Suddenly we had a deluge of press to cope with, trips around book-shops, advanced distribution to set up, extra print runs. But these were good problems to have. It was exciting. It was fun. We were doing something good for the world. We had to learn a lot very quickly and sometimes it felt we were on a treadmill that was going ever faster . . .

Elly recalls the time as a breathless episode in all their lives:

It was astonishingly exciting, the learning curve (which had already been pretty huge, simply in terms of setting up a very modest press) was ramped up to a degree that was sometimes quite hard to keep up with. And mistakes were made – disagreements were had. But by and large, we did okay.

Just before the Goldsmiths Prize winner was announced,

Henry quit the publishing company he had co-founded. He agreed with his co-directors that he would stay on part-time in some sort of associate role, although this didn't work out. It was a dispiriting end to a brief and productive alliance but, he says, there were 'personality clashes': 'We didn't know each other at all when we started and then had massive workloads and massive success very quickly, and I could see a huge meltdown coming, so I walked quite happily.'

To return to the month of publication – I thought my short review (coupled with the irresistible power of the sticker) might encourage a few curious readers to investigate further but, much as I admired the book, I was as pessimistic as any mainstream publisher when it came to likely sales. Even though the handful of people I knew who had by now read it had all been eloquent in their praise, I still couldn't imagine it ever appealing to a wider audience, or even that such an audience existed. In any case a tiny outfit in Norwich wouldn't have the resources for marketing or distribution if the book did acquire a following.

For a small independent publisher a surprise bestseller can be a mixed blessing. Although little or no money is coming in (that takes time), overheads rise dramatically – new staff must be recruited, operating costs escalate, printing and warehousing and distribution need managing and orders have to be processed; there's more paperwork, more stress. Success is really not what small publishers set out to achieve, except in the abstract. And a *huge* success, as was the case with *A Girl Is a Half-formed Thing*, is likely to mean making a deal with a larger publisher, one with the capacity to deliver mass-market paperbacks; it means international rights and e-books and promotional tours and marketing campaigns. Large publishers tend to represent everything that small independent presses set out to oppose, so it can be a fraught experience on both sides when a partnership is brokered.

Eimear had agreed to give a reading on 8 June at the Stoke Newington Literary Festival. She was (she later told me) nervous about making her first public appearance as an author, even at such a low-key event, jointly arranged by Galley Beggar and three other small independent publishers. The line-up included 3:AM (who produce an excellent online literary magazine with the strapline 'Whatever it is, we're against it'), Influx and Lonely Coot, each aiming to showcase their books and authors.

I was intrigued, and although I tend to avoid literary festivals I made my way on a warm Sunday afternoon to an above-ground dive (if you can picture such a thing) called the Mascara Bar. It was at the top of a long road leading up from Stoke Newington and I arrived, out of breath, a few minutes before the announced starting time. A cluster of smokers was gathered outside, looking more like hungover regulars than book-loving festival-goers. The interior of the Mascara Bar was mostly shadow and it took a while for my eyes to adjust to the gloom. Shafts of sunlight were thick with floating dust motes.

The publishers had set up tables at the back of the room next to a low stage, stacked with samples of their wares. I bought a drink and found a seat near the front. A few dim spotlights faintly illuminated a static glitter ball. The carpet felt sticky underfoot. I glanced around, wondering if Eimear McBride was present and whether I'd have the chance, or temerity, to tell the author how much I'd admired her book, and that she should look out for my review in the *TLS* and that I'd be interested in anything else she'd written. I wanted to show off a bit, I expect. The room began to fill up as the smokers drifted inside and either lounged on the sofas or propped themselves against the wall. A speaker tapped the microphone, which screeched, and then with over-amplified plosives introduced the first reading, by a young woman who wasn't Eimear McBride. I didn't catch the names of the publisher, the writer or much of what she said as the sound was terrible and the background hubbub distracting. I sat through two or three more turns before somebody (later revealed to be Sam Jordison of Galley Beggar Press) introduced the next author. A surprisingly young woman detached herself from a small group on a sofa in the darkness behind me and made her way to the stage. She appeared nervous and, holding a copy of the as-yet-unpublished paperback, she began to read at once, without any preamble and without using the microphone, the first three pages of *A Girl Is a Half-formed Thing*.

The surrounding hubbub subsided and – this is no false memory, no exaggeration – the cash registers stopped pinging and kerchinging and the whole room became quiet. Everybody paid attention. She read confidently, a little too fast but with beautifully modulated fluency. Her voice made the text fresh and new and alive. The embedded rhythms had a musical quality, a pulse and a beat. It was spellbinding. She finished her reading, flashed a wide smile and, clearly relieved it was all over, made her way back to rejoin her friends. There was loud applause and a few whoops.

I'd now seen and heard the author – an attractive woman in her thirties with a southern Irish accent. She had masses of red hair and a friendly, open, untroubled expression. I suppose I was agreeably disappointed, because what I'd been expecting was – well *what*, exactly? Somebody more like the protagonist of the novel? Somebody *damaged*?

I was itching to get away and sat fidgeting through the next reading. Then there was a break in the programme and lights were switched on. As I turned to leave I approached the author (who was standing with two friends, former colleagues from the Wellcome Trust) and stammered an introduction. We both babbled inconsequentially for a few minutes about Joyce. Yes, she admired him very much of course. Had she read any Ann Quin? She had not. I made a commonplace crack about the dangers of writing a second novel, and how it's much better to plunge straight into writing a third. I told her how much I admired her book without trying to sound too enthusiastic. She seemed pleased at the prospect of a *TLS* review, if rather taken aback. We shook hands, and I blurted out something complimentary that was heartfelt but probably sounded like bullshit. We parted and as I stood blinking in the bright late afternoon sunshine, I realised I hadn't asked her to sign the advance copy in my bag.

The *TLS* editor Peter Stothard decided to 'splash' *A Girl Is a Half-formed Thing* on the front cover of the following week's issue and this caused quite a sensation in Norwich and in Ireland, where the *Irish Independent* reported the story on 23 June under the excited headline: 'Irish writer's brilliant debut earns coveted spot on cover of *TLS*'. Recognising the likely effect on sales in Ireland, Galley Beggar Press hastily began to arrange launch events in the Republic.

I was surprised, the day after my review appeared, to receive a friendly email from the author, the very first email I'd received from any writer I'd reviewed. She said some nice things about my review, and I was pleased to hear that she felt I'd been right about what she set out to achieve, and about her use of spare vocabulary and intricate phrasing. She said she'd been surprised to meet a *TLS* reviewer in what she called 'a strip club' (although I'm pretty sure it wasn't a strip club).

I was relieved to learn from the author that my review wasn't wide of the mark. We began exchanging often lengthy emails – hundreds of them – over the ensuing months. Many of these were the basis for the interview which forms Chapter 4 of this book. I have quoted sparingly from others, and always with the author's permission. The period of our most frequent and lengthiest exchanges turned out to be the calm before the storm – by the end of the year she had won the first of many big literary prizes and was about to become, after a decade of rejection, an overnight success.

The first really important critical push came from Adam Mars-Jones. He's the only novelist and critic I know quite well socially, so it seemed a good idea to pass him my advance copy of *A Girl* when we met at my partner's fiftieth birthday party in late May. I may have babbled too enthusiastically. I wasn't especially sober at the time, and nobody else was either.

When I bumped into Adam a few months later at a noisy

literary bunfight he gently roared in my ear: 'You're quite right about McBride!' No further words on the subject were exchanged until I read his long and thoughtful piece in the *London Review of Books* (8 August 2013), the first serious consideration of the novel. It's a masterclass in how to write about writing, and here it is in full:

All your walkmans fizz in tune

To go on a starvation diet in terms of the comma (including the inverted ones that designate speech), as Eimear McBride does in her remarkable, harshly satisfying first novel, may not seem a particularly drastic discipline, set beside such feats as avoiding the letter e (Perec's *La Disparition*, Englished by Gilbert Adair as *A Void*) or telling Ophelia's side of the story using only the words she's allotted in Shakespeare's play (Paul Griffiths' *Let Me Tell You*). She compensates by scattering full stops with a liberal, even a raisin-loaf-making hand, but it's more than enough to shake things up.

Commas bred freely in the favourable conditions of proto- and early modernism. The priority for many writers seemed to be deferring grammatical closure for as long as possible, subjecting direct statement to parentheses and qualifications of every kind, and keeping the maximum number of plates spinning with flicks of punctuation. It would do Henry James' vision more violence to translate his books into an English deprived of the intermediate stops than to render them in a comma-rich Esperanto. The novels of Proust and Mann would lose much of their intellectual flavour if commas were put on the ration . . . meanwhile Céline took away the sting of finality from the full stop itself with his obsessive use of the ellipsis, making it no more than a sort of super-comma – or the equivalent of Tristram Shandy's dashes. A reluctance to abide by the arbitrary curfew of the sentence-end and the paragraph-end is strong in Broch, Bernhard, Bolaño.

There were short sentences before Hemingway, but it was Hemingway who made the short sentence part of both a literary and a moral agenda, a matter of looking at the world frontally and without distracting elaboration – seeing things as they are, as if words could ever do that, and giving precedence to described actions over spelled-out feelings. Hard-bitten understatement became a way of being in the world without illusions. Short sentences in this tradition have an impersonality that codes itself as male (odd that you can disown personality while continuing to insist on gender).

Hemingway's style, with its anti-aestheticising aesthetic, is still influential, not only on Raymond Carver but on Cormac McCarthy, at least in some of his books. McCarthy dispenses with the apostrophes in shortened forms like 'doesnt' and 'wouldnt', though the need for clarity requires him to keep it in 'can't' – and the impression of an imperative sparseness suffers from chafing so inconsistently against typographical convention. (James Kelman has the same parsimonious way with an apostrophe.) If the short sentence can be characterised as masculine, that doesn't mean that the long sentence is any less so, symbolically, though in Molly Bloom's section of *Ulysses* Joyce proposed endless unpunctuated flow as an archetype of femininity, a visionary notion at the time even if it has come to seem rather quaint.

Reversing the formal procedure of Molly Bloom's monologue, chopping up its continuousness with frequent full stops, putting the emphasis on sentence fragments, would give some sense of the impact of *A Girl Is a Half-formed Thing*: 'It's only the first time. After that it's just. The ordinary. Do it. And think no more about it why can't you? Kiss a man. Without going and marrying him. First. You sometimes love to. Wildly. When you feel that way. So nice. All. Over. You. You can't help yourself. I wish some man. Or other. Would take me sometime. When he's there. And kiss me in his arms. There's nothing like a kiss. Long. And hot. Down. To your soul. Almost. Paralyses you.' Even with this drastic syncopation Molly is more at peace with her emotions than McBride's unnamed narrator, who often shoots out sentences that are as blocked in their rhythm as they are molten in feeling.

In the earlier, day-lit episodes of *Ulysses*, Joyce used sentence-fragments to cue the transitions from narration to interior monologue. A passage like this of Eimear McBride's is recognisably of that lineage: 'That water. Smells like onions. Growing in the hot tap. Flake of scale there. Mine. Rough skin. Scalp. Hard water soap doesn't lather and shampoo going down the drain. Gully lets the cold in like an open door.' The difference is that McBride's book is all interior monologue, with only incidental description of any out-side world, and fragmentary sentences outnumber full ones. Speech is faithfully notated, and sometimes also the not-speech that Joyce treated with hardly less respect, in the case of sea sounds or a cat's voracious miaowing – so that 'Thoo pthoo' mimics the dental and plosive sounds made, as a by-product, when someone spits out stray strands of tobacco while smoking a roll-up.

There's a 'you' in the book as constant as the 'I', the narrator's brother, addressed from inside the womb on the opening pages. Birth is seen as a diminishment of faculty ('I saw less with these flesh eyes') if not a fall from grace: 'Dividing from the sweet of mother flesh that could not take me in again.' Before 'I' was born 'you' had already had cancer, either halted by the wonder-working power of prayer – the mother's chosen version – or else gone into remission after aggressive therapy ('Scared and bald and wet the bed'. 'I' can feel the tumour lurking, 'cosy kernelled in your head', though the mother has chosen not to see the signs and 'turned her good eyes blind'.

The word Hugh Kenner chose, in *The Stoic Comedians*, to describe the style of phrase-making in *Ulysses* was 'unmortared'. Joyce brought together words that seemed to have no affinity and made them fit flush against each other, leaving no gap. He built dry-stone walls of language, held up by their own weight. That isn't at all Eimear McBride's approach. There's a lot of give in every sentence, and a re-fusal to be bound by formal grammar. Her prose couldn't reasonably be described as vague – perhaps 'indeterminate' is the better word, with its overtones of quantum physics. There's a reluctance to yield up exact meanings that is reminiscent of poetry, but she's not lyrical, and she avoids the stasis that announces poetic moments, the halo of hush round beauty.

McBride is closer in her aesthetic to Jack Butler Yeats than to Wil-liam, with her preference for smudges and streaks, abrupt smears of language, avoiding the sort of brush-stroke that vanishes, its job done, into the likeness of the thing represented. Her prose has a texture and a sculptural texture, so perhaps what she holds in her hand is closer to a palette knife than a brush.

This is an extreme prose idiom, but extremity isn't exciting in itself, only when it's well controlled. The prevailing shortness of the sentences puts a limit on how far the reading eye can stray. The navigation may not be the easiest, but you're never more than a few words away from the marker buoy of a full stop. McBride takes the biggest risks in the shortest sentences ('My thud cheeks up', say, or 'Chew it lurks me'). Those who have read E. E. Cummings' poem 'Anyone lived in a pretty how town' (with up so floating many bells down) know how quickly inverted formulations and games with parts of speech can become twee. It doesn't happen here.

One of the effects of the constantly broken rhythm is that any sustained utterance becomes shocking in itself. At one point the mother launches into a half-page list of complaints about her son, starting: 'He's got this job but won't get a lift with yer one and he won't give me his pay now and won't move to his own and he won't help around the house and he won't fill the buckets clean the fire and his bin is full of sweets and he's getting tub now . . .' It's as if she's giving birth to a whale among all these thrashing and broken-backed sprats. Elsewhere it's prayers that have a solidity and weight unlike anything in the narrator's own experience. They seem to be made of marble, oppressive or comforting or both at once.

This timeless provincial Ireland of suffering, sentiment and bigotry, with sexual shame both a form of background radiation and a recurrent lightning-strike, risks seeming generic: 'In the post office they'd say he was a real type of gent. Held doors for women. Kind to dumb animals. Gave generously to the plate on Sundays and could teach you a thing or two about a godly life. Gave up the drink for his mother on her death-bed. Bad he was and all with it. He says himself it was the hardest thing he ever did but if you're bad to your mother you'll never have luck. He doesn't know about that but he knows what's right. Never touched a drop again after. All those children too and each one a regular communicant . . .' There are few novels that even try to broker their reality without a heavy reliance on detail, the established preference being for the deluge of specificities, as if one more brand name would finally do the trick. Here the period of the setting only emerges obliquely. An early reference to a man's hair being gelled rather than oiled suggests the 1980s, a hint confirmed when the narrator's new schoolmates listen to the personal stereo of the day: 'Those herd. Such bovine singing heifers. Come don't hate me. All your walkmans fizz in tune . . .' The *Encyclopaedia Britannica* the narrator consults even has an entry on Sexism.

It's at school that 'I' learns to separate emotionally from her brother, who can't compete intellectually. She doesn't stay the younger for long. He longs for 'the comrade nudge of adulation' but she can't bear watching him being mocked as he tries to play football during the lunch break: 'That bad eye I know cannot keep up with a ball nor does it see one of them and his doing you for the crowd. Behind your back. For their laughter is a mighty thing to invoke. Your little limp. Sometimes the way you shake your head. It's brilliant that the worst one on the whole field doesn't know it. See him do it. For their roaring. For their great lads fun.'

A virtual first-person narration in fiction is like a video camera at the central character's shoulder. A true first person is like a hand-held camera – only this one is like a micro-camera attached to the narrator's head, shooting off in new directions with every nod and nervous movement. Other characters, including mother and brother, are consistently developed but can never be free-standing in a book that is written like this. And though it may be an exaggeration to say that you get used to this way of writing, you learn to trust it.

Young writers are routinely advised to find their voice, but for Irish writers voice is as much the problem as anything else. To indulge the national stereotype of garrulousness is one sort of trap, but it's possible to react against it too much. Dublin was described (by James O'Reilly) as a place where the only listeners were exhausted talkers, and Dublin talk is a big part of what keeps *Ulysses* afloat, with even the supposedly repellent figure of Buck Mulligan failing to cloy as he's meant to – though disembodied voices aren't enough to give *Finnegans Wake* much in the way of breath and a pulse.

You could see Beckett's career as a long struggle against his own charm and eloquence. His intermittent practice of writing texts in French rather than English was a drastic sort of blarney-filter, debarring him from parochial material and quirks of speech.

Yet he never quite abandoned the cadence, the fall of a sentence shaped by a breath, without which his negations would lose their vitality. Even in *How It Is*, no picnic for the reader, he doesn't outlaw the consolations of rhythm from his prose: 'the fingers deceived the mouth resigned to an olive and given a cherry but no preference no searching not even for a language meet for me meet for here no more searching.' As to whether it's admissible to combine a rigorous philosophical pessimism with the ghost of a lilt, well, that's either the clinching proof of Beckett's humanity or a bit of a cheat, depending on your point of view. In stage works he fought to limit the actors' potential for expressiveness, preventing them from loading the carrier frequency of his words with the noise of their own personalities – just you try winking across the footlights when playing Mouth in Not I, with only a small area of your face left visible. He went to great lengths to strip the humanity from the speaker in that play, who possesses nothing but the words she disowns (by making out she's recounting someone else's experience), and then reconstituted it in the neuter figure of a listener downstage audience left – the Auditor – raising its ungendered arms at specified moments in 'a gesture of helpless compassion'.

Coming after Joyce and Beckett, archetypes of plenitude and abstention, was for generations of writers (not just Irish ones, of course) something that combined the difficulties late-nineteenth-century composers faced after Wagner with the ones their twentieth-century successors experienced following Webern. Where to go when all the options from extreme expansiveness to uttermost compression have been explored and contradicted? There's nothing to prove that Eimear McBride has given Beckett a moment's thought, though given that she studied at Drama Centre London, according to the back flap of the book, it seems likely that she's given him more than a moment.

She opens up space where there shouldn't really be any, by bruising the cadence and roughening up the grammar. The charged inconclusiveness of 'I look him back from looking right at me', for instance, reproduces those aspects of the encounter. A group scene can be rendered more or less all at once: 'People stoking up the range and crossing over teapot stretch to pour a pan of sausage out.' The book is much fuller in its intensely cohesive fragmentation than a more conventionally finished literary product. The overlapping emotions don't settle down, and combine differently on re-reading.

Eimear McBride takes particular risks with her presentation of dialogue, withholding not just the marks that Joyce called 'perverted commas' but any help from the layout of the page. James Kelman indents his dialogue as a matter of course, and Irvine Welsh, following Joyce, accords his readers the additional courtesy of the continental

dash. McBride lets the registers mix within the paragraph, with results that are mostly worth the effort: 'I make my breakfast. Eat that.
Don't look. Don't be letting my face get warm. I've done worse much
more times again but. Drink up. Say I am going out. But love. But
love. So much to do. Sandwiches and cakes. All hands on deck. Too
many Mammy in here. Anyway you know well I can't cook . . .' The
repeated 'But love' turns out to be the mother's reproach for selfish-
ness, muted for company's ears, yet it isn't entirely divided from the
sense it first seemed to have.

At fifteen and sixteen McBride's 'I' and her best friend lose themselves in books and fantasise accordingly: 'Read Milton and feeling
moved discuss the heavens and the earth and the film stars we'd do
with a chance.' Then there's Scott Fitzgerald, 'know that I must drop
the F. Think American twenties just divine and I'd be Zelda if I
could. Think suffering's worth it. To be mad a fine exciting thing to
be for those short times in those mad years. Wearing pearls and drink
champagne and bob my hair and show my knees.' There's something
a little jarring about the relative richness of detail here – or perhaps
it's just the surprise of authors having names when family members
don't. The light dropping-in of 'suffering's worth it' is relatively conventional irony-building by McBride's standards.

Perhaps these innocuous literary references don't quite fit because
the book itself is so laudably unliterary, in its favouring of the provisional over the definitive. First and second thoughts jostle against
each other, in 'Where God is looking in he isn't if he was.' or 'Your
will be done not mine no let mine let mine.' 'Half-formed' certainly earns its place in the title, though the chosen phrasing has a
misleading whimsicality, a jauntiness very foreign to a book that is
an exhilarating read against the grain of its predominantly negative emotions. These sentences seem to have been grown from seed,
without reference to previous traditions of putting words together.
Even when there's a strong convergence with Beckett ('Go on go on
you can go on') it seems remarkably unselfconscious, less a matter
of stepping in someone's footprints than of sharing a shoe size. In
recent years ownership of the Irish-inflected 'go on' has been a sort
of tug-of-war between the ending of Beckett's *The Unnamable* ('You
must go on, I can't go on, I'll go on') and the hectoring housekeeper
in *Father Ted* as played by Pauline McLynn. It's nice to feel confident

that Mrs Doyle's victory won't be permanent.

By virtue of not being 'correct' McBride's way of writing avoids the alienating effect that comes with an educated manner handling volatile material. The beauty of Joyce's *Portrait* becomes over-sleek towards the end, and no doubt this is part of the design, to indicate that Stephen needs to be laid open by new experiences before he can fulfil himself. The final shift to diary form breaks up the rhythms and allows for a more conflicted rhetoric. Eimear McBride herself tries to pull out yet more stops towards the end of the novel. Violence to the person of the narrator is accompanied by violence done to the font, with upper-case letters bursting out in the middle of words. There seems no point in the author reaching for a sixth gear when she's been in top a lot of the time since page one and holding the road but just barely. If your technique is adequate to evoke the experience of a foetus sitting in the womb, already knowing her brother has cancer, then it seems safe to say it's up to most things and shouldn't be tinkered with.

There's also a shrewd, reader-conscious side of McBride canny enough to step back when her volatile book threatens to get out of control. The mother may be referred to as 'she' in early sections but she becomes 'our mother' or 'Mammy' at family gatherings where a little more help is called for. In a crucial passage of dialogue late in the book McBride briefly recants her page-layout protocol and indents for clarity on this special occasion.

If every book was as intense as this, reading literature would be even more of a minority pursuit than it is already. *A Girl Is a Half-formed Thing* makes that rapturous lament *By Grand Central Station I Sat Down and Wept* look like *Hotel du Lac*. But then you wouldn't want to go to *Not I* every night of the week. It's hard to imagine another narrative that would justify this way of telling, but perhaps McBride can build another style from scratch for another style of story. That's a project for another day, when this little book is famous.

To be on the receiving end of such a lengthy, erudite and wide-ranging review was something of a shock and the author emailed to admit 'I can't tell if I've just had a pat on the back or a puck in the ribs'. Her mixed reaction was understandable, as only on a second reading does Mars-Jones appear unequivocally enthusiastic. After some reflection she said she disagreed with his view that the title had some whimsical association, pointing out that 'half-formed' was closer to 'malformed' than he allowed, but the review was, she admitted, 'astounding'.

She found this review particularly helpful when it came to describing her book from the outside, as it were, which proved something of a challenge in the in early interviews. All first-time authors tend to find it hard to talk in public about their writing, to explain where they're coming from and what it is they're trying to say. In this case the author had to talk about a new book that was already ten years old. She had clearly been thinking hard about her approach to writing when she sent me this, soon after the *LRB* review appeared:

> I might say that if Joyce's characters generate language and Beckett's are generated by language, I was aiming for the tiny spot between, just before thought and impulse become language, which makes the answer to your 'Is it stream of consciousness?' question No, maybe closer is stream of pre-consciousness. Both sub- and un- seem too far down.

In the weeks that followed she developed and refined the 'stream of pre-consciousness' idea until it became an essential term for anyone attempting to describe this new way of representing human thought.

'Definitely a genius'

On several occasions the author has said that the turning point for the book was Anne Enright's review in the *Guardian*, which was published on 20 September 2013. In the first paragraph of the review Enright reports that, asked by her husband while she was still reading the book if the author was a genius or just very good, she replied: 'Well, she is definitely a genius. But I don't know how good she is, yet.' By the end of the book she had no doubt: the writing is 'direct, simple and free of intertextual tricks and, after a while, the language becomes its own kind of object. The narrator is better at hearing things than telling them: there are riffs of reported speech and scraps of banter, and these are put to virtuoso use in building scenes and describing action.' If the book is sometimes hard to read, this is 'for the best reasons: everything about it is intense and difficult and hard-won'. This novel, which had spent nine years going the rounds of publishers' desks before it found a home, is, Enright declares, 'an instant classic'. It is 'completely modern in its sensibility and completely old-fashioned in the way it triumphantly ignores the needs of the book market'.

Early in the review Enright makes an interesting point, in her sarcastic aside about there being 'no female contenders' for the role of genius, about the role of women in modernism. A lot of women writers were and are regarded precisely as that, from Jane Austen, George Eliot and the Brontës to Virginia Woolf, Iris Murdoch and Doris Lessing. There are few literary geniuses *period*, and some of them are women and some of them are not, and while writers certainly have a gender, books don't. When I first saw the name Eimear McBride in print I was un-sure whether this was a male or female writer, a confusion com-pounded by the fact that the small-print author's copyright in my advance copy was in the name of Simon Gough, her Galley Beggar predecessor. So I started reading with a *particularly* open mind because I had no choice. This is relatively uncommon for a reviewer, and rather unsettling because all you have to go on is your judgement. There's nothing to write against. In the case of *A Girl Is a Half-formed Thing* we need to apply Wordsworth's dictum (cribbed from Coleridge) that 'every great and original writer, in proportion as he is great and original, must himself create the taste by which he is to be relished'. Look at that again, and tweak the pronoun.

Norwich . . . Dublin. Castlebar . . . London

A Girl Is a Half-formed Thing was launched four times – in Norwich, Dublin, Castlebar and London. The first launch, on 27 June 2013, was held at the Book Hive and was a relatively low-key affair for friends and family and supporters, buoyed by the *TLS* coverage and increasing press interest in Ireland. For the Irish launches the author was accompanied by Galley Beggar Sam. The original plan for a modest event in the author's home town had been augmented by a grander occasion in the capital, and the Dublin launch was scheduled for 9 July in the Hodges Figgis bookshop in Dawson Street. McBride was delighted by the choice of venue as Dublin's oldest bookshop, founded in 1768, features in the pages of *Ulysses* ('The virgin at Hodges Figgis' window on Monday looking for one of the alphabet books you were going to write. Keen glance you gave her'). As usual there was a very tight budget, as Sam recalls:

> It was all done on a shoestring (I managed to wangle a gig reviewing Dublin hotels when we were there, or I would never have been able to afford it. Eimear pretty much paid her way too, out of her own pocket – and was very understanding about that).

(In fact it was the delayed payment of her small advance that enabled the author to pay her way. The whole Galley Beggar enterprise was run on the flimsiest of shoestrings.)

> It started off because a bookshop in Castlebar was interested in holding an event for Eimear – which I'll get to. But I thought if we were going there, we should try to get some interest going in Dublin. Pretty much on spec (and on the strength of your review) I called up Hodges Figgis, thinking I might as well start at the top. And damn me, if they didn't say yes. They were incredibly supportive. They gave over an evening to launching the book there, advertised it really well and got one whole load of books in. Right in the centre of the biggest shop in Dublin. And after Eimear gave her reading an astonishing man called Alan Crilly stood up and said, 'This is the book I've been waiting for . . .' He then spoke about just how important the

book was, how it was the first thing that moved modernism forward that he'd seen for years, how the voice was entirely authentic, and how it was daring and brilliant. It almost brought me to tears. He also – wise man – said everyone had to buy four copies. One to read and carry around. One to keep forever. Two to give to friends . . . because they're going to want to read it.

Every writer needs, and some even deserve, a supporter such as Crilly. I tracked him down and we exchanged some emails. He describes himself as a 'middle-aged middle manager in a software company, with an overwhelming interest in literature and little time to pursue it'. He's a devotee of Joyce and Beckett and admires such contemporaries as Will Self, Lee Rourke and Tom McCarthy, but feels the latter 'share a tendency towards too much clarity and exposition', adding that he'd 'waited a long time for Eimear to extend Beckett's genealogy in English prose'.

He wrote to me to describe the launch in Dublin:

My recollection is fallible but I think I can outline the essence of the event. To begin with attendance, when Sam suggests in his July 2013 blog post that 'There was a good turn out on one of the hottest days the city has seen for years', he's being elegantly allusive – there were very few people there. As I recall, there was a small group of Eimear's friends and possibly in the region of six civilians, possibly only four. Sam is certainly correct about the weather, it was an extraordinary summer's day, but the event was also under the radar for most people and none of the 'usual suspects' in Dublin publishing were present.

Sam spoke first, offering a brief introduction, and then Eimear read, certainly including the beginning of the book because I noted the resonance of the word 'girleen' at this point, which had evaded me on first reading. The reading was followed by a Q&A. I was both achingly aware of the historic nature of the event and desperate that the novel would receive due recognition in its first publication so I felt compelled to contribute . . . I dominated the Q&A, making some fragmented contributions and asking almost all the questions, and then we repaired to the drinks and signing.

Crilly compared a Hodges Figgis shindig for the Tramp Press launch of *Dubliners 100* a year later in June 2014:

> This was attended by a significant proportion of the Dublin publishing community, including most of the contributors; Eimear, in her absence, represented the distant star around whom that evening revolved. I chatted to Rob Doyle about the recent resurgence in Irish fiction and specifically about Eimear's success, which he expressly cited as inspirational. Donal Ryan was also there, having earlier in the year been very gracious in a joint interview with Eimear on RTE Radio's *The Book Show* when, despite his undoubtedly superior sales figures, he deferred to Eimear's work as 'a stylistic benchmark for literature in Ireland and England'. Everyone at that more conspicuous launched would have deferred to her.

There followed a review of the book by the poet, critic and journalist John Boland in the *Irish Times*. This was both penetrating and (given its popular newspaper context) impressively thorough and considered. He started by warning readers that this novel offered nothing in the way of consolation or redemption, before going on to praise the 'exhilarating linguistic effects' of a book 'bracingly alive with sardonic humour'. He hazarded that the book had 'autobiographical underpinnings' and ended with a view that would come to annoy the author, that the book was 'a one-off'.

Another early champion was the arts journalist and broadcaster Sinéad Gleeson, who interviewed the author in Dublin. Gleeson was one of the first journalists to get behind the book at this critical stage in its history and has remained an enthusiastic supporter.

Following the launch Alan Crilly embarked on what we might call a programme of guerrilla marketing:

> On the ground in Dublin, I tramped around independent bookshops in the early days asking them to stock the book (Books Upstairs opposite Trinity College was the one which actually did), worked with John O'Sullivan to broker the review and interview for the *Sunday*

Times, approached a friend at a national radio station to try to arrange an interview, which I don't believe came about, and generally accosted friends and strangers alike about the book. The level of personal investment the novel engenders is, I think, testament to a rare confluence of elements in Eimear's writing.

When writing this chapter I searched for a single substantial review by a critic who did not admire the novel. The only negative review I could find was a piece in the *Irish Independent* (7 October 2013) by Desmond Traynor, an Irish writer and journalist. He didn't like the book and didn't think much of the author either, delivering some nasty *ad feminem* insults when not deploring the novel's 'obtuse use of language and idiosyncratic punctuation' and condemning the subject matter as 'tediously conventional'. His take on the girl's experiences is conventionally misogynist – her rape by her uncle is described as a seduction, what follows this as 'an affair', and he reduces the girl's complex behaviour to a crass and insulting summary: 'She likes being beaten up.' Then he turns his attention to the author: 'There is a long and complex history of Irish writers making good in England by presenting versions of the Irish experience which merely cater to and reinforce English perceptions and prejudices of Irish stereotypes.' Traynor might pause to reflect on why a novel he describes as cynically concocted to appeal to 'certain readers across the water', a novel that in his view caters for English readers by deliberately reinforcing Irish stereotypes, should have taken almost a decade to find a publisher.

Two days after the launch the author and her publisher left Dublin and travelled west to Eimear's home town. Sam takes up the story:

As for Castlebar, it was astonishing. This was before Eimear won any prizes, but already they knew they had a champion among them. It was triumphant. The bookshop was completely rammed and everyone was there. Old friends, teachers, neighbours, priests, journos . . . Eimear was signing over copies to nuns. God alone knows what they made of it! Her friend Jarlath made another wonderful speech about the book's qualities, and how well it captured a time and place he knew very well . . . It was a crush. It was hot. I was dripping with sweat (everyone told me the weather wasn't normally like that in Castlebar) and then we retired to the pub. There's a place there that does Guinness in special 2/3 pint glasses that got me into a bit of trouble. That stuff was pretty damn tasty. I also very much enjoyed being gently ribbed as the clueless arty publisher from England . . .

The pub was Johnny McHale's in Chapel Street Lower, a favourite of the author's. It's an unspoiled traditional pub famous for serving a 'meejum' of Guinness, a unique measure somewhere between a half and a pint. Sam also explored the town and walked beside the stretch of dark water that features in the novel's final pages:

Going there was like walking into the pages of the book – especially when I went out to the local lake. Anyone who has read the book must regard that stretch of dark water, like me, as a place of near religious significance.

The London launch on 18 July 2013 was prompted by increasing press interest in the book. The venue was the London Review Bookshop in Bury Place, Bloomsbury, and a crowd of around a hundred friends, family and well-wishers packed the shop on a warm summer's evening. There were short speeches by Henry Layte and Sam Jordison, and I'd been invited to make a few carefully prepared off-the-cuff remarks. Then Eimear read beautifully from the opening pages of the book and from the wake episode. We chatted for while, clumsily passing a microphone from hand to hand, and both of us failed completely to remember the correct wording of Joyce's well-known note to his patron Harriet Shaw Weaver explaining the language of *Finnegans Wake*.

What followed a few minutes later would be dismissed as implausible by any sane editor. After the formal part of the launch was over, as the drink flowed and the noise level rose, a young woman introduced herself to the author as Kate Creelman, saying that she had grown up 'surrounded by modernist writing'. Her maternal grandmother, she explained, was the aforementioned Harriet Shaw Weaver – patron of Joyce, Eliot and other, less illustrious beneficiaries. In the 1920s Weaver owned a suffragist publication that, improbably, employed Ezra Pound as its literary critic. He changed its name to *The Egoist* and they published *A Portrait of the Artist* in serial form. She added that the family had a collection of correspondence between Joyce and Weaver.

Creelman, a Norwich lawyer, was engaged to (and is now married to) Simon Gough's son, which explained her presence at the London launch. Harriet Shaw Weaver bankrolled Joyce and his family over the years to the tune of £1.5 million. She got a bargain and has an honourable place in literary history as somebody who made things happen. Just as her name will always be linked with that of Joyce, Henry Layte and his Galley Beggar co-founders also have a place in the history of literature as idealistic and independent young publishers who took a huge risk, and did the right thing.

4   'Write good books and try not to die'

The first part of the following interview is based on a series of email exchanges with Eimear McBride in August 2013; it was printed in *The White Review* in May 2014. The growing interest surrounding her, complex negotiations with publishers, the demands of a young daughter and work on her second book were all excellent reasons for her to turn down my request, or to reply to my questions very briefly. In fact, her answers were thoughtful, unguarded, expansive and illuminating.

This was a unique opportunity to conduct a lengthy interview with an author on the brink of national and international fame. When the exchanges came to an end she reflected on the value of an exercise which had seemed, from her perspective, premature. She wasn't yet used to the degree of interest her book would soon come to attract but later said that the interview was 'a very useful exercise to have completed before all this unexpected life took off'. The interview appears here in its original form with some minor editorial changes and the reinstatement of sections that did not appear online. There are inevitably some overlaps with other parts of this book, but I want to preserve the original interview in this, its first appearance in print.

Let's begin with your family background. Were your parents first-generation exiles? What prompted them to leave Liverpool and return to Ireland?

Yes, they were first-generation but always saw themselves as temporary exiles and, while that attitude wasn't so unusual among Irish immigrants, it proved true in their case. They were only in the UK from 1970 to 1979, but returned to the Republic rather than the North because of the Troubles. Sligo just happened to be where the job came up. My father was a psychiatric nurse. Both of my parents were nurses. In the UK they worked in a number of institutions for what was then termed 'the criminally insane'.

Was there any sense of loss and dislocation?

I was only two at the time so not for me. For my parents and older brothers the return was difficult enough, economically certainly, then being strangers in a place where belonging was prized above all else. It's probably not much of an exaggeration to say that, in spite of all the years the family lived in Tubbercurry, we were still considered strangers when we left.

What was on offer culturally in Sligo and Mayo when you were growing up?

The source of most of my cultural experience growing up was the drama class I attended from age nine. Ireland was a hotbed of amateur dramatics in those days so I got to see a lot of Synge, though not much else. There was no proper library in Tubbercurry but my parents put a big emphasis on reading so no trip to Sligo town was complete without a visit to Keohane's bookshop. Better still were the occasional trips to Galway or Dublin from which we'd all return with as many books as we could carry. Castlebar was different. It was a much larger town. There was a bookshop, an old flea-pit cinema that played recent releases, a library that was very willing to order in if they didn't have, and the Linenhall Arts Centre where you could see small-scale touring theatre and dance. I think the first Pinter I ever encountered was there and I remember it being particularly exciting because there was a parental warning about bad language on the poster.

You once mentioned 'lots of early writing'. Terrible or not, what sort of things did you write?

I tried to write novels, or stories, even as a small child. 'The

Fastest Eagle in Sandom' springs to mind – I was 7 or 8 at the time. It was about an eagle, living in a place called Sandom, who could fly very fast. There may also have been illustrations and a puppet made out of dead pheasants' wings. But teenage poetry aside, that's the only form I've ever really been interested in.

You plagiarised *Death in Venice*?

Yes, I was around 14 and was so bowled over by it that I immediately set out to write my own version – unfortunately it hadn't occurred to me that Castlebar wasn't particularly pestilential, at least not in that way. I can't remember very much about it now except that an image from it (the plagiarism) shows up in *Girl*, in the final scene with the uncle – long divorced from Thomas Mann by that stage I should add.

Were you interested in other literatures?

I read a lot of Russian literature and quite a lot of German, also writers like Milan Kundera and Henrik Ibsen. Actually, it occurs to me now that most of my reading was in translation in my teens. I think it was a way to connect with some kind of world beyond my narrow own. Though I do remember D. H. Lawrence being a phase too and the Brontës and Edna O'Brien. I was very fond of biographies as well. And I was mad about Tennessee Williams. *Streetcar* particularly.

Back when I was interested in poetry, I was all for the Russian Silver Age: Pasternak, Akhmatova, Tsvetayeva, etc. As a teenager – which probably goes without saying – I liked Emily Dickinson and Sylvia Plath. Growing up in Sligo meant that wherever you looked, Yeats was on the horizon. Luckily I liked that. Later, at Drama Centre, we had an epic poem voice project and were assigned Pushkin's *Eugene Onegin*. I remember really hoping I'd get to play Tatyana but ending up with the death of Lensky instead. Even now I remember the difficulty of having to drum up enthusiasm for the utter drama-sucking dryness of the translation. It put me off translated poetry altogether.

Years later, sitting, quite drunk, in the tiny kitchen of the flat in St Petersburg with a few equally drunk Russians, someone began to recite it in the original. I could hardly understand a word but I still understood more than I had. Now I can't remember the last time I bought a book of poetry and it was mostly likely something I thought of as a gap in my reading rather than anything I was particularly interested in.

What was Drama Centre like when you were there?

What I remember most from my first year was being really poor and really happy. Right from the start it was like breathing properly for the first time in years. It was a very broad, very literary training. If anything, it was a slightly laborious one for an actor, and certainly involved fewer jazz bands and more Nietzsche than one might have expected, but it turned out to be an excellent training for a would-be experimental writer and all that running around in a toga was great preparation for the humiliations of publishing.

I assume that you made close readings of Beckett at Drama Centre.

We never touched Beckett there. He operated outside the ethos. The director was obsessed with obscure Restoration tragedies, Racine and Molière, while the acting teachers mostly plumped for 20th-century Americans or 19th-century Russians.

What about your theatre career after graduation?

My actual career extended to some warm-propping, a bit of telly and a bedevilled production of Mishima's *Madame de Sade* directed by William [Galinsky]. I think the day I was called to audition for a BBC costume drama and thought 'Oh fuck!' instead of 'Where's my bonnet?' was the day I realised I didn't want to be an actress any more.

You've said elsewhere that the playwright Sarah Kane was an influence.

The week my brother Donagh died was the same week Sarah Kane killed herself. I didn't know her work very well then but I often thought of her because of that and because they were the same age when they died. Then a short while after I started work on *Girl*, I happened to see a production of *Crave* and it was like lightning. I went home afterwards and immediately read all the rest of her work. I'd say that I share some of her thematic preoccupations – as well as a religious upbringing – but what I most admire about her writing, and tried to adopt in my own as a result, was the purity of her intent and the ferocity of her approach. What I mean by purity is her lack of cynicism. Her work is utterly confrontational and uncompromising. She stretches both characters and audience, out to the very edges of their humanity to see what they can see, and I find something incredibly beautiful and admirable about that.

Were you writing much during the Drama Centre years? And was there a connection between your decision to leave acting and your commitment to being a writer?

I continued writing the whole time I was there but the decision to leave acting came in the year my brother was dying, which began about six months after finishing Drama Centre. At first I decided that I just wanted a break. With everything else, I was finding it hard to cope with the rejection. Then when he died I was so shattered, my confidence was so shattered that I just couldn't face it anymore. I think as a child, after my father died, I'd somehow managed to entangle the idea of being an actress with some notion of immunity from all future pain, so when my brother died, that fantasy was destroyed and I was left very lost for a very long time after.

In a newspaper interview you were reported as saying: 'I really didn't want to write about this, but in some ways it was cathartic. A year after my brother died, I went to Russia for two months because I wanted to be alone. I was in St Petersburg, with the White Nights of summer and

no darkness. I had insomnia for months so I wandered around, looking at everything. Then it hit me that I wanted to work towards writing.'

There were a few factual errors in that interview and also in the use of the word 'cathartic'. I actually spent four months in St Petersburg but, yes, I was alone. I didn't go with anyone or have anyone I knew waiting for me. I had a job teaching English a few mornings a week which paid the rent for a room in an old *communalka* on Liteniy Prospekt owned by a very nice elderly Russian couple. It was a difficult time for me and a lonely time but very useful in terms of piecing myself back together and extremely rich culturally – which certainly helped with the task in hand. It was over the summer months so the White Nights were in full swing for much of my time there. They're very beautiful in St Petersburg but can be quite disorientating and I ended up with roaring insomnia. So I spent a lot of time just walking the streets at very odd hours. It didn't 'hit me' that I wanted to work towards writing; I was already doing that anyway. It just shifted something into place which helped me to make the leap from scribbling when the mood took hold, to being serious about what I wanted to do. I was really only starting to write there, not in a particularly organised fashion or with any particular end in mind. I was just feeling around in the dark to see if the words were still there – I hadn't written much since leaving Drama Centre in 1997. I don't know if any of it still exists. I destroyed a lot of writing when we moved from Beaconsfield Road to Campbell Road.

What drew you to Eastern Europe?

I'd been interested in Russia since my early teens and was and am a big fan of Russian literature. I wanted to see St Petersburg for the romance of Peter the Great and Diaghilev and Dostoyevsky. Growing up in Holy Catholic Ireland, my keenness for Russia and Eastern Europe probably contained more than a drop of contrariness too . . .

How did you earn a living after you returned from Russia?

Those years were mostly spent temping and usually of the lowest variety. Working on switchboards, filing, data entry, photocopying, licking envelopes. It was the dogsbody work of office life and at the mercy of people who knew it. It was all pretty terrible – though in retrospect, useful – until I pitched up at the Wellcome Library – which was after I'd written *Girl* and really wasn't bad. It would have been great if only I'd been able to write alongside it. During that period I also managed quite an interesting journey to Khartoum and a bizarre road trip through the northern Sudanese desert with William and a bunch of Sudanese actors (William was researching Tayeb Saleh for an RSC new-work show), plus we spent some time in Egypt when he was on the judging panel for the Cairo Theatre Festival – you've not seen Sarah Kane until you've seen her in Armenian . . .

So you settled in London, completed your first book, but then returned to Ireland?

I was completely settled in London. I'd lived there for thirteen years at that point and had never imagined leaving. Then William was offered a job running the Midsummer Festival in Cork. Prior to that he'd been a freelance theatre director but that was beginning to lose its charm and by 2006 he'd arrived at a point where he wanted to change direction. I was reluctant to go back to Ireland but a combination of circumstances, ranging from not having time to write to narrowly escaping being stabbed to death on my doorstep, persuaded me that change of any kind would be better than staying where I was. We spent four years in Cork. It wasn't really the place for me and the only saving grace of this period was being able write full-time again – this was where I began my second novel. So when the Norfolk and Norwich Festival job came up, I was really hoping he'd get it. He did and so we moved to Norwich in 2011.

When did you first begin writing A Girl? Did you abandon something else when you began the novel?

I started writing in the autumn of 2003. In the previous June, our house in Tottenham had been burgled and about two years-worth of my longhand notes were stolen. At the time I was distraught but in retrospect it was a good thing. Starting afresh meant there was no temptation to worm in any half-dead 'great ideas', which made way for something more immediate.

Do you write in longhand? Or on a laptop? Do you have any kind of regime?

I began work in longhand but when William's brother-in-law gave us an ancient desktop Mac – which took about thirty seconds for the words to appear once you'd finished typing – I moved to that, mostly because of losing the previous work and the difficulty of keeping up-to-date copies of longhand. I started work around nine and went through to four or five most days. I was very strict about it because the time was gift I didn't want to waste. It was a good habit to get into and I still work that way now. I did three drafts of *Girl* in six months so I suppose I wrote and re-wrote quite quickly. For the first draft, when I still didn't know if I would be able to write at all, I gave myself a 1,000-words-a-day rule and stuck to it. Every morning I re-read the previous days' work, cut everything I didn't like – the majority, usually – then continued from the most interesting line. The second draft involved reshuffling some sections, more cutting and a few fillings out. The third draft was mostly tuning, with the addition of only one scene, as far as I can remember. Then nine years later I did another draft, cutting a further 8,000 words.

Perhaps you could say something about the composition of an episode. The grandfather's wake, for example?

When it comes to describing the writing of the wake section

− and this is not the answer you will be hoping for − the first draft is almost exactly as it appears in the final version, so I can't say anything about it. I decided to include it purely as a way to move the plot forward and − somewhat depressingly − it appears to have written itself.

It is, for want of a better word, a transgressive episode − a dispassionate look at a continuing tradition − the laying out of the body and so on.

As far as it being transgressive to an Irish audience, I think this is to do with the fact that although Irish literature teems with wakes, descriptions of the old methods of preparing the corpse − packing the cavities etc. − are few and far between. Nowadays, even for the traditional laying out in the home, bodies are usually professionally prepared by an undertaker. So I wanted to note the unsavoury old ways before they disappear.

The prose of *A Girl* has a cinematic quality and it often puts me in mind of rough cuts and out-takes without the slickness of a final edit. Could you say more about films and film-makers who have influenced you?

I can't remember a time when I didn't watch films. I can't say there were specific films or film-makers who influenced me as a writer though, not in terms of *Girl* anyway.

Your spare, highly focused approach puts me in mind of Robert Bresson in particular, an austere Catholic film-maker.

I wouldn't say I particularly align myself with Bresson's aesthetic and I don't think it could be argued that my work is comparably austere, but the underlying aim of stripping away layers of artifice is one I identify with, not accepting the accepted impurities of form. That may be about the unshieldable nature of the Catholic conscience but I doubt it. Irish Catholicism is all about accepting impurities of form.

Impurities of form? Is purity always something to aim for? And to what extent does purity mean 'less' rather than 'more'?

I suppose the impurity in this instance refers to traditionally accepted drawbacks in any given form. For Bresson, one of those was the theatrical style of acting expected in films at the time. He dealt with it by stripping the actor out, almost completely, and the effect is powerful. So, yes, I do think purity is something to aim for and I can't think of an instance when it means more rather than less.

In a radio discussion of A Girl Is a Half-formed Thing the Irish reviewer John Boland said: 'There's no reassurance here. There are no consolations. There are no redemptions.' Do you agree? Is there any role for redemptive fiction?

Whether or not the reader finds redemption in *Girl* depends on what they understand by redemption. For him it seemed to mean a happy or at least hopeful resolution, which the reader will certainly not find. As the novel itself states, 'There is no God here', so redemption in any Christian sense is automatically precluded. For me, though, redemption is about transcendence, of the past, of the situation and of the self, consciously achieved through the will of the individual, all of which does occur by the end, in my opinion. And while I am not as good an atheist as I would like to be, this idea is significant to me. In the year after my brother died I remember reading all of George Eliot and finding a great deal of comfort in her ideas about the individual's capacity for transformation. Now the reader may not find that the girl has become – and I shudder to say it – 'a better person' by the end of the book but she has, undeniably, become herself.

Is it fair to describe your book as an act of commemoration, or eulogy?

There is a particular cruelty in the grief for someone who's died young, before they've had children or appear to have made any permanent mark on the world, and those left behind often struggle to create some kind of memorial to redress the balance. *Girl* is, in part, my attempt. My brother Donagh lived a very quiet and unassuming life. He survived his initial brain-tumour at the age of five but my parents were warned he would only receive a clean bill of health after twenty years had passed. Twenty did and two after that, it returned. He was quite an easy-going person, struggled at school, trained briefly for the priesthood and in the last few years of his life took great pleasure in his job as a care worker. He died aged 28 and the loss of him is the single most devastating experience of my life. So while *Girl* may not say much about Donagh's own life – and the brother is a fictional character – it does try to say something about the awful unfairness of his death and at least leave some track of how much he was loved behind.

How predetermined was your approach when it came to omitting almost all temporal and topographical detail? Did you exclude from the outset, or include then delete? Was this a gesture (as the posh critics put it) towards universalism? Or is it that grief and remorse have no temporal boundaries?

It was there from the start and a kind of universalism – socialist rather than posh though – was certainly my aim. If I'd known how to place the story outside of time and space I would have. I think I probably could have written it plausibly enough but all the linguistic tricks in the world would have struggled to make that choice breathe.

Your punctuation is a radical development – the elimination of commas. More radical, I think, than the violent typographical outbreaks in the final section. What came first – the elimination of commas, or a decision to punctuate heavily with full stops?

I decided to punctuate mainly with full stops in the first draft and that was because there's nothing like misplacing one to indicate something else is going on in a text. The principle just got extended as the drafts went by. In fact, during the tortuous copy-edit it was once suggested I use a semicolon, which I couldn't for fear its solitary inclusion would bestow more significance than the tatty sentence merited.

'Chew it lurks me' is one of many compacted but immediately comprehensible and naggingly memorable phrases. Did you arrive at such formulations directly, or was there much of a honing process?

I find English a pretty blunt tool most of the time but studying other languages at school – Irish, German, French – and later learning a bit of Russian (though none to any great success I should add) offered plenty of ideas about alternative options to straightforward, grammatical writing. Also, I was interested to see how far it was possible to push word order and structure while still remaining comprehensible and – more importantly – engaging. Specific to the writing of *Girl* was the positioning of the narrative voice and I knew to achieve that effect I would have to make the language work in a different way. It seemed to me that when attempting to tell a story from a point so far back in the mind that it is completely experiential, completely gut-reactive and balancing on the moment just before language becomes formatted thought, English needs to be made to pick up its feet and move. This clearly wasn't going to be the place for *bon mots* or delvings into the farthest reaches of the *Oxford English Dictionary*. Every word had to be drawn from whatever would exist in anyone's basic active vocabulary and this was the rule I pretty much stuck to. When I needed the language to do more, it had to come from the way a phrase was constructed. Luckily these sorts of phrases pop into my head all the time and I get a lot of nerdy pleasure in thinking of sentences then forcing the words to arrive at the same destination via an alternative route, so I can't claim any great technical process is at work there. Of course there's a huge amount of honing involved too, but that's the best explanation I can offer of the basic plan.

Passages of Catholic liturgy occur intermittently, as well as hymns and snatches of the Bible. These in their relatively grammatical coherence seem to offer a sort of textual stability in the maelstrom of thoughts and feelings.

As with other aspects of *Girl* this was an attempt to explore how opposing truths can nevertheless remain true, simultaneously. The girl is comforted by the ritual and hopeful of the magical solutions offered by religion while her personal experience of it is mostly oppressive and destructive. And further, she often seeks comfort in it from the very aspects of herself that have become problematic because of how her religious upbringing informs her view of that self. (Something of the Church persuading women to cannibalise themselves in there too.) From an aesthetic point of view though, I find most of the included prayers very beautiful, so that, along with their fittingness and alien integrity, suggested another useful method of punctuation.

Since your technique is (crudely out) to place the reader inside the narrator's mind at a point before thought becomes (inarticulate) speech, was the decision to anonymise the narrator, and her brother and mother, made at the outset?

Yes, I began with the intention everyone would be anonymous but hadn't decided if that would change as the story progressed, and was equally dubious about my technical ability to sustain the conceit. However, the further I went the clearer it became that the epiphany, which a sudden flurry of names would require, was not about to happen for her and I had, in fact, made a rod for my own back.

What response(s) do you expect to elicit from your readers? Does that response figure at all in your writing? Do you write with any notional reader in mind?

I have no expectations about reader response to the story itself and, from the outset, had none in mind that I hoped to provoke. It's quite interesting to now — finally — be in a position to hear reader's responses — the diversity of which can be both delightful and alarming! And while I'd say I had no notional reader in mind, I was always aware that I wasn't just 'writing for myself' — which I consider one of the laziest, ill-conceived pieces of advice ever offered to writers. (If you want to 'write for yourself' keep a diary.) This is not to say I think a writer should ever write to please readers, but the logical end point of 'writing for yourself' is *The Making of Americans*, possibly even *Finnegans Wake*, and while it was important those experiments were carried out, they proved to be kamikaze missions leaving no viable legacy for the next generation. In trying to find a new origin of perspective and coercing the language into working in a way that might plausibly suggest it, I was attempting to take what I considered to be the successes of that era, then turn them inside out to achieve the opposite effect. So while – in my very undereducated opinion – the non-specialist reader finds those books obtuse and alienating, I wanted mine to go in as close as the reader would reasonably permit. I wanted the simplicity of the vocabulary to allow the more complex construction to slip in under the radar so that the decoding would take place within the readers themselves, almost as though they were experiencing the story from the inside out rather than the outside in. All of which is a long-winded way of saying that even though every word selected and phrase constructed was held to a standard that was mine alone, the idea of communication was absolutely central – which was probably also the reason I was willing to take an editorial note about the opening. On the technical side, Mammy etc. came about because of residual theatre-sense – directors don't ask actors to deliver grand soliloquies with their backs to the audience. And while writers shouldn't shy away from asking readers to work a bit, they should also offer a stick for the hill.

A Girl is an assault on 'that most holy and catastrophic of constructs, "Female purity"' (as you say in your introduction to George Egerton's *Wedlock*). This leads to a question about your own position. Would you describe yourself as feminist? Post-feminist?

Feminist, decisively so, particularly in my personal reading of *Girl* and the exploration of sexuality. I am slightly surprised that no one's raised any flags about this aspect of the book so far – apart from one online reviewer who seemed to think there was some ambiguity about whether a grown man having sex with a 13-year-old constitutes rape or seduction. In a way, I don't want to say too much about the sexual element of the story because it's extremely difficult to do so without having to use the very narrow, moralistic vocabulary available for discussion about sex. What I will say is that a 13-year-old having a crush on a 41-year-old and therefore allowing him to do what he wants to her will probably feel complicit in that act, but is not and cannot be, and those unfounded feelings of complicity may ultimately prove as destructive as the initial violation. The later 'violations', however, are more complex – although certainly the product of the first. This is why I would describe it as feminist rather than post-feminist. Her sexual behaviour is not that of someone at peace with their sexuality and she generally utilises it for every reason but the two basics: physical pleasure and/or closeness to another person. There isn't a single description of her deriving either from any of her encounters. The best she achieves is a moment of absence from her own inner turmoil which mostly leads to yet greater disconnect within herself. She is not someone enjoying the hard-won fruits of sexual liberation, she is almost the opposite. The product of a system that could offer nothing to women but sexual shame, ignorance and servitude.

What happened after you completed the original draft?

I finished the third draft of *Girl* in the summer of 2004, so between then and publication in the summer of 2013, she had quite a bumpy ride. There was the glitzy agency who said they 'might' offer representation if I re-wrote it to their exact specifications and the publisher who said he was only interested if he could sell it as a memoir. Then all the major publishing houses turned it down with glowing refusals – although it was nearly taken up by two who shall remain nameless only to be vetoed later on the grounds of being unmarketable. A small press in Dublin showed interest for a while and then also backed off as they couldn't 'afford to take any risks'. When I pulled them up on this they said they'd reconsider, were just waiting to hear about their Arts Council funding and would be in touch. They never were. So eventually *Girl* was consigned to the drawer and over time I made some embittered peace with that.

Then along came Galley Beggar Press, a tiny independent outfit right on your doorstep in Norwich.

By the time William and I moved to Norwich in February 2011, I was pretty much resigned to *Girl* not going anywhere and was trying to keep the weight of that off my second novel. We'd only been here about three months when William arrived home one evening saying he'd been talking to the fella in the Book Hive [Henry Layte, proprietor of the independent Norwich bookshop] who'd asked what I did, said he was thinking of starting a press and wondered if I'd let him read *Girl*? Then followed several months of Feydeau when neither Henry nor I emailed each other because William had misinformed both about who would. Luckily a chance conversation during which I was roundly cursing Henry as yet another time-waster revealed the mix-up and we got in touch. Our first meeting took place on my 35th birthday and finished with the – by now – ominous sounding, 'We're waiting to hear about our Arts Council funding'. I expected to hear no more and didn't, until the following year, when Galley Beggar had just published their first book [Simon Gough's memoir *The White Goddess: An Encounter*; McBride's novel was their second publication]. Things went on swiftly from there.

I'd like to know more about your influences. Negative influences also – the type of writer/writing you most dislike.

Well, I hate a moral and I'm not much keener on an inspirational tale of survival against the odds. I find the current vogue for heavyweight middlebrow fairly depressing too, but suspect this has more to do with what publishers are willing to publish than what writers are offering. *Girl* was recently turned down by a large publishing house in the US because they feared '. . . that broad-mindedness is a thing of the past and that McBride's brilliant and moving novel will suffer in the marketplace as a result'. I can't count how many responses I've had in that vein and I don't think they're just a problem for me personally. Responses like that are a problem for everyone interested in serious writing. I will be eternally grateful to Galley Beggar for the risk they took in publishing *Girl* and for possessing the imagination to see beyond the narrow perimeters marketing departments offer to their giant international counterparts. That they have generated so much interest on a marketing budget of almost nothing is testament to their hard work but also to the fact that there is an audience out there for this kind of writing, and while *Girl* isn't going to make millionaires of any of us, it has a place and a value too. Publishing shouldn't be about seeking out next year's rip-off of last year's hit. Both readers and writers deserve better.

We've touched on this – are you especially interested in any experimental writing of the past? Do you have a sense of being part of a continuity?

I wouldn't say I'm interested in experimental writing purely for the sake of it but I am generally interested in modernist writing. This is mostly fuelled by romantic notions about experimenting with form and ignoble nosiness about the writers themselves, but also by admiration regarding their will for unseemly, almost antisocial literary adventure – which publishing houses and creative writing courses are still trying to kick out of writers to this day. In that sense I feel part of a continuity. I don't have the cheek to claim any other.

Do you see yourself specifically as an Irish writer?

No. I'd like to set up my stall up as a European writer, but I don't know if it's up to me. I probably belong in the diaspora set because I only have clarity from a distance.

'Silence, exile and cunning'?

The silence, exile and cunning bit is a little worn out by now. Ireland has a history of rejecting at the teat. One day, you simply reject back and get on with it. There is no greater freedom than getting on with it.

★

A Girl Is a Half-formed Thing won the inaugural Goldsmiths Prize three months later and the author began her rapid ascent to the first rank of contemporary writers. She was much in demand, and had just returned from an exhausting promotional tour of North America when we resumed our email exchanges in December 2014. It gave the author a chance to reflect on a year during which her book had won a succession of major prizes and (more importantly) been the subject of ecstatic reviews on both sides of the Atlantic. Her book had been adapted for the stage and she had recently completed the recording of an unabridged audiobook for Faber.

To start with: something about recording the audiobook. Did the acting background kick in?

I certainly wanted to do the recording myself and thought that I was well enough equipped for the task in hand. Of course this may have just been my own control-freakery at work but it felt like the opportunity to have my final say on the matter.

It's more of a performance than a reading. Is that overstating it?

Is there a difference? I read the text as I heard it in my head during the writing.

You've said that the real tipping point for *A Girl*'s success was Anne Enright's review in the *Guardian* (20 September 2013). What are your thoughts about 'genius'? And about 'classics'?

Anne Enright made it clear she was using the word 'genius' in the context of its older meaning, as a term to describe someone operating on the edges. I also think she was also using it to provoke the old boys of the literary world, who rarely apply it to women. What actually affected me in the review though was the implication that I had not sold out, and coming from someone like Anne Enright, whose work and career I respect enormously, it felt like a huge validation of all those seemingly wasted years. Only time will tell if the book is a classic or not but if it's still being described as such in fifty years then I'll be very happy indeed.

A *Girl* already features on several college syllabuses and you can expect more academic attention in the years to come. How do you feel about this?

Like most writers I want my work to have a long life and academic attention is a way to help ensure that. However, I wouldn't want the book to become ghettoised by academia. I put a few literary games in there but only for fun and I don't consider them important to understanding the text. *Girl* was written to be flesh and blood and that is the connection I most hope it continues to make.

What are your thoughts about longlists, shortlists and literary prizes?

They're great! What can I really say about this when *Girl* has managed to reach the kind of readership I would never have dreamt possible because of the various prizes and listings it has received? Book prizes aren't definitive in the manner of sporting competitions and I don't think anyone believes they are, but drawing readers' attention to work which may otherwise fall through the cracks is the remit of many prizes and *Girl* is proof that they can do this in a way good reviews, and even expensive marketing campaigns, cannot.

And your recent shortlisting for the new post of Irish Literary Laureate?

It's very flattering but somewhat premature. I have a great deal to prove to myself before I would consider feeling entitled to that kind of role.

[On 29 January 2015 the Taoiseach, Enda Kenny, TD, announced Anne Enright as the inaugural Laureate for Irish Fiction. She was chosen by a panel chaired by the poet Paul Muldoon from a shortlist of 34 nominees.]

Would such an honour (if it is an honour) be compatible with your alignment to European (as opposed to simply Irish) writing?

Well, this goes to the heart of the overly fraught and vaguely tail-chasing question of what it means to be an 'Irish' writer, but I think it's safe to say that the broad shoulders of Ireland's literary wealth are more than capable of carrying all our varieties along with it.

You appear to have taken on the role of a major writer, and the associated brouhaha, very confidently. How do you feel about reading to large audiences and making public appearances?

It probably helps that I don't see myself as a major writer, more as someone who had a lot of bad luck then, suddenly, a lot of good luck. Just coping with the travelling means I have almost no energy left for neurosis and I found that – after the first terrifying few – I quite enjoyed doing the events themselves and talking to readers. Literary parties are another matter entirely . . .

Is critical acclaim a mixed blessing?

At the beginning I thought so. The critical eyebrow-wriggling about what I'd manage to do next – would it be radically different or more of the same, with all the implied disappointment at either outcome – gave me the fear. Then I realised that I had almost come full circle and that the success of *A Girl* had given me as much freedom to do what I want with my next book as its failure had before. The critical acclaim has been wonderful but I lived without it long enough to understand that it exists outside and makes very little difference to what I'm after as a writer.

You donated part of your Baileys Prize money to the Book Hive in Norwich to allow free distribution of novels in response to the then-Education Minster Michael Gove's contentious decision to ban non-English novels from the National Curriculum. Can you say something about that?

It was a small and easily made gesture of disgust at a lazy and ignorant decision. For a Minister of Education to consider banning non-English novels was a gratuitous act of self-serving little-Englandism which was beneath his office and a betrayal of the students whose education he was supposed to help shape. The nature, scope and remit of literature are boundless, to pretend otherwise is to display a fundamental misunderstanding of this and, for a man in his position, was unforgivable.

Do you now see yourself (however reluctantly) as a 'public figure'? What role do/should writers have in public life?

No I don't, and I have no interest in becoming one. I try to answer what questions I am asked, nothing more. I'm sure writers do have a place in public life but in what manner and to what degree is a matter for the individual's conscience and talent.

Any thoughts on working in the theatre in the future (as a writer, I mean)? Does collaboration appeal?

I'm not a natural collaborator – which is why acting never really suited me – but I would be interested in working in the theatre again. We'll see.

Do you ever feel that you no longer 'own' the book? By which I mean how do you feel now the Girl has a life of her own?

No, she's still mine but, like the parent of any late developer, I'm pleased she finally has a life of her own. It probably helps that I've rarely come across interpretations of the book that I have seriously objected to. There have been one or two but they're usually so self-evidently ridiculous as to not cause me any great concern. I've been working on the second novel for years now so that's where all my deep feeling resides.

There was a bidding war for rights to A Girl. Can you say a little about that, and how you settled on Faber?

This is really a question for Sam and Eloise at Galley Beggar. It was their decision to sell the mass-market paperback rights and they conducted all meetings with the interested parties. They settled on Faber and I was not directly involved in the negotiation of the terms of that contract, nor was I a signatory to it. My role was to sign an amendment to my original contract with Galley Beggar enabling them to legally make the deal which, at their request, I did. Personally I think they made a good decision and have been very happy with the outcome.

Faber's marketing of the book after the Baileys was astonishing – the advertising on the sides of London buses, I mean. What did you make of that?

The buses were the last thing I ever expected. Books like mine don't usually end up on the sides of buses but why not? Screw payday loans and celebrity biogs. I think it was both imaginative and a tremendous display of belief on Faber's part and I hope to see Beckett on the 79 from now on.

Could you tell me something about how you manage your commitments, or how they're managed on your behalf.

Before Faber took over, the Wylie Agency helped a lot with booking and organising travel, and still do with most of my overseas commitments but I was responsible for paying all of my own travel and accommodation costs. After the Faber deal Rachel Alexander and Lauren Nicoll took over most of the UK and Irish stuff and saved me from the incredibly time-consuming organisation.

Something, briefly, about translators and foreign rights. Has this come up yet? Do you/will you work closely with translators?

This has only just begun and, so far, involves me translating the text in plainer English then trying to give a flavour of how the changes subtly alter it. I have no idea if I'm any use or not but it's an interesting process. Usually it's no more than a sentence or a specific phrase. For example, a translator sent this query: '"Gull the engine. Gull the traffic going by." Gull?' And I replied: 'This is the phrase to "Gun the engine" or "rev the engine" mixed with the noise of a seagull.' I haven't pre-emptively selected any passages, I haven't had time to consider these things much this year. I suspect less is more in this context. I hear the audiobook is a useful translation aid.

Reviews. Are there any you'd single out as especially astute? I'm thinking especially of the US coverage.

I think I enjoyed Joshua Cohen's in the *New York Times* the most. It was so well written and a great survey of literature too.

Can you compare responses in the US to over here? Responses from readers, I mean – the ones you've met.

I haven't picked up on any remarkable differences. US readers possibly find the language more readily accessible but not really. The only serious difference I've noticed is that Australian female interviewers are refreshingly eager to get into the nuts and bolts of the sexual aspect of the book in a way no one anywhere else has been. That's been challenging but is also an insight into where Australian women feel their battles lie.

The scenes of violation are fierce and troubling but they leave little to interrogate or uncover (at least in a critical sense). They are what they are – what can anyone add to that?

I very much disagree with that statement. I think the girl's conflicted relationship with her own sexuality is one of the most interesting aspects of the book and also the one which separates it out from its potential stable-mates in the Irish misery-lit genre. The interviewers I refer to recognised this and wanted to discuss it further, which I very much appreciated the opportunity to do.

What difference would early recognition have made? In your twenties, say?

I can't say. I can never know and I don't really think it matters anyway.

Other novelists have told me that it's a different thing to write as a writer (rather than as an aspiring writer, if you see what I mean). There's a natural tendency for established writers to write about writing, or to have writers as characters, because this is what they know most about. Your thoughts on this?

No, I don't really understand so have no thoughts on this but, if I start writing about writing before I've published at least two more novels, I hope someone will take me out and shoot me.

So what's your game plan?

Write good books and try not to die.

5   Right now. Next now. What I'll be?

Folio, Goldsmiths

When Dame Stella Rimington, former Director General of the Security Service (better known as MI5) and chair of the 2011 Man Booker Prize judges, remarked that what she and her fellow judges were looking for was 'readability', she enraged those in the literary world who believed that the Booker had a nobler remit. 'Readability' – the very word was enough to make the literati shudder, coming from the same perky lexicon as 'wow factor' and 'tingle quotient' and 'this summer's must-read'. When Eimear McBride won the inaugural Goldsmiths Prize two years later, Sam Jordison reflected:

> I think we partly have Stella Rimington's disastrous chairmanship of the 2011 Booker to thank. We're enjoying the backlash against the idea that books should be judged mainly on 'readability' . . . Rightly or wrongly, that year's Booker prize galvanised people into shouting about the rewards and delights of challenging fiction.

But first, the Folio Prize – established in 2013 to reward novels 'unsurpassed in their quality and ambition' (in the words of the prize's founder, the agent Andrew Kidd), precisely what the Booker was now failing to do. Until the Folio Society ended its short-lived sponsorship in 2015, the prize was run by the Folio Prize Academy, made up mostly of writers and critics, which played the decisive role in selecting titles for the shortlist. The winner of the inaugural Folio Prize in 2013 was *Tenth of December*, a collection of short stories by George Saunders, but that *A Girl Is a Half-formed Thing* had been shortlisted was no small honour for a debut novel from a tiny independent publisher.

The other new prize set up in response to changes in the Booker, particularly its opening up to writers from outside the UK and the Commonwealth, was the Goldsmiths, organised by the University of London in association with the *New Statesman* magazine. It offered a prize of £10,000 'to reward fiction that breaks the mould or opens up new possibilities for the novel form', recognising and rewarding 'daring, innovation and experiment'. Only authors published by UK houses were eligible to enter and the inaugural shortlist, whittled down from a longlist of 123, was a mixture of well-established heavyweights and intriguing newcomers, labels that applied as much to the publishers as it did to the authors. The heavyweights were Jim Crace, David Peace and Ali Smith. The newcomers were Lars Iyer, Philip Terry and Eimear McBride. This was certainly an interesting shortlist, and speculation was, if not heated, agreeably intense. It was a rare pleasure to see Galley Beggar Press, with only two books in print, up against the mighty Faber and Faber.

Jim Crace's *Harvest* (published by Picador) was also shortlisted for that year's Man Booker Prize; Philip Terry's *Tapestry* (Reality Street) was a collection of stories structured around the weaving of the Bayeux Tapestry, employing a phonetic mock Anglo-Saxon dialect; Lars Iyer's *Exodus* (Melville House) was a mordant road trip around what remains of university humanities departments; David Peace's *Red or Dead* (Faber and Faber), was an account of the life of the Liverpool Football Club manager Bill Shankly, rendered in incantatory prose that was, depending on your taste, a brilliant subversion of sports biography using minimalist techniques or simply infuriating. (I admire Peace's writing very much but couldn't stand this novel.) Ali Smith – who would win the following year's Goldsmiths and Costa Book Awards, and the Baileys, *and* be shortlisted for the Man Booker for *How to be Both* – was on the first Goldsmiths shortlist for *Artful* (Penguin), a blend of essay and fiction which seemed to me the strongest contender, although its status as a novel was questionable.

The prize judges were the novelist, playwright and critic Gabriel Josipovici, Jonathan Derbyshire, the managing editor of *Prospect* magazine, and the novelist Nicola Barker. Tim Parnell, chair of the panel, praised all of the shortlisted books as 'strikingly original', and said that 'all of them refuse the ready comforts of convention. Making full use of the resources and possibilities of the novel form, each writer has found the distinct idiom that their story demands.'

Some weeks before the prize-winner was announced there were public readings at Goldsmiths College. This was the first public reading I'd seen by McBride since the afternoon in the Mascara Bar and I recall three things: the burst of applause as she rose to read, the intense concentration of the audience and of the other shortlisted writers as she read, and the second tremendous burst of applause when she finished reading and returned to her seat. In the panel discussion that followed Ali Smith said she couldn't recall 'a sexier evening' and Jim Crace expressed his irritation at the recent opening up of the Booker: 'Each prize has a flavour. That's what we've lost. We'd not say the Commonwealth Games should be opened up to Americans.'

Nobody really expected *A Girl Is a Half-formed Thing* to win the Goldsmiths, least of all the author herself. At least the prize-giving ceremony would be something to look forward to – a good night out, with plenty to drink. But one knowledgeable observer was more optimistic. Adam Mars-Jones, a veteran of such literary brouhaha, emailed me to say: 'I'd think she has a very good chance of the Goldsmiths, since prize choices always have a rhetorical element that says "This is what our prize is about" – and the "story" of *Half-formed* is strongly appealing, the travails of rejection and then marginal publication . . . I'm aware that this is a cynical argument, but it wouldn't be a cynical result.'

Things took an unexpected turn when *A Girl Is a Half-formed Thing* suddenly became the bookmakers' favourite. I risked a self-conscious tenner – my first ever bet – at odds of 3/1 and then settled down to await the announcement of the prize-winner in mid-November, aware that I now had a financial stake in the result. My spirits rose when one of the judges, the novelist Nicola Barker, went public with the following view of the novel:

> Imagine being repeatedly slapped in the face, only quite lightly to begin with, by a delicate little hand wearing a large and ornate signet ring. You want to turn away, to lash out, to resist, but the little hand is so dogged, so persistent, and the ring has caught your eye, somehow, and you just want to study it, to focus in on it, because you know that it is strange and special and very beautiful. But as the little hand continues to slap it becomes more painful and your cheeks gradually start to sting and to redden. Is it a pleasurable feeling? No. Well, yes. Is it startling? Certainly. And afterwards? When it's all finally over? The devastating bruises, spreading and flowering across your flesh in their terrible palette of blue, green, black, purple . . . *A Girl Is a Half-formed Thing* is at once the slap and the gasp after the slap. It is, in a single word, breathtaking.

On 13 November 2013 Tim Parnell announced the winner at a reception in Goldsmiths College. First, he introduced the prize itself:

> As it happens, we decided not to use the term 'experimental' in describing the brief of the Goldsmiths Prize, but chose instead to stress the quality of originality expressed in the very name of the most popular of literary kinds: the novel. To call a work of fiction 'experimental' is to imply that it somehow deviates from the genre's natural concerns, structures and idioms. Yet a long view of the novel's history – one which takes in the rich period before certain conventions calcified in the nineteenth century – suggests that the novel is most itself when writers make use of its near endless resources and possibilities and are prepared to challenge and surprise their readers. This has nothing to do with form for form's sake. As should be clear from the books on our shortlist, form is not the enemy of content but rather its closest ally. Nor should it be confused with the tarnished notion of 'innovation' associated with glib marketing. Overused conventions quickly become clichés, so that they lose the power to speak, and to make it new is to offer a powerful antidote to the numbing effects of habitual perception.

He discussed each of the shortlisted books, including *A Girl*:

> Eimear McBride's *A Girl Is a Half-formed Thing* is not an easy read. It
> is nearly always disturbing and frequently upsetting. It is also utterly
> compelling as it maintains a seldom-encountered level of emotional
> intensity throughout its 200 pages. If ever a novel gave the lie to the
> notion that formal inventiveness necessarily precludes feeling, it is
> this one. In a perfect marriage of form and content, McBride has
> created an idiolect, dominated by sentence fragments, which enacts
> the narrator's pained and traumatised responses to a hostile world
> with remarkable power and clarity. It is a masterpiece of sustained
> poetic prose.

When he announced that 'the winner of the Goldsmiths Prize
2013 is *A Girl Is a Half-formed Thing* by Eimear McBride' there
was a huge burst of applause after just the first two words of the
title. Eimear made her way through the crowd, onto the stage
and into the bright spotlight. Moments after receiving the prize
an absolutely delighted author spoke to a television film crew:

> For a long time I thought I would never have this book published,
> and I felt quite depressed about the state of publishing as a result. To
> have a prize like this is a really wonderful thing to encourage writers
> to be adventurous, to encourage publishers to be adventurous, and
> readers to be adventurous.

She now had a platform and over the following weeks (and
as the prize-winning acceptance speeches began to accumulate)
repeated this message, calling on readers and publishers to raise
their game, to take risks and to support new writers.

Remembering that Tim Parnell had made a point of not referring to Goldsmiths-shortlisted novels as 'experimental', I asked
him how he would describe *A Girl Is a Half-formed Thing*:

> If it weren't for the fact that the category has little or no descriptive
> power, I'd call it simply a novel because I think McBride writes with
> a keen awareness of what the form has been and can be. If pushed
> further, I'd describe it as a novel written in the modernist tradition,
> because it is that in both particular and general ways (the debt to the

idioms and methods of Joyce and Beckett is clear and acknowledged; and McBride shares the modernist commitment to making it new and to finding ways of telling that fit the particular demands of the tale).

Parnell emphasised the 'emotional intensity' that McBride brought to formal innovation, in sharp contrast with the often bloodless and intellectual quality of much experimental writing. I asked if this had been a factor:

> Yes, this is one of the most distinctive and, for many readers, ultimately winning, features of *A Girl*. I have more appetite than I think you have for the more 'intellectual' forms of 'experiment' associated with, say, George Perec, and the various traditions of literary self-consciousness, but McBride's book is one of very few formally innovative novels in which technique is deployed better to communicate its harrowing story. I suppose the same might be said of Joyce and Beckett, but McBride is perhaps closer to Woolf and Faulkner in this (especially the latter, where literary self-consciousness is never an issue).

Asked if *A Girl* had helped to define the 'profile' of the Goldsmiths, Parnell replied:

> It has certainly helped to do that, although I don't think any one book can or should define a prize. I hope that the prize's profile will emerge with greatest clarity when we have had, say, ten winners. That said, we were incredibly lucky to launch in the year in which *A Girl* was published and it's hard to think of a more suitable or worthy winner of the inaugural prize.

Wylie, Faber, Coffee House Press

Following the Goldsmiths, Tracy Bohan of the Wylie Agency, which represents a roster of big-name writers, travelled from London to Norwich to sign up the Irish literary sensation. This marked an end to the long relationship with David Grossman.

The Wylie Agency, based in one of the large Georgian town

houses of Bedford Square, is a stone's throw from the offices of the publishers Faber and Faber. Hannah Griffiths, Faber fiction editor, first became aware of *A Girl Is a Half-formed Thing* when she read Anne Enright's *Guardian* review. Over lunch at the Faber offices early in 2014 Tracy Bohan told her that she was now representing the author and the possibility of acquiring rights to the novel from Galley Beggar Press was raised. Hannah had not yet read the novel but was aware of the excitement it was generating. She was certainly interested and on 16 January headed home after work with an e-file copy of the novel. Within a week Neil Belton, Faber's editorial director for non-fiction, had also read the book and loved it. A consensus was building within the company and Hannah, intrigued by the novel's long history of non-publication, looked up the relevant emails in the Faber archive and found that it had originally been submitted to them in January 2007. Now, in 2013 and in the wake of a major literary prize, Griffiths made a confident presentation to her colleagues.

Following Anne Enright's declaration of the author as a genius the reviews were rapidly accumulating – and they all followed the Enright line:

'[A]n immensely arresting novel. McBride is fully deserving of all her accolades; the question now is what she can produce next.' (*Sunday Times*, Pick of the Paperbacks)

'A novel that redefines the novel – that not only takes us on an emotionally dense rollercoaster ride through the perils of intimacy and family life, but delivers the whole extraordinary story in a syntax that is flat out new and terrifyingly and wondrously imaginative.' (Kirsty Gunn, *Herald Scotland*)

'A remarkable achievement.' (John Boland, *Irish Independent*)

'A brutal and brilliant debut . . . This book will arouse powerful emotions in anyone who accords it the respect of reading with attention.' (John P. O'Sullivan, *Sunday Times Ireland*)

'McBride's Joycean inventiveness depicts the girl's entire self, the prose cutting through to her feelings, impressions, thoughts and half-thoughts. The short, choppy sentences, and the novel's bleak vision are also reminiscent of Samuel Beckett.' (Joanne Hayden, *Sunday Post*)

'The author's use of language is so unique, so instantly inimitable that McBridean deserves to be an adjective . . . Writing like this doesn't come about too often, and when it does it should be lauded.' (Toby Lichtig, *New Humanist*)

'The virtuoso violence of McBride's expression feels instinctive rather than artful, the only way to tell a story that can hardly bear to be told . . . *A Girl Is a Half-formed Thing* is a familiar Irish tale told in transfigured Irish style, a lyrical prose-poem on horror and human endurance.' (Alexandra Coghlan, *The Monthly*)

In response to the growing interest Sam and Elly, now running Galley Beggar, engaged literary agent Jack Ramm to broker a deal with a major publisher. Jack circulated the manuscript widely and a number of big publishers expressed serious interest. Faber soon became the front-runner and a series of meetings was arranged. Further negotiations took place via email and phone calls. Although the author was regularly briefed by her agent and had final approval of any deal, she played no role in the negotiations. There is no standard model for publishing partnership agreements, but Ramm says there were no particular problems in brokering the deal between Faber and Galley Beggar.

On 17 March *The Bookseller* reported the deal and quoted Hannah Griffiths:

This extraordinary debut novel has already attracted considerable attention and found many fans thanks to the great work of Galley Beggar Press. We are coming on board as partners to help take the book to even more readers, to build on this extraordinary momentum and support its continuing life in both paperback and ebook. Faber feels like a natural home for a novel with such a clear modernist influence and given Faber's own history with Irish writing.

The momentum did not let up. Three months later in early June the book was included in a strong shortlist for the Baileys Women's Prize for Fiction. Launched in 1996 as the Orange Prize, the Baileys is second only to the Man Booker in terms of prestige and monetary value. Any woman writing in English is eligible, regardless of nationality, country of residence, age or subject matter. In addition to *A Girl Is a Half-Formed Thing* the 2014 Baileys shortlist consisted of *Americanah* by Chimamanda Ngozi Adichie, *Burial Rites by* Hannah Kent, *The Lowland* by Jhumpa Lahiri, *The Undertaking* by Audrey Magee and *The Goldfinch* by Donna Tartt

At the Royal Festival Hall on the night before the prize ceremony all the authors were present on stage apart from Tartt, who had other commitments. Her place was taken by the actor Charles Dance, presumably because no woman could be found capable of reading from *The Goldfinch*. As each shortlisted writer rose to read there was polite applause, but when Eimear McBride stood up there was such a roar of approval from the audience that she looked momentarily taken aback. She read from page 54 onwards ('Come running by the lake. Fall down. I am also too old for that I should be smoking drinking now'). You can find a recording of this reading on the internet – a spellbinding performance to a hushed and attentive audience; there's not a cough or a shuffle. She sat down to more thunderous applause.

The following evening, less than twelve months since her first public appearance in the Mascara Bar, Eimear McBride was announced as the winner of the 2014 Baileys Prize. She stepped up to receive her 'Bessie', the stylish trophy created and donated by the artist Grizel Niven, along with a cheque for £30,000. The applause died down and she spoke briefly:

> We're writers . . . but we're all readers first and to be a reader is a fearless thing and to win the Women's Prize is particularly wonderful because to be a woman is to be a very fearless thing these days too.

The deal with Faber – who after the Baileys Prize immediately rushed a further 25,000 copies into print – was well-timed and a great success, not least in getting a huge number of books printed and distributed and managing the media storm, foreign rights, promotional tours and so on. It was good news all round, but the remaining Galley Beggars were not entirely happy. They were chiefly disgruntled by what they saw as the lack of any GBP presence on the Faber cover, having believed that their impish logo would appear alongside the Faber colophon, and that their name as co-publisher would appear on the copyright page. They felt they had been excluded from the book's history. When they made their concern known, the Galley Beggar logo was added to the Faber edition, and has since appeared on all copies. In the future Galley Beggar Press plans to go it alone and avoid the complications of co-publishing. They now have greater financial autonomy, better access to finance and, most importantly, more experience. Still a small independent with an increasingly impressive list of debut authors, they navigated the pitfalls of early success and learned from the experience, as Sam confirms:

> We came out of this with a deal that was (though only if you *have* to co-publish) a decent deal for everyone. So I guess I would like there to be a warning: that if you're going to go into this as a small publisher, you need to remember that this is big business for most people – and that you need to fight your corner, because the other parties aren't going to be looking out for you.

Following the Baileys win the usual full-page ads were placed in national newspapers, but Faber were reluctant to accommodate the long lead time required to get posters up in stations on the London Underground system, so they took the unprecedented step (for them) of advertising their prize-winning acquisition on the sides of London's double-decker buses. 'Read it and be changed' – Eleanor Catton's clarion phrase accompanied a blow-up image of the book's cover, in the type of campaign usually associated with mass-market blockbuster authors. It was an unusual experience, in the summer of 2014, to travel around the capital on a mobile billboard promoting an avant-garde novel.

The inaugural Goldsmiths Prize had been the first in an increasingly high-profile succession of literary awards which, by the middle of 2014, seemed to have attained its own momentum and led one commentator to suggest that, if she bothered to turn up, McBride stood a good chance of winning that summer's Wimbledon Open tennis championship. Here are the awards for which the novel was shortlisted; with the exception of the Folio and the Dylan Thomas, the book won in each case:

2013 Goldsmiths Prize
2013 Geoffrey Faber Memorial Prize (awarded in 2014)
2014 Folio Prize shortlist (won by George Saunders for *Tenth of December*)
2014 Baileys Women's Prize for Fiction
2014 Kerry Group Irish Fiction Award
2014 Desmond Elliott Prize (for debut novelists)
2014 Dylan Thomas Prize shortlist (won by Joshua Ferris for *To Rise Again at a Decent Hour*)

No other debut novelist has ever swept the board like this, and even to be shortlisted for any of these awards would have been an outstanding achievement. Of particular importance are the lesser-known awards – the Desmond Elliott and Geoffrey Faber Prizes, which come with relatively modest prize money but have potent cultural associations. Such success was a powerful vindication, and McBride surely reflected on the similar tribulations endured by James Joyce during the nine years he took to find a publisher for *Dubliners*. Nine years of rejection and neglect: they had this in common.

An idea of the rapid escalation in the number of public commitments that followed the Goldsmiths can be seen in the author's schedule for the following twelve months, although this gives only a partial idea of what was going on. There were many other more informal appearances, readings, interviews and so on, for national and international print and electronic media, and her schedule, hectic as it was, cannot show the many unclassifiable encounters at readings and signings that make up the public life of a successful writer. It doesn't show the huge amount of time spent unproductively on trains and planes and in taxis, waiting for connections at stations and airports, getting from one venue to another, packing and unpacking and trying to remember where on earth you're expected to be tomorrow. Finally, it doesn't show McBride's evolving presence as an all-round literary practitioner – reviewing for some leading UK publications, writing commissioned articles (on Joyce, among others). Amid all this she found the time to write 'Ivy Day in the Committee Room' for the *Dubliners 100* anthology and continue work on her second novel.

Following McBride's first reading at the Mascara Bar in June 2013, her commitments for the rest of that year were limited to launches in Norwich, Dublin, Castlebar and London, plus five other low-key events in London, Norwich and Dingle. During 2014 her commitments included, in addition to more than a dozen London engagements, events in Liverpool, Bristol, Dublin, Galway, Listowel, Carlow, Cork, Edinburgh, Cheltenham, Swansea, Cambridge, Belfast and, of course, Norwich. And there were many festivals abroad: Indonesia, Oslo, Auckland in New Zealand, Sydney in Australia, Bali, Calgary and Toronto in Canada, and San Francisco, Seattle, Austin, Washington, DC, and Boston in the US.

Things became a little calmer towards the end of 2014, but the following year saw the first translated version appear in Dutch, as *Een meisje is maar half af*, and this involved a week in Holland with the now-familiar round of interviews, readings and signings. After that the focus would be on completing the final draft of *The Lesser Bohemians*, with publication scheduled for autumn 2016.

Girl on the road

A Girl Is a Half-formed Thing was published in the United States on 9 September 2014, but there had already been some early critical reactions to the novel before it appeared. One of the first extended US reviews was by Eric Karl Anderson, blogging as 'The Lonesome Reader', who published a lengthy and thoughtful consideration in April 2014, noting presciently:

> There are such powerful character voices cutting through the text that they can be naturally transformed into a theatrical monologue. For instance try reading these few lines silently and then say them out loud: 'And my head is good for secrets. I can bang it on the wall. It takes the nervous out and no one bothers for it at all.' Doesn't the meaning subtly develop and change? If nothing else, it allows you to appreciate how unusually beautiful the writing is. Whether you choose to read part or all of this book aloud yourself is up to you, but I'd recommend trying it.

Following official publication the mainstream American reviewers began to take an interest. Things got off to a bad start when Ron Charles, former staff critic at the *Christian Science Monitor* and now book critic of the *Washington Post*, delivered his review on 16 September. After rehearsing the now-familiar story of the author's long search for a publisher and describing her book's success as 'a minor literary legend', he went in for the kill, describing the book as 'an extraordinarily demanding novel that will fascinate dozens of American readers', 'a migraine in print' presented in language 'as clever and effective as it is opaque and confusing'. At the end of the review he painstakingly typed out a decontextualised passage guaranteed to dismay the average reader, just for the sake of a wisecrack.

Ron Charles produces 'The Totally Hip Video Book Review', an online series for his employers at the *Washington Post* in which, sometimes accompanied by his wife, a high-school English teacher, he 'hams it up with sight gags and intentionally bad jokes. It is a satirical look at current books in the news and the art of book reviewing.' Behind all the cavorting there's something rather despicable, and his condescending estimate of the size of an American audience for serious experimental fiction is a giveaway. He condemns the book for not being snapped up by 'big New York publishers' without pausing to reflect that this is not something he should be too cocky about.

Worse was to come in another early review posted by Russell Smith of the *Globe and Mail*. Under the headline 'A column is a half-formed thing' he decided to amuse his readers with a ham-fisted pastiche which served only to confirm that there's much more to McBridean prose than short sentences, inverted syntax and lots of full stops. Here's how Smith begins: 'Book. There. There new book. You all talk. About the book. There is so much talking.' He carries on like this for 800 words.

Things improved after that. Heller McAlpin's online review on the NPR Books website praised 'this raw, visceral, brutally intense neo-modernist first novel', and two days later Lisa Moore's piece (also for the *Globe and Mail*) described the novel as 'shockingly honest, devastatingly beautiful'. She made an illuminating comparison with William Faulkner's *The Sound and the Fury* and the tenderly anxious relationship between Caddie and her vulnerable younger brother Benjy. A week later Joshua Cohen in the *New York Times* delivered a brilliantly lucid review following an excited introduction: 'Lord above, it's a future classic. After only a chapter or two, the style is justified, and the reader converted.' Malcolm Forbes in the *Star Tribune* hailed as 'spellbinding' a book whose 'creative and emotional power renders us awe-struck', an example of 'brave, dizzying, risk-taking fiction of the highest order'. There followed the now-obligatory comparisons with Joyce and Beckett.

At the end of the month *The New Yorker* review by James Wood appeared online, a piece equivalent to Anne Enright's watershed *Guardian* review the previous year. He called the novel 'blazingly daring'. I wanted to include this terrific piece in full, not least because James Wood is my favourite critic, but the permission fee is beyond this book's budget so you'll have to go online and look it up for free. It's good.

There were many other print and online reviews and it soon became impossible to keep track. Some of these were of great interest, such as those by Jenny Hendrix and Lisa Moore (the author of *Caught*). Annie Galvine in the *Los Angeles Review of Books* (7 October 2014) was among those who saw *A Girl* as part of a high modernist tradition dating back to Joyce and Woolf in its attempt to find a language for the 'vicissitudes of consciousness', and she compared it favourably with *A Portrait of the Artist as a Young Man*. Galvine believes that what makes the novel part of an enduring canon of women's writing is the fact that the author 'never self-censors when engaging with the pain, the abjection, and the desperation generated out of situations in which a woman is granted little more than her body and her words to use as weapons within imbalanced power structures'.

Sara Weinman, writing for *Maclean's Magazine* online, took a literalist perspective when she said that the novel was 'the most acute depiction of post-traumatic stress disorder', and I was pleased to learn that a copy of the novel was acquired by the library at the Wellcome Institute, Eimear's former employers, for just that reason. Weinman also acclaimed it as a literary 'miracle' and a 'devastating, ferociously original debut'.

There were a few dissenting voices. Writing on 15 September in the *Chicago Tribune*'s Sunday book section, Diane Leach said that she 'didn't like it, and feel heretical admitting so'. Inside the girl's head is, she says, 'not a pleasant place to spend time'. She also seemed to think that 'Mammy' is a name. She finally backtracked, comparing the novel to 'a shot of blackest espresso: sharp, jolting, and acidic. This isn't necessarily bad; I'll take it any day over a romance novel.'

In October Coffee House Press organised a promotional tour of North America, starting at Green Apple Books in San Francisco on the 22nd ('In conversation with Anisse Gross'), then in quick succession Seattle, Austin, Washington, DC, Boston (in conversation with Madeline Miller, whose debut novel, *Song of Achilles,* had won the Orange Prize in 2012) and finally New York City, the author arriving on the 30th for an event at the Irish Arts Center on West 51st Street, a conversation with Rivka Gelchen. After a day's rest she appeared on 1 November at Word Bookstore on Broadway with a Hallowe'en linked event, 'Art & Monsters with Eimear McBride and Jenny Offill', chaired by Isaac Fitzgerald.

After which the exhausted author flew home. Her life had changed immeasurably in the previous twelve months and taken her way beyond my orbit, or the orbit of most writers. She was now an internationally acclaimed headliner. I asked Elizabeth McCracken whether, following the spectacular success of *A Girl,* she had any advice for her friend about balancing – or juggling – commitments as a professional writer: 'I'm lousy with that kind of advice, except I know you have to do it. And also (particularly in a time so full of demands, and with a little kid) she should also give herself a break till she finds time.'

The accumulative nature of the internet, its content rapidly out-distancing the most diligent researcher, contributes to what Walter Benjamin called the 'aura' of artworks and what I prefer to call the novel's *sillage*. This is the French word for the vapour trail left by a jet aeroplane, or the lingering aroma of perfume left behind by its wearer after they leave the room, and I'd like to apply it to the cultural vapour trail of *A Girl Is a Half-formed Thing*.

Alert to the least whiff of pretension, the author said she thought the term should be 'silage', which to be sure also leaves an aromatic trace, but I've always liked the French word, and when it comes to assessing the impact of any new work of art on the world at large it seems to me just right: a fragrance that fades – because the reviews and the profiles and the interviews, the media interest and the awards are not intended to last beyond their moment. Yet – to pursue the metaphor – long after the vapour trail has faded the aeroplane is still in service somewhere, resting on the tarmac or making new trails; long after the aroma of Givenchy's *Vol de Nuit* has dissipated, its far-away wearer picks up the lovely bottle and prepares for another adventure.

Speaking of perfume, it was a close reading of *A Girl Is a Half-formed Thing* that prompted my short-lived interest in the kind of scents that are marketed to teenage girls. The girls on the school bus with their fizzing walkmans favour impulse (the lower-case rendering the word less emphatic, like a barely-noticed aroma), so I looked it up because with a writer like Eimear McBride nothing is thoughtless or accidental. Impulse is a body spray manufactured by Fabergé, part of the colossal Anglo-Dutch company Unilever, based in Rotterdam and London. First introduced as a 'perfume deodorant' in South Africa in 1972, Impulse arrived

in Britain and Ireland in 1981 and was promoted with the slo-
gan 'Men can't help acting on Impulse.' Six variant scents were
introduced in the United States: Always Alluring, Delightfully
Daring, Instantly Innocent, Mysterious Musk, Possibly Playful
and Suddenly Sassy; other products have since been added to the
range. There's a rich seam here for both cultural anthropologists
and satirists.

Sillage also includes all those things other than writing novels
that require the attention of a successful novelist: the readings
and the signings and the interviews, the literary journalism, the
writing of blurbs and reviews, participation in panel discussions,
judging prizes, contributing to broadcasts and so on. Some of
this is distracting and some of it of interest, especially when it
throws light on an author's reading preferences. McBride is very
well read and a thoughtful critic of other writers' work. She
has a particular admiration for a writer still little known in the
English-speaking world, Agota Kristof (1935–2011).

Kristof left her native Hungary at the age of 21, following
the 1956 Spring Uprising, and went with her husband to live
in Switzerland. Working in a clock factory, she began slowly
to write in French and her first book, *Le Grand Cahier* (*The
Notebook*), became an international success. Four of her books
are published in English by CB editions – *The Notebook* (1986),
The Proof (1988)*, The Third Lie* (1991) and *The Illiterate* (2004).
I recommended *The Notebook* to Eimear as it seemed to me
Kristof's novel shared some of the concerns and approaches of *A
Girl Is a Half-formed Thing* – the anonymous narrators (identical
twin boys), the unspecified rural setting, the sudden explosions
of violence and troubling sexual encounters. Kritsof's prose is
precise, restrained, pared down, with an intense emotional undertow. Eimear reviewed *The Notebook* and *The Illiterate* for the
Times Literary Supplement (9 April 2014), her second appearance
in print, following a review of Frank McGuinness's *Arimathea*
for the *Guardian*. On several occasions after that, in interviews
and in print, she confirmed her admiration for the writer and

the novel – thus aligning herself with a European experimental tradition. She discussed *The Notebook* at length with the American author and art historian Noah Charney in an interview for *The Believer*, an online literary blog: 'I found it profoundly disturbing, incredibly well written, and very brave. And the fact that it was written by a woman – it has a startling brutality and ferocity about the style that I find very inspiring.'

In that same interview she spoke warmly of three other Irish writers as if, having aligned herself with the European modernist Kristof and established her primary affiliation, she could now look closer to home. She cited *In Night's City* (1982) by Dorothy Nelson (a powerful account of a daughter coming to terms with the death of her abusive father), Donal Ryan's *The Thing about December* and *The Spinning Heart* and (surprisingly, given her claimed aversion to poetry), Martin Dyar's collection *Charney*. Elsewhere she has reviewed *The Wake* by Paul Kingsnorth, Sigrid Undset's *Marta Oulie: A novel of betrayal* and Niall Williams's *History of the Rain,* and she has expressed in interviews her admiration for, among others, the Australian writer Elizabeth Harrower.

The proliferation of online appearances can overwhelm the researcher. David Foster Wallace summed up the problem when he said: 'There are four trillion bits coming at you. 99 per cent of them are shit, and it's too much work to do triage to decide.' The other one per cent cannot be ignored but I gave up keeping a close track of McBride's online appearances when it became impossible to do so. A few things from what will be known as 'the early years' are certainly worth preserving. Here's McBride responding to a question about her 'all-time favourites' on a website called *Slightly Bookist*:

> It's probably boring to say *Ulysses* but it never stops being the truth. Thomas Mann's *Doctor Faustus, Middlemarch,* Dostoyevsky's *The Devils, Tender is the Night, Nineteen Eighty-Four.* This is a very hard question to stop answering.

Her reply is tantalising because it appears in a format that doesn't allow for expansion, and so we may feel short-changed. Does Orwell feature because her father read *Animal Farm* to her when she was very young? What is it about *Middlemarch* that particularly prompts her admiration? Why *Tender is the Night*? But there's no time to dwell on such matters because the next question is already snapping its fingers impatiently for a punchy answer.

I'll confess to having a soft spot for this superficial approach, and would contentedly fire hundreds of such inane yet potentially revealing questions at any writer I admire. Pen or pencil? Milk or plain? Favourite Hitchcock? Last time you bounced a cheque? Can you drive? Do you smoke? Any tattoos? Cats or dogs? *TLS* or *LRB*? Both? Neither? This could be fun, for a while, for me at least. Such questions don't dig deep, but they cover a lot of ground quickly. They can break the ice, or form it. The best of these exchanges appeared in the *Financial Times* when the author was interviewed by Carl Wilkinson. She confirmed that her husband was her 'first reader and harshest critic', that her bedside reading was *The Animals: Love Letters between Christopher Isherwood and Don Bachardy*, Samuel Beckett's *Worstward Ho* and a collection of Henry Green novels; that her favourite place in the world was Bertra Beach in County Mayo, near the mountain of Croagh Patrick; that she wishes she had written *The Brothers Karamazov* and that she relaxes 'with white wine and *Battlestar Galactica*'. Best of all, given the *FT*'s role as the financial establishment's house journal, was the final exchange. Asked 'What is the best piece of advice a parent gave you?' the author responded: 'That the acquiring of wealth was a waste of a life.'

In a May 2015 *Guardian* feature later covered by *The New Yorker*, she was among a group of authors invited to name their favourite word. She chose 'yoke', not in the familiar sense of a wooden bar used to hitch oxen together but, as she defined it, 'a term of indeterminate identification applicable to any and all objects or people', i.e. an all-purpose word meaning thing

with 'its showier cousins' yokeymabob, yokeymajig and yokeybus (forms of jocular elaboration that linguists term 'radiant
particularisation'). She adds a warning: '[Y]oke and yokeybus,
when attached to people – which yokemabob and yokemajig
should never be – carry slight intimations of obstinacy; I have
fond memories of being described as a Divil of a yokeybus by an
elderly neighbour when I was a small child.' The word 'yoke'
and its variants do not appear in *A Girl Is a Half-formed Thing*
but in the *Guardian* piece the author added that 'when applied to
grown women, yoke's slang synonym is probably wagon, which
is used to describe any manner of awkward or disagreeable female: intransigent ex-wife; equal-rights campaigner; pro-choice
advocate and so on'.

In another *Guardian* profile she confirmed her abiding admiration for 'the Tindersticks back catalogue' and records by Bill
Callahan, Will Oldham and Nick Cave's 'The Mercy Seat'. She
said she liked to listen to the Stooges in the car and Bach on
the plane ('in case it's the last sound I ever hear'). Her favourite
films include *Taxi Driver*, *The Godfather* parts 1 and 2 and *The
Turning Point* (directed by Herbert Ross in 1977 and starring
Anne Bancroft). As a family choice she opted for 'the wonderful Stuart Staples/Dave Boulter-produced *Songs for the Young at
Heart* album. Thank God for it.'

The perfect specific

'Snipcock and Tweed' is a strip cartoon about publishing by
Nick Newman that has been running at the foot of the 'Literary Review' page in the satirical magazine *Private Eye* for many
years and usually consists of a terse exchange between the two
eponymous publishers. Snipcock is short, portly and bearded, in
double-breasted suit and bow tie, while Tweed is more ascetic,
wearing half-moon spectacles and a tweed jacket with leather
elbow patches, looking rather like the *Eye*'s former editor Richard Ingrams. Occasionally one or the other will be seen outside

the confines of their Georgian offices, usually guzzling wine at a book launch or trade fair.

A cartoon in the issue dated 13 June 2014 portrayed Snipcock in front of a pile of books and behind him a poster announcing the winner of the 2014 Baileys Prize for Women's Fiction. Addressing the trophy-bearing author, Snipcock, brimming wine glass in hand, blusters: 'How can we possibly have failed to spot that your book was so brilliant?' To which, in the second frame, our author replies: 'Elbow. Publishers. Know. Their. Don't From. Arses? Their.'

By the time the Newman cartoon was published the reputation of *A Girl Is a Half-formed Thing* had already transcended its readership (actual or hypothetical) to become in some way public property and to 'stand for' something. Newman, an established *Eye* regular, is particularly adept at exploiting 'the perfect specific', a term which is useful in discussing the cultural resonances of the McBridean style. When Newman wants to represent, say, an Australian or American tourist he'll show the former in a wide-brimmed hat with dangling corks and the latter in a stetson (cigar and camera optional); a football supporter will invariably appear in a striped scarf, sporting a large rosette and carrying a rattle; civil servants always wear pinstripe trousers and bowler hats; Frenchmen in berets wheel bicycles festooned with onions; Scotsmen wear kilts and artists wear smocks and carry easels. When was the last time you saw a football fan with a rosette? But these comfortingly threadbare stereotypes still enjoy a certain currency, at least in cartoons. The images are seldom disparaging and never, these days, racist, but allow the cartoonist to make a point, and the reader to get it without too much effort. Perfect specifics are non-verbal cultural signifiers around which a certain consensus has formed. They are harmless (unless they represent, say, a bearded man in turban holding a copy of the Koran and therefore might conceivably depict the Prophet Mohammed, but that's another issue). The name 'Snipcock' carries with it a whiff of anti-Semitism and the character is reportedly based on Tom Rosenthal, the flamboyant Jewish publisher. Newman's take on McBride is crudely reductionist (big hair, frock, curves, lips) but you'd find it hard to make a case that his work is offensive.

That Eimear McBride's style is instantly recognisable suggests to some that it is easily imitable. Several readers posting their comments on Amazon attempt to do so (as they put it) 'in the style of the book itself' and of course fail utterly even to approximate what it is that makes McBride's language so powerful and effective. It's not simply a matter of jumbling up grammatical sentences into two-word fragments and then rearranging them like fridge magnets, as the cartoon McBride does to a flabbergasted Snipcock. It's not about word inversion at all, and it's certainly nothing as simple as writing in plain English and then mucking about with it.

When Newman has a cartoon McBride say 'Elbow. Publishers. Know. Their. Don't From. Arses? Their' we are invited to infer that the author *actually speaks like that.* She doesn't, of course. Although it wouldn't be so far from the truth to say she *thinks* ungrammatically, because we all do. At least that's what I thought until I read this angry comment on the Goodreads website by somebody we'll call Bob: 'I don't care what the author was trying to accomplish, the writing style is inane and moronic. I believe we all think in fully-formed sentences, so this stream of consciousness made no sense[.]' Bob is free to believe that of course, and perhaps there are certain psychotic states in which that actually happens, but despite his confident assertion there's absolutely no reason to suppose that our consciousness is based on Fowler's *Modern English Usage.* Thought is natural, writing cultural. Speech is natural, rhetoric cultural. These are reasonably straightforward distinctions. *A Girl Is a Half-formed Thing* is a cultural object that makes claims to represent the natural. The technique may be highly artificial (and we need to give full weight to the meaning of 'artifice' and think of Joyce's 'great artificer', Icarus) but the effect is not – at least to readers who engage with the prose to the point where (as Beckett would say) 'the hooks go in'.

Private Eye's anonymous contributor 'Bookworm', the novelist and critic D. J. Taylor, lives near Norwich and is a Book Hive regular. Taylor took over the regular spoof Diary feature from Craig Brown for an issue when McBride fever was at its height, and produced a pastiche of the kind of reading lists favoured by the quality newspapers, assembling the choices of, among others, A. S. Byatt, Hanif Kureishi, Andrew Motion and the Labour Party leader Ed Miliband. The herd instinct of the British literati is neatly skewered as each of them, having made a first and usually pompous or self-serving choice, then opts for *A Girl Is a Half-formed Thing*. Here's 'Ed Miliband': 'Look, I'm sure I read something in the *Observer* about some Irish woman who imitates James Joyce. Surely that would go down OK, wouldn't it?'

This says something about public figures' fear of being left behind in a consensual stampede. It also says something about a function of literature in a celebrity culture, of celebrities endorsing a highbrow novel as a means of confirming their own cultural status and affiliations. Finally it says something about the way experimental or subversive art is swiftly co-opted by the establishment, rendered (at least in this satirical context) briefly safe.

The new serious

It was the late critic and novelist Gilbert Adair who observed, in his collection of essays *Myths and Memories* (1986), that regardless of the unquestionable brilliance of Henry Moore's sculptures there might just be something a tiny bit kitsch in his signature 'hole', the aspect of his work easily exploited as a perfect specific by any cartoonist wishing to represent something unambiguously 'modern' and 'challenging' to an artless audience alert to pretension. This, Adair suggested, plants a tiny seed of doubt even in (and perhaps especially in) the mind of any admirer of Moore's work.

I'm happy to admit that I owe Gilbert Adair a double debt – for the term *sillage* and for introducing me to the term 'perfect specific' (which I believe he in turn took from Oliver Sacks). Both terms appeared in two of the many brilliant essays included in *Myths and Memories*. Few cultural commentators can match Adair's range, knowledge and intelligence. He wrote in a way I like to think I think, and is much missed. I want to rope in Adair for a third and final time, because he summed up the shortcomings and attractions of postmodernism in a short piece in *Flickers: An Illustrated Celebration of 100 Years of Cinema* (1995). Writing about Clint Eastwood's *Unforgiven*, he references Umberto Eco's *Reflections on the Name of the Rose,* in which Eco, describing the genesis of his most celebrated novel, defines the postmodern attitude 'as that of a man who loves a very cultivated woman and knows he cannot say to her, "I love you madly", because he knows that she knows (and that she knows that he knows) that these words have already been written by Barbara Cartland. Still,' continues Eco, 'there is a solution. He can say, "As Barbara Cartland would put it, I love you madly."'

Thus, Adair argues, the speaker avoids any false innocence and, in stating clearly that it is no longer possible to speak with true innocence, he is nevertheless able to say what he wants to say to the woman: that he loves her sincerely in an age of lost innocence, an age in which sincerity has been compromised by a pervasive and ironic self-consciousness. I'd suggest that McBride has shown us a way in which we can say, unironically, 'I love you madly'; or (if we adhere to the Adair/Eco principle) she has given us an alternative to the ironic detachment of 'As Barbara Cartland would say, "I love you madly"' (which is me quoting Gilbert Adair quoting Umberto Eco quoting an imaginary suitor quoting Barbara Cartland). In other words she has given us a new literary standard against which human experience can be measured. More, she has introduced feeling to modernist writing, combining virtuosity with tenderness. She has brought life to the avant-garde, and brought the avant-garde to life.

She has also enriched the debate surrounding modern literature by pointing to the way in which publishers neglect their readers, or are misled into catering for some hypothetical popular audience with unambitious tastes:

> I think the fact that this book has done so well is proof that there is a readership for fiction of this kind and of course I hope that might encourage publishers to let more difficult fiction out there and to really stop patronising their readers. I think to suggest that readers are too stupid or lazy to understand work of this kind is really an abuse of the relationship between publisher and reader.

A generation of writers – and of readers too – born in the 1980s and 90s are united in their loathing of the way art has become an alternative economy for the super-rich. There's a reaction against the self-conscious playfulness that plagued (and defined) much writing in the 1980s and a wish to recover values that have been squandered – commitment, political engagement and a high-minded sense of the non-material. Wherever I look I see a new seriousness in the arts, a renewed commitment to craft, to tradition and to highbrow cultural values, now stripped of their elitist connotations – in the work of poets and writers and artists still in their thirties who are at home with new media and technologies and exploiting them the hilt, but who are not in thrall to them. They seem to share a profound understanding of the modernist tradition and a sceptical take on the gimcrack ironies of postmodernism.

A rant by Will Self in the *New Statesman* (15 September 2014) seemed to me a watershed moment in contemporary cultural discourse, marking as it did the belated realisation by a leading writer of his (and my) fifty-something generation that the game is up, and that said game wasn't worth the candle. Self described a showdown in an LA cafeteria in which he asks the proprietor to turn down the overwhelming music. The proprietor refuses so Self has to eat his breakfast waffles to the sound of trip-hop. This annoys him and when one of his sons shouts something sympathetic over the racket Self says, 'Really, it's OK. After all, it's my generation that's to blame for this bullshit culture.'

The incident prompted Self into bilious reflections on his generation, 'the pierced and tattooed, shorts-wearing, skunk-smoking, OxyContin-popping, neurotic dickheads' and their complicity in the commodification of counterculture. Getting into his stride, he berates the 'twats' who insist that there is nothing to choose between high and popular culture, who embrace a doctrine of relativism that places advertising and fine art on the same level, and finally describes cultural criticism of the kind he and his peers perpetrated as – and I'm sorry for this – 'jetted slurry from our dickhead arseholes'.

There is another cultural tendency to set alongside Self's tattooed, shorts-wearing dickheads. The journalist and cultural commentator Marc Spitz has identified what he calls 'the first great cultural movement since Hip Hop, a new aesthetic that's both old-fashioned and completely modern, created and adopted by teens, twenty and thirty-somethings (and even late Baby Boomers like myself)'. He calls it 'Twee' and traces its origins to the post-war 1950s in Walt Disney movies and such writers as J. D. Salinger, Sylvia Plath, Dr Seuss, Maurice Sendak and Judy Blume. Generation Twee has adopted a culture of 'calculated precocity' embodied in (and I take this from his publisher's website) 'Vampire Weekend, Garden State, Miranda July, Belle and Sebastian, Wes Anderson, Mumblecore, McSweeney's, Morrissey, beards, artisanal pickles, food trucks, crocheted owls on Etsy, ukuleles, kittens and Zooey Deschanel'.

I've heard of Morrissey of course. Everybody's heard of Morrissey. Wes Anderson rings bells. Beards and 'artisanal pickles' suggest the hipster quarters of Hoxton and Shoreditch, both well off my radar. Crocheted owls on Etsy ('a peer-to-peer e-commerce website focused on handmade or vintage items') sound cute if inessential (and I'll confess to owning a crocheted finger puppet of James Joyce, on my desk beside me as I type. It was a gift). 'Ukuleles, kittens and Zooey Deschanel' all seem mimsy enough and I've just learned to my horror that Zooey Deschanel, aged 35, runs a website called giggles.com and says things like 'I wish everyone looked like a kitten'.

'Generation Twee' – infantilised, incurious, silly – resemble the Eloi, those elegant childlike adults in H. G. Wells's *The Time Machine*. The Eloi are, you'll remember, reared and slaughtered for food by the subterranean Morlocks, brutish creatures descended, surely, from Will Self and his fellow dickheads. Whatever the zeitgeisty value of Twee it's as likely to be remembered by future generations as the 1920s bestsellers listed in the next chapter. Or it may be remembered fondly and ironically by its adherents as they lapse into middle age. But it is so heavily commodified, so related to the acquisition of material 'stuff' rather than human experience, that it will hold no residual value, offer no consolation, no assurance.

Eimear McBride is certainly no representative of 'Generation Twee'. She is a young woman still and with wide-ranging cultural tastes (*Battlestar Galactica* and Tarkovsky's *Nostalgia*, The Tindersticks and Agota Kristof). She's part of the intelligentsia, whatever that is, and, like it or not, now part of the literary establishment. There are times when I am keenly aware of the fact that she belongs to the generation after mine, the one that's taking over from tattooed dickheads, and thank the stars for that.

About interpretation

Cartoons, parodies, online reviews, newsprint Q&As, readings and signings and panel discussions – *sillage* trails in different densities behind the book and its author. One young woman was so moved by her reading of *A Girl* that she had a line from the book tattooed on her body, then posted an image of the fresh dermal inking on her Facebook account. At the other extreme from facetiousness (and all the more likely to be pilloried by hacks at the *Eye*) is the academic world, and writers whose aim is not to simplify (as Newman and his *Eye* colleagues do) but to complicate and problematise. There are a number of essays and articles on McBride and her novel and these will multiply as the book becomes embedded in college syllabuses.

I made several false starts when looking at the novel from an academic (but not an academic's) perspective. I thought I might be on to something with a consideration of what's called 'performative writing' – a form of critical writing about performance, and particularly performance art, which claims to be a form of performance in itself. Its practitioners assert that it's a better way to capture the ephemeral nature of a performance, and to pin down the thoughts that pass through the mind of the viewer during and after a performance. It's associated with feminist writers, and a notable exponent and advocate is the theorist Peggy Phelan. In *Mourning Sex* (1997) she says that performative writing 'enacts the death of the "we" that we think we are before we begin to write. A statement of allegiance to the radicality of unknowing who we are becoming, this writing pushes against the ideology of knowledge as a progressive movement forever approaching a completed end-point.'

'The radicality of unknowing who we are becoming' is language on its last legs, a fridge-magnet lexicon. If something of import is being set down here it doesn't survive the process. When I read stuff like this – and I don't often, because I value my sanity – my critical spirits droop and my critical hackles rise, not because it is aimlessly self-regarding and grotesquely written, and of no interest to anyone beyond a small circle of like-minded practitioners, but because it seems to me to be anti-life and essentially silly and lightweight. Phelan's supporters and followers – I know some of them and admire their work very much – would denounce me for being even more silly and lightweight, and perhaps I am being arrogant when I insist that if something is unintelligible to me then it's not my intelligence that's being called into question but that of the writer. I am sure that to her admirers my objections to Phelan's approach resemble the objections of those online reviewers who angrily denounce McBridean prose. But – to come to the point – I mentioned performative writing to the author as a possible approach to her work because I thought she might have come across it during her time at Drama Centre. This, I thought, might have been an influence, if remotely, but the author told me she had never heard of performative writing and could therefore hardly be influenced by it. So why include this digression? It's because I admire the French essayist Ivan Rioufol's aphorism 'I believe in what I see. The doctrinaire see what they believe in' (*'les doctrinaires croyait qu'ils lisent . . .'*) – and I hope my reference to performative writing may serve to pre-empt such approaches, anticipating a tendency among doctrinaire academics to regard novels as their own 'found documents'.

I was also interested in the extent to which McBridean pre-consciousness might find a parallel in current scientific and philosophic thinking about what's known as 'the hard problem' – the question of what actually constitutes consciousness. When I tentatively suggested to the author that this might be a fruitful line of enquiry, she replied: 'As you know "my innovations" do not have a root in the scientific understanding of pre-conscious speech! But I'll leave you to amuse yourself.'

Of course there's no reason why creative artists should not arrive at an understanding of the human condition which others have reached by scientific means, but I understand why Eimear McBride would wish to distance herself from the hermetic and counter-literate world of academic writing about writing, and am keen to do so myself. The point of this digression is to suggest that too much academic critical writing is, as it were, all gong and no dinner. It has the shape of robust enquiry but not the content. There will be brighter, sharper minds than mine, tenured academics all, who will engage with her work, and one hopes the results will be worthwhile, or at least literate. I do not wish to suggest that McBride is in any way anti-intellectual – she has a sharp and original intelligence that leaves me floundering. But I want to give it one more shot, and go back to consciousness.

'The hard problem' is one that presents itself in different ways and at different times to all of us. What is consciousness and how can it exist in a material world – a world of things? Is consciousness just another 'thing'? If not, what is it? What do we mean by it? Is it the same for all of us? How can all the electrical charges in our brain produce our subjective sense of the world and our place in it? Who are we anyway?

The easy problems are all to do with biology – how the brain works, what happens when we sneeze or have a stroke or epileptic fit. But whenever we start to think seriously about the easy problems the hard problem is waiting to pounce. Perhaps it's really a question best left to neuroscientists rather than philosophers, but writers such as Eimear McBride suggest the multiplicity of human consciousness – that it's complex, unstable, contingent and ever-changing. It hardly seems a radical proposal to suggest that our 'personality' (for want of a better word) responds to, is formed by, context. This is certainly the case with language: there's really no such thing as 'good' or 'bad' language – the only worthwhile measure is one of appropriacy.

Before we leave this brief consideration of the literary treatment of consciousness we might consider *A Girl Is a Half-formed Thing* in terms of what Marco Roth calls 'the neuronovel'. In a 2011 article for the Brooklyn-based literary magazine *n+1*, Roth traces the origins of the form to Ian McEwan's *Enduring Love* (1997), the first in a series of novels by very different writers each investigating what Roth calls 'a cognitively anomalous or abnormal person'. He cites Mark Haddon's *The Curious Incident of the Dog in the Night-Time* (in which the main character is a boy with an autistic disorder); Richard Powers's *The Echomaker* (facial agnosia and Capgras syndrome, in which the sufferer believes friends and family have been replaced by impostors); McEwan's *Saturday* (Huntington's disease) and Rivka Galchen's *Atmospheric Disturbances* (Capgras syndrome again). To these can be added many genre novels which feature, for instance, amnesia and bipolar disorders. What connects them all is an interest in the workings of the brain rather than the mind.

The neuronovel reflects, says Roth, a movement by authors away from traditional theories of personality and a return to the study of the brain itself. This tendency mirrors a decline in the status of Freudian and Lacanian psychoanalysis and the increasing popularity of psychiatric drugs such as Prozac. Compared with most novels of the past century or so, including those which exploit a 'steam-of-consciousness' approach, the neuronovel (according to Roth) has 'little interest in society, or classes, or individuals interacting, or of individual development alongside or in opposition to historical forces'. Along with the loss of society and the loss of religion the neuronovel explores the loss of self – although it is not that selfhood no longer exists, but, he argues, that selfhood is no longer the prerogative of novelists. The study of selfhood is now the property of specialists working within their own professional disciplines. I'm sure Roth would agree that human consciousness is too complex a subject to be left to scientists and philosophers. ('Only art can contain an idea,' wrote the poet Les Murray.)

Roth gloomily concludes that the rise of the neuronovel, far from expanding literature's purchase on the cultural imagination, 'appears as another sign of the novel's diminishing purview'. *A Girl Is a Half-formed Thing* isn't, by Roth's definition, truly a neuronovel because the girl does not suffer from any cognitive disorder. There is clearly evidence in her behaviour of post-traumatic stress, at least for readers with a taste for such a diagnosis, but she is in no way abnormal.

Girl, interpreted: the stage adaptation

Interviewed by JoAnna Novak during her American tour in 2014, McBride confirmed the importance of theatre texts in her reading:

There's lots of gaps in my reading, but I've read a lot of theatre texts and classic plays and so I've kind of gone through the ages in that way instead, and that's been useful because it's . . . I think I've got away with feeling a bit less precious about language and about literature in a way and you know, having a much more physical approach to it and what it can do.

On reading *A Girl Is a Half-formed Thing* in January 2014, the Chicago-born director and founder of Dublin's Corn Exchange Theatre, Annie Ryan, was struck by its potential as a dramatic monologue. She emailed the author, saying that she'd like to chat about the possibility of adapting the novel for performance. The Corn Exchange company's wide-ranging repertoire includes Beckett, Chekhov, Eugene O'Neill and Tennessee Williams, adapted novels (Nabokov's *Lolita*), site-specific work (Joyce's *Dubliners*) and original work, often in collaboration with Ryan's partner, the writer and translator Michael West. Michael and William Galinsky had met at a writer's retreat in Aldeburgh and became reacquainted in Cork, where William was running the Midsummer Festival. The two couples met for dinner one evening, during which Eimear sat quietly – neither Annie nor Michael had the slightest idea thrn that she had written a novel.

That one meeting at least meant that the proposal to adapt the novel for the stage did not come out of the blue. Annie sent a 'very strong letter' outlining her plans for a stage production. She suggested that the novel was performable, but might not be stageable. She had not yet arrived at the form the final production would take and recalled: 'The only thing I knew at that stage was that it would be a one-woman show, because the book is in her mind. I knew that I wanted to do this . . . to be true to the book as much as possible.'

The author agreed to the adaptation on condition that the text could be cut but not otherwise changed. With this restriction in mind the director began to work through a Word file of the novel using grey highlighter to show what could be cut. She pared the text back to just 90 minutes, which seemed a limit to the endurance of both the performer and an audience. The reduction continued through many drafts. It was a collaborative process between author and director, with Annie very open to the author's concerns while McBride (as she herself put it) 'tried not to be dog in the manger about the cuts she obviously needed to make'. Eimear's role throughout was consultative and she attended rehearsals and an early preview. She was deeply impressed by Aoife [pron. *Ee-fer*] Duffin's performance to the extent, she recalled, that she was like any other member of the audience, unaware of cuts to the text.

Rehearsals were intense. After one particularly distressing scene everyone in the room burst into tears for 20 minutes. The crew did yoga during theatre runs to help them cope, but Aoife was often in tears and inconsolable. After several short runs the performance is still gruelling and makes extraordinary demands on her memory and physical stamina. One thinks, of course, of what Billie Whitelaw went through when directed by Beckett in the Royal Court production of *Not I*.

Duffin comes originally from Castlegregory, a village on the Dingle Peninsula in County Kerry. Her accent — quite unlike that of Mayo, where the novel is set — is natural, unforced and distinctive, by turns mild and harsh. She studied acting at Trinity College Dublin and, while she has a substantial background in theatre, film and television, she is probably best known for appearing in *Moone Boy*, an Irish television comedy co-written by and co-starring Chris O'Dowd and set in the small town of Boyle in County Roscommon, 50 miles east of Castlebar, in the late 80s/early 90s (a temporal overlap with *A Girl Is a Half-formed Thing*).

When I saw the production for the first time it occurred to me that I'd never really thought much about the girl's physical appearance. If I think of her in visual terms all I see is pain and tears and snot and cuts and bruises. Duffin's presence on the bare and dimly lit stage is dark, austere, taut and vulnerable. Her achievement is that she manages to hold our attention throughout yet is never distractingly visible as she seamlessly incarnates the girl and the characters the girl engages with. There is, in other words, no intrusive mediation by the performer, who 'disappears' in the same way the author does in the novel. The experience for the audience is unusually intense.

The play opened at the Samuel Beckett Theatre, part of Trinity College Dublin's School of Drama, Film and Music, as part of the Dublin Theatre Festival, on 25 September 2014. This is a black-box performance space with an audience capacity of around 200. There were not many reviews of the first run, but they were all sensational. The *Guardian*'s Helen Meaney praised a 'courageously feminist production' and compared McBride's exploration of female sexuality to work by Marina Abramovic and Sarah Kane: 'Startling and upsetting to witness, through Duffin's magnificent portrayal it travels through raw revelation of pain to a calm aftermath.'

I saw the production for the first time at the Norfolk and Norwich Festival in May 2015. I had expected the presence of a performer, however brilliant, would come between the audience and the text; she would be the object of our scrutiny and whatever happens to the girl would happen to *her*, not to us. Our relation to the text would, I thought, be passive because the 'I' of the novel would become the 'she' of the stage. I was also concerned that the loss of so much of the text would be a fatal reduction – the audiobook, read by the author, runs for more than seven hours and not a line is superfluous. In the event, the production left me breathless. To be part of a 300-strong audience made the experience a very different one from reading the novel alone.

Aoife Duffin gave one of the most powerful theatrical performances I've ever seen, She incarnated the girl as a foetus (briefly), then as a newborn baby, toddler, gauche teen and troubled young woman. She also played every other character with astonishing virtuosity: the mother (particularly impressive), the dying brother, the bigot grandfather, the predatory uncle, a bunch of callous schoolboys, university students, gormless evangelical Christians and others, many others. This was a superb display of physical acting – subtle, detailed and constantly inventive – and was a gruelling experience for both Duffin and her audience.

I'd been invited by the festival organisers to chair a post-show discussion and was joined on stage by the author and director. We explored, briefly, the genesis of the production and the overlap between Stanislavskian approaches to acting and writing. We were later joined by Aoife and there followed many insights into the creative collaboration that had led to this richly rewarding piece of theatre.

The experience of working on the Corn Exchange production was, despite some early uncertainty, a happy one for the author. I asked her whether she would consider further collaborations or even a return to the stage.

> A few years ago, I did the English-language version of a play called *The Bath of Baghdad* in collaboration with an Arabic translator, which I enjoyed enormously. It was all the pleasure of working out the language without any of the pressure of generation. So I could certainly imagine collaborating in that way again. I quite fancy having a crack at Pushkin – since he's proved so elusive in translation, so far – but again it would have to be in collaboration with a translator. I could never actually write with anyone else though. I'd never endure the intrusion! I could imagine trying to write for the theatre at some stage, which is a collaboration of sorts. I don't harbour any delusions about being a playwright but if a project came along which I found interesting and where I thought I might have something to offer, I could be persuaded.

Cover girls

The book's physical appearance is the most visible evidence of its cultural presence and to date it has appeared in four different covers. The original Galley Beggar Press edition was only the second publication to appear in their distinctive house style, devised by Niki Medlik – matt black wraparound covers with red and white lettering and the tiny Galley Beggar imp in the bottom right corner of the front cover. The author's name was in a spot colour and there's a pull quote from the book itself in white and grey, with right-hand justification.

The decision to use spot colour for the author's name was Medlik's:

> The style for the cover was already set, so it was just going with my gut feeling for the second colour. I was a bit nervous of whether it would be OK for Eimear, but she loved it and was great to work with – really appreciative and good fun. I struggled a bit with reading [the novel] because of the style, until I heard her read it, and then it blew me away. I was very lucky to believe in the books I was designing the covers for at GBP.

At Faber Donna Payne and an art team of five produce an impressive 350 book covers each year, and at any given time she might be working on 30 or so different designs, each cover taking between two weeks and three months to complete. She reads a lot of Faber titles and before designing a cover will skim the book to get a feel for its tone but generally doesn't want to know the details because she wants to approach the book as a designer and not a reader. She makes the point that people increasingly browse for books online and at the Kindle store, and it's therefore important to take into account how a book cover will look as a tiny thumbnail, so there's a tendency for covers to become cleaner and simpler.

For background to the Faber paperback cover, here – reproduced in full, with his permission – is Jonathan Gibbs's post from his regular Friday Book Design Blog for the *Independent*. (Gibbs's own debut novel, *Randall*, a sharp satire on the British art movement that begins with the premise that Damien Hirst died in 1989 at the height of his powers, is published by Galley Beggar Press):

I love the new cover for Eimear McBride's Baileys-winning – and Goldsmiths-winning and Kerry Group Irish Novel-winning – *A Girl Is a Half-formed Thing*. This is the mass market paperback, from Faber, following its first publication by tiny Norwich indie Galley Beggar Press (who are, full disclosure, my publisher also). But I think it does a brilliant job of representing a remarkable and challenging book without selling it short.

With its fractured syntax leaping at you from the first page, McBride's book is on the face of it a hard read, but is actually far easier than you'd think, once you immerse yourself in its flow of 'pre-cognitive' language. Its subject matter – a girl growing up in suffocatingly religious rural Ireland, and suffering sexual abuse from a family member – could so easily have led to 'misery memoir' stylings, or floaty 'woman seen from behind walking through cornfield' pastoralia.

I spoke to Donna Payne, art director at Faber, who talked me through the process of designing the cover: 'Eimear gave me a very open brief with just a couple of pointers on what she wanted to avoid. No images of tough sexualised girls – one such image had accompanied a newspaper article about the book and it felt very wrong and at odds with the complexity of the writing and with 'the girl' herself – who is never named, much less described.' She also said the publishers' powers-that-be 'afforded [her] the rare luxury of designing from the heart with the reader rather than the retailer in mind' – though personally I can't think of any retailer who'd be disappointed by what she came up with.

First up, the font – rather bizarrely named Lust Slim, Payne tells me – which just about catches the right degree of retro. It's a modern font, but recalls the early 80s setting of the book. As Payne says, its use was inspired by old *Jackie* magazines and 'cheap make-up packaging'.

I also like the jumbled tumble of the title – or, in fact, not a tumble; it's more that it seems to be building itself upwards, stacking itself like a tower that just might fall, but also shows resilience and strength, the author's name acting as a kind of pedestal, keeping it stable.

And, below that, the apple.

Ah, the apple! That most symbolic of foods – it could stand for innocence (the apple the schoolchild offers the teacher) or experience (the one that the serpent pushes Eve's way).

Says Payne: 'The apple as a symbol for femininity is a familiar one.

But the way in which the book questions and perverts any traditional notion of what it means to be a girl led me to look to images of spoiled, over-ripe fruit. And also that idea of something beautiful and familiar which is perceived as 'not quite right' or 'perfect enough' – for me, also described how other people view the girl's learning disabled brother – a relationship at the very heart of the book and absolutely tied in with her emerging identity.'

It's not just that the fruit is over-ripe, the bruise of the apple is carried over into the faux water damage to the cover itself – which you could just take as a reference to the damp walls of an old, cold house in the country, or as a nod to the water that pervades the book, especially in the lake so crucial to the plot's unfolding.

All in all a great cover – and with news that Faber are printing 25,000 additional copies of it following the Baileys win – the likelihood is that you'll be seeing a lot more of it.

But, here I've got to say that McBride's book has been rather well served by its covers before and beyond this one. The original edition, from Norwich's Galley Beggar Press, follows a strict design template the publisher uses for all their first-run books: matt black cover, text-only but for a tiny Galley Beggar imp, with the author name in a spot colour, and the title and pull quote from the book itself in white and grey. It's a great look that harks back to great independent publishers of the last century, and it's one that absolutely matches the modernist rigour of McBride's prose. In a way it's the perfect match.

But *A Girl* is coming out from Coffee House Press in the US, too, and they have taken an equally interesting, equally successful approach to their design. [Late note: In fact this cover is licensed from the Australian edition, for Text Publishing, where the design is by Australian designer W. H. Chong.] There is something of the Franz Kline about the doodle, also something Japanese. All three covers are admirable responses to a book that could scare readers off and, worse, could scare publishers into not wanting to scare them off, and so betraying the book itself.

The first foreign-language edition – *Een meisje is maar half af* – was published in Holland in March 2015 by Hollands Diep. This features a cover image by the Belgian photographer Lara Gasparotto. It shows the pale back of a dark-haired girl, perhaps pubescent, with rounded shoulders. Around her head dark clouds surround a patch of water light, a vague halo. There's landscape and perhaps a hint of water to the right. It's hard to say what's happening, or has happened, or is about to happen – the girl avoids or evades our objectification. The lettering covers her back, echoing the shape of her torso, the title again a 'jumbled table' but no longer supported by the author's name. This appears above the title, although whether this is a Dutch design convention or a reflection of her star billing I couldn't say.

A final example of what the author insists is the novel's cultural silage: in April 2015 the American actress Sarah Jessica Parker arrived at a New York television studio to appear on *The Late Show with David Letterman*. She was photographed in a Theory 'Vintan' jumpsuit from the Spring 2015 collection 'in a deep forest-green hue'. Fashion pundits admired 'the relaxed simplicity and loose silhouette of the look, to which she added her own SJP signature flair via a lighter jade-green blazer, statement necklaces, and her eponymous SJP heels'. Her final 'accessory piece', held in her left hand, was the Coffee House Press edition of *A Girl*.

7 Nicer is not what I'm after

> My quibble with a lot of modernist writing is that it is very closed to the reader and demands a lot of study. There are great rewards but they don't help you in any way. And I felt – and also because I am interested in language, very specifically in rhythms – I really wanted to give the reader something in return for making the effort. Because I understand that when you open a page and there are lots of sentences with two words and some of them end with the word 'the', that that is slightly alarming and possibly off-putting. But I think if you give it a go, you do get something that helps to pull you through, and the rhythm is certainly part of that, so at least you know that there is a thread that you can connect to.

The above comes from McBride's interview with the Australian journalist Romana Koval. McBride's writing may appeal to a minority (which is by no means the same thing as an elite) and is certainly not for everyone. But it is is, to make a nice point, for anyone. Anyone, that is, prepared to overcome their wariness and scepticism and engage with something new and strange and – at first sight – 'difficult'. There are no barriers to entry.

O, rocks! she said. Tell us in plain words.

Molly Bloom's impatient response to her husband's ponderous explanation of the word 'metempsychosis' comes to mind when considering the place of *A Girl Is a Half-formed Thing* in the modernist literary tradition. I'll use plain words, although plain words aren't always the best words – as the art historian David Brown used to say, 'art is complex because life is complex'. In presenting human consciousness in simple prose Eimear McBride builds on the achievements of earlier writers, and by her own admission is particularly indebted to James Joyce and the stream of consciousness technique (which Joyce didn't invent but could be said to have perfected). When writing about Joyce it can be difficult to use plain words.

In what follows I want to consider where McBride's novel stands in relation to the modernist tradition of which she is now an important part and this will involve digressions, but not into critical theory. My approach is subjective, unsystematic and partial. I am an unreliable authority and I'm certainly no academic. This is just as well, as the author has made her own position clear when it comes to scholarly analysis and interpretation: '*Girl* is in no way influenced by critical theory of any kind.' She says she has 'a life-long phobia for that kind of self-regarding nonsense', adding briskly: 'I have no interest in writing which revolves around [. . .] in-depth explanations about the impossibility of language to mean anything.'

That so much academic writing about literature should be so aggressively unliterary (the prose equivalent of a musicologist being tone deaf) is enough to put you off reading, or at least reading academic writing. Equally, that *A Girl Is a Half-formed Thing* was rejected by publishers for a decade because they either couldn't see its value or, having seen it, didn't know how to proceed, is a terrible reflection on the state of our literary culture. But have things changed much since the heyday of modernism?

Shelf life, and afterlife

Here's a list of ten novels and a question: what do they all have in common, apart from being out of print and completely forgotten?

If Winter Comes by A. S. M. Hutchinson
The Sheik by Edith M. Hull
Gentle Julia by Booth Tarkington
The Head of the House of Coombe by Frances Hodgson Burnett

Simon Called Peter by Robert Keable
The Breaking Point by Mary Roberts Rinehart
This Freedom by A. S. M. Hutchinson
Maria Chapdelaine by Louis Hémon
To the Last Man by Zane Grey
Babbitt by Sinclair Lewis
Helen of the Old House by Harold Bell Wright

These were, according to the American trade magazine *Publishers Weekly*, the ten top-selling works of fiction in the United States in 1922 – the year that *Ulysses* was published. I've heard of the Western writer Zane Grey but only because he's cited as an influence by the hapless Holly Martins as he flounders through a British Council lecture in Carol Reed's film version of *The Third Man*. Booth Tarkington's name rings a bell because Orson Welles adapted her novel *The Magnificent Ambersons* for the screen, and brilliantly. Frances Hodgson Burnett is an Edwardian figure best known for her children's stories *Little Lord Fauntleroy* and *The Secret Garden*. *The Head of the House of Coombe* is not one of better efforts. *Babbitt* I've never read. Sinclair Lewis (who won the Nobel Prize in Literature in 1930) is a once highly regarded satirical writer, but I have to admit that I've never read any of his books, or any other books by any of the writers on the list. Most of the names mean nothing to me.

Let's spread the net. Of the one hundred top sellers of that entire decade listed in the same trade journal very few are still in circulation. Of these I've read only Erich Maria Remarque's *All Quiet on the Western Front* (1927) and *Gentlemen Prefer Blondes* (1925), the comic novel by Anita Loos much admired by Joyce. Both of these, significantly, were made into popular films, which may have contributed to their extended afterlife. The rest of the hundred-strong list features a clutch of once-popular heavyweight middlebrow authors – Thornton Wilder, Sinclair Lewis (again) and John Galsworthy (who won the 1932 Nobel Prize in Literature) – but I haven't read any of their 1920s works and in most cases the titles are wholly unfamiliar. The rest of the best-selling books are almost all genre fictions. This is an American list but the British equivalent would be similar.

Here are ten other novels, all from the same decade:

A Passage to India (1924)
Mrs Dalloway (1925)
The Trial (1925)
The Great Gatsby (1925)
The Sun Also Rises (1926)
To the Lighthouse (1927)
Lady Chatterley's Lover (1928)
Decline & Fall (1928)
A Farewell to Arms (1929)
A Room of One's Own (1929)

They've never been out of print and are so well known that there's no need to identify the authors. Every one of them has also been made into a film, and in certain cases more than once, which may enhance their currency or simply confirm their initial appeal. You will have heard of them all and, I'm sure, have read most or all of them.

What these books and their authors share, to a greater or lesser extent, is a commitment to modernism, to complexity, to fresh ways of thinking and writing. All the authors are in one way or another examples of the Burgessian 'B-writer' I mentioned in Chapter 2, writers concerned with the potential of language to explore some aspect of the human condition. They all wrote 'difficult' books which broke with convention and were read at the time by a small audience. It's my guess that the accumulated readership for each of these novels by now equals and quite possibly outnumbers the combined readership of the ten forgotten best-sellers listed earlier. What are we to make of this?

My second list is, in two senses, *partial* – both incomplete and subjective. I have omitted *À la recherche du temps perdu* as only five of its seven volumes were published in the 1920s; and there's no poetry at all, so no Eliot or Pound. I could add many more books of equal quality, but I think I've made my point – that great books last but bad ones, however popular, don't. For Peter B. Kyne, Harold Bell Wright and Joseph C. Lincoln read Dan Brown, Jeffrey Archer and John Grisham; for Ethel M. Dell read E. L. James. These writers and their novels – not all of them by any means negligible – will all be forgotten, and quite soon. These books will die along with their readers.

Was there ever a more productive decade for serious literature than the 1920s? I don't think so. When it comes to backing the innovative and the unfamiliar, have today's publishers learned any lessons from history? Have they hell. But then it's not simply the fault of the publishers. Consider a third list – the *New York Times* Best Seller List for 3 October 1976 (the week Eimear McBride was born):

1 *Trinity* by Leon Uris
2 *Sleeping Murder* by Agatha Christie
3 *Dolores* by Jacqueline Susann
4 *Touch Not the Cat* by Mary Stewart
5 *Ordinary People* by Judith Guest
6 *Slapstick* by Kurt Vonnegut
7 *The Lonely Lady* by Harold Robbins
8 *The Deep* by Peter Benchley
9 *Storm Warning* by Jack Higgins
10 *The Navigator* by Morris West

It was the same top ten the week before that, and the week after that. My point is not that bestsellers are generally rubbish. All of these books were written by hard-working authors who in one way or another can be said to have made their mark: Jack Higgins has published more than 80 novels; Harold Robbins sold 750 million books in 32 languages, and *The Lonely Lady* was made into a Hollywood movie in 1983 (starring Pia Zadora). All of these authors, male and female, sold a lot of books to a huge audience of appreciative readers, but apart from Vonnegut they were all critically ignored or snobbishly derided. None of these bestsellers is truly atrocious (with the exception of those by Harold Robbins and Jacqueline Susann), or even particularly offensive to a modern readership, but how many are even in print? One reads Jacqueline Susann now with self-conscious irony, enjoying her kitsch campness. Of course the minute a reader begins to patronise this kind of fiction, the minute any condescension or irony enters into the engagement, the moment it becomes, in those awful phrases, 'a guilty pleasure' or 'so bad it's good', then any real claim to value, however slight, is lost.

Much of what I say here about books applies equally to films and plays and songs of the period. The movie stars of the 1920s are, with a few durable exceptions, mostly forgotten; stage actors likewise are remembered only by a handful of audience members, themselves on the brink of oblivion. The popular music of the age is no longer much in circulation except as a signifier of the epoch in films and on television. It's become a niche interest for specialists and is no longer – surely the most reliable sign of currency – hummed or whistled.

The reason for this extended digression is that many readers, myself included, were excited, when first encountering *A Girl Is a Half-formed Thing* and listening to its author in interviews, to discover the kind of modernist writing and type of author we most associate mainly with the 1920s was again in circulation. Of course there have been many experimental novels since *Ulysses* and *Mrs Dalloway*, and some great ones, and not only in English and not only by men, but they have never been popular and a whiff of elitism therefore clings to such writing. ('Elite' in this case has nothing to do with wealth or social position, it just means a very small number.)

McBride's novel, some of us thought optimistically, might just cross over into the literary mainstream, introducing the general reader to the fierce pleasures of experimental writing, exposing them to something challenging and worthwhile. This seems to have happened, and is continuing to happen, and this is surely a good thing. In her interview with JoAnna Novak the author explained the line of reasoning that led her to take on the earlier modernists, to re-boot the franchise:

> Joyce was a huge influence on me like every Irish writer – probably every writer – and so modernism was certainly where I felt I was coming from and I felt that tradition had been closed down sort of unfairly, people felt that it was done, it had nothing left to say, which I really disagreed with, and I think particularly as a woman I felt there was a lot of room left there . . . that modernism could be a really useful tool for talking about female experience and in a very unsentimental way . . . taking a tradition which has – especially with Joyce and Beckett being the sort of great figures of it – a quite male lineage, although there are a lot wonderful female modernists, all the glory went to the men, obviously . . .

What I find exciting about Eimear McBride's arrival as a major writer is summed up when she says 'that modernism could be a really useful tool for talking about female experience', with the implication that all the achievements by male writers to date had not exhausted the potential of the modernist novel. The modernist project is far from complete and there is still plenty of work to be done.

Boys' Own modernism

In discussion with a group of undergraduates at Wolverhampton University on 18 February 2015, McBride made an off-the-cuff remark that bears closer examination: 'My novel shocked the old men who think they own modernism.' Who are these elderly self-appointed proprietors? Critics? Ageing modernist novelists? Can anybody really be said to 'own' modernism? Would anybody in their right mind want to?

McBride has also said that experimental women writers have been airbrushed out of the picture. More, that women have not to date been seen as making a great impression on modernism. Is that really the case?

Wikipedia is a useful measure, not as a reliable or objective source but as a kind of cultural barometer. Look up 'avant-garde artists' and, under the heading 'authors, playwrights, actors and theatre directors' you'll find a list of 56 names of which JoAnne Akalaitis (founder of the theatre group Mabou Mines) is the first. There are just seven other women: Jayne Cortez (African-American poet and performance artist), the poet Mina Loy, the actress, writer and director Judith Malina, novelists Anaïs Nin and Gertrude Stein, the theatre director Ellen Stewart and Virginia Woolf. That list says more about Wikipedia protocols than women of the avant-garde, but however these lists are compiled the same gender imbalance is apparent in other categories – in architecture, music, theatre and so on. The only avant-garde practice in which women emphatically predominate is in dance and choreography, with 16 of 23 citations. Why *is* that?

Another lengthy Wikipedia entry, for 'experimental literature', mentions only Woolf, Stein and the Puerto Rican writer Giannina Braschi (born 1953). Braschi is the author of *Yo-Yo Boing!* (1998) and modestly describes herself as the 'granddaughter of Alfred Jarry and Antonin Artaud, bastard child of Samuel Beckett and James Joyce, half-sister to Heiner Müller, kissing cousin of Tadeusz Kantor, and lover of Witkiewicz [the Polish poet who died fifteen years before Braschi was born]'. The lack of any female literary forebears in her background tells its own story, but Braschi's choice of antecedents reflects one reason women have failed to make their mark in avant-garde literature – she is complicit in her own exclusion because she does nothing to challenge the male hegemony. She also, in common with most of us, has a talent that doesn't bear comparison with that of her chosen antecedents.

For a snapshot of the situation in academia, we can look back to a two-day conference in Manchester entitled 'Contemporary Experimental Women's Writing' in autumn 2013, four months after the publication of *A Girl Is a Half-formed Thing*. There were panel sessions devoted to, among many others, Christine Brooke-Rose, Angela Carter, Anna Kavan and Ann Quin (an intriguing double act) and Muriel Spark. A laudable aim of the Manchester event was to counter the bias found in the recently published Routledge *Companion to Experimental Literature* (2012), edited by Joe Bray, Alison Gibbons and Brian McHale, which claimed to cover 'the history of literary experiment from the beginning of the twentieth century to the present' yet in which only one of the 36 chapters was on women's experimental writing.

The conference organisers hardly needed to point out that it wasn't just the Routledge account that overlooked and undervalued women's contribution to experimental writing. Discussions surrounding literary experiment after postmodernism focused largely, they claimed, on such writers as J. M. Coetzee, Dave Eggars, David Mitchell, David Peace, Thomas Pynchon, W. G. Sebald and David Foster Wallace. To redress this the conference call for papers listed 'experimental women writers who have, to date, received relatively little critical attention'.

What strikes me is how narrow the range of writers under consideration is, and how conservative. According to the organisers the 'canonical authors' are Angela Carter, Ali Smith, Jeanette Winterson 'and others'. These are three very gifted authors, although Carter is no longer among the living and the other two are in their fifties. They are, in a sense, establishment figures. There was a paper on Catherynne M. Valente (born 1979, a best-selling American author of 'challenging folklore-based fantasy') but otherwise little acknowledgement of living writers under fifty or genre fiction or fan fiction or new media. It's churlish to focus on omissions, but I think a challenge for women writers (and their readers) is to extend their reach beyond their gender and beyond the anglophone world.

In the original opening paragraph of my review of *A Girl Is a Half-formed Thing* (which was rightly cut as an unnecessary piece of throat-clearing) I wrote:

> There are not many experimental novelists, and very few of them are female. Leading the field are Gertrude Stein, Virginia Woolf and

Dorothy Richardson (whose *Pointed Roofs* developed a stream of consciousness technique seven years before the publication of *Ulysses*). More recently Christine Brooke-Rose, Marguerite Duras, Eva Figes, Ann Quin, Nathalie Sarraute and a handful of others have explored and expanded the novel's formal potential. Eimear McBride is of their number and, on the strength of this brilliantly accomplished first book, equal to the best of them.

I stand by that. As a freelance hack I regularly pitch suggestions to various editors, prompted either by review copies of forthcoming books or by my own ramshackle range of interests (fiction, biography, poetry, cinema, photography, architecture). It's a living. I am always pleased and relieved when the *Times Literary Supplement* runs anything I contribute because it reviews only around 2 per cent of all the books it receives each week. I think that's worth repeating – only around two in every hundred books received at the offices of the *TLS* are reviewed in their pages. Few of those are novels, and even fewer are debut novels.

In 2015 Toby Lichtig, then acting fiction editor at the *TLS*, wrote about female presence in literary journalism for the *Los Angeles Review of Books*, a thoughtful response to accusations by Katherine Angel (also writing in the *LARB*) that literary magazines are 'bastions of androcentricity'. (O rocks!) Angel attacked 'the shocking paucity of women of authority and expertise across all media' and 'the disturbing preponderance of men (their reviews and their books) in literary magazines'. She's quite right, although Lichtig gently insists that the situation has changed, and continues to change, and that in the case of *TLS* fiction reviews at least there is a surprising equality. A 2013 survey showed an overall ratio in the *TLS* of 71 per cent male reviewers to 29 per cent female; in the *LRB*, 82 per cent to 18 per cent; and in the *New York Review of Books,* 81 per cent to 19 per cent. So there's nothing near parity but, as Lichtig points out, the significance is not in the ratio but the volume. Over a two-year period the *TLS* had a 66 per cent to 34 per cent male–female divide in non-fiction, but complete parity in the fiction pages. Lichtig finally makes the point that eminent writers and subject experts tend to be from an older generation, probably going to university in the 1960s or 1970s, an era in which women faced even more barriers than they do today and fewer entered higher education. This will change as we old guys drop off the perch.

Change is certainly under way, says Lichtig, and is 'quicker in English literature, where women have for many decades been well-represented; slower in the worlds of analytic philosophy or military history'. He adds something entirely new to me – that men 'pitch' more regularly than women and that male pitchers tend to be more persistent, returning after a rejection. I can vouch for that, but am surprised at this easily remedied difference. Literary history certainly is male-dominated, and the further back you go the more pronounced the dominance. Yet, writers aside, the modern publishing industry has a very high female presence. In 2013 Julie Crisp, commissioning editor at Tor Books (specialists in genre fiction), wrote in a blog post entitled 'Sexism in genre publishing: a publisher's perspective' that 'every genre publisher in the UK has female commissioning editors and 90% of the genre imprints here are actually run by women'. Taking a sample of 530 submissions to Tor, she provided a gender breakdown according to genre:

	Women	Men
Historical/epic/fantasy	33%	67%
Urban fantasy/paranormal romance	57%	43%
Horror	17%	83%
Science-fiction	22%	78%
Young adult	68%	32%
Other (difficult to categorise)	27%	73%
Total	32%	68%

This is a snapshot of genre fiction, not groundbreaking experimental writing (although I'd be interested to see what crops up in that 'difficult to categorise' slush pile). It suggests that in an industry largely staffed by women, men predominate in supplying the raw material for publication.

Faced with a dispiriting lack of experimental artists of any gender in Irish culture, the composer Jennifer Walshe set about creating her own early history of the Irish avant-garde, scrupulously researched, carefully documented with books and manuscripts and photographs and paintings, and completely fictitious. – an elaborate highbrow prank. It's worth a look if you want to learn more about such imaginary figures as Zaftig Giolla (a 'musician-composer-poet-field recordist' from Galway obsessed with Futurism) or the Guinness Dadaists ('the Irish language is a material which can be broken into fragments which can be mobilised against all sense and meaning'). There is of course no reason a renaissance in modernist and experimental writing should not feature many more female authors – and female readers.

Stream of (pre-)consciousness

The prose of *A Girl Is a Half-formed Thing* is routinely described as a 'stream of consciousness', but it really isn't anything of the kind. To call it a monologue is also inadequate because although throughout we are given the narrator's view of what happens, there are many different voices which have their own separate presence – especially those of the brother, mother, grandfather and uncle.

'Stream of consciousness' is an approach to rendering human experience from the inside, as it were, and is most commonly associated with Joyce, in *Ulysses*. Most famously in 'Penelope', the final episode in which Molly Bloom's drowsy nocturnal thoughts are presented like this:

> who knows is there anything the matter with my insides or have I
> something growing in me getting that thing like that every week

when was it last I Whit Monday yes its only about 3 weeks I ought to go to the doctor only it would be like before I married him when I had that white thing coming from me and Floey made me go to that dry old stick Dr Collins for womens diseases on Pembroke road your vagina he called it I suppose thats how he got all the gilt mirrors and carpets getting round those rich ones off Stephens green running up to him for every little fiddlefaddle her vagina and her cochinchina theyve money of course so theyre all right I wouldnt marry him not if he was the last man in the world

Adam Mars-Jones said in his review of *A Girl Is a Half-formed Thing* that this approach, once considered revolutionary, now seems rather quaint. He may be right, although it still makes a strong impression on the first-time reader and is never likely to be consigned to what the art historian Robert Hughes called 'the mausoleum of the nearly-new'. Mars-Jones in his review even went so far as to punctuate part of Molly Bloom's un-punctuated monologue to give an impression of the McBridean approach, while admitting this failed to convey the power of McBride's words, 'as blocked in their rhythm as they are molten in feeling'.

When Joyce's copyright expired in 2012 a former barrister called Robert Gogan took it upon himself to punctuate *Ulysses* 'properly', making it, he claimed, accessible to the common reader. He didn't change a word yet the project for some reason took him six years to complete. I'd argue that readers who give up on *Ulysses* are less discouraged by Joyce's punctuation than by (say) 'Ineluctable modality of the visible' and 'agenbite of inwit' and 'Bronze by gold heard the hoofirons, steelyringing Imperthnthn thnthnthn' and 'Deshil Holles Eamus' and even 'metempsychosis' (O, rocks!). Simply sprinkling around a few commas and italics won't alter that. The first episode, 'Telema-chus', is particularly hard going as Stephen Daedalus has the inflated, self-consciously wordy rhetoric of a pretentious young intellectual, although anyone who has first read *A Portrait of the Artist as a Young Man* will have his number. An awareness of the Homeric substructure can also make the first-time reader anxious – is she expected to have a working knowledge of the *Odyssey*? Should she read it first? If, on the other hand, you're more interested in virtuoso writing than mere cleverness, then this is the book for you, and to hell with the undercarriage.

What Joyce does, and not just in Molly's case, is to present his main characters' inner thoughts as an integral part of the novel's narrative. Here's Leopold Bloom, preparing his sleeping wife's breakfast early on a warm and sunlit 16 June:

Another slice of bread and butter: three, four: right. She didn't like her plate full. Right. He turned from the tray, lifted the kettle off the hob and set it sideways on the fire. It sat there, dull and squat, its spout stuck out. Cup of tea soon. Good. Mouth dry. The cat walked stiffly round a leg of the table with tail on high.

—Mkgnao!

—O, there you are, Mr Bloom said, turning from the fire.

The cat mewed in answer and stalked again stiffly round a leg of the table, mewing. Just how she stalks over my writingtable. Prr. Scratch my head. Prr.

Mr Bloom watched curiously, kindly the lithe black form. Clean to see: the gloss of her sleek hide, the white button under the butt of her tail, the green flashing eyes. He bent down to her, his hands on his knees.

—Milk for the pussens, he said.

—Mrkgnao! the cat cried.

They call them stupid. They understand what we say better than we understand them. She understands all she wants to. Vindictive too. Cruel. Her nature. Curious mice never squeal. Seem to like it. Wonder what I look like to her. Height of a tower? No, she can jump me.

There's nothing remotely difficult about any of this, although it is certainly sophisticated. Robert Grogan might diligently impose conventional speech marks where Joyce opted for a continental dash, but simply repunctuating the passage won't make it any easier to understand because it's already easy. That we dip in and out of Bloom's thoughts during his encounter with the pussens is no longer a challenge to the average (and even below-average) reader, if it ever really was. The compression ('Height of a tower? No, she can jump me') keeps us on our toes, and there are times when Joyce really makes us work hard – though seldom as hard as we do when following the labyrinthine plots of the average forensic thriller. That's a different kind of hard, and offers a different kind of satisfaction.

We may not immediately register the sexual undertow of the pussen's stiff-tailed navigation of that table leg (I certainly didn't, until it was pointed out to me), and we may struggle later on with some of the less immediately absorbing and entertaining passages. I always want to skip the 'Eumaeus' episode, in which Bloom and Stephen stagger to the cabman's shelter and the language becomes deliberately laboured and plodding, although by this stage in the novel the author has long-since earned the right to do whatever he chooses.

A commonplace observation by otherwise literate people is that Joyce's great book is not for them because they are simply too common-sensical and down-to-earth to waste their time on such a pretentious and overblown work. They won't be taken in – and those of us who do read the book and continue re-reading it are pretentious, gullible and 'clever-clever'. They have a point. Gilbert Adair observed that 'clever-clever' isn't double clever but actually *half* clever, and to his detractors Joyce is, and will always be 'clever-clever', too bright for his boots, a show-off. He can leave even his admirers (and *especially* his admirers) with a nagging sense of inadequacy. Perhaps too many of us first attempt to read *Ulysses* at the wrong age. It was only in my late thirties (the age at which Joyce was writing his greatest novel) that I began to read the book properly, and I've been re-reading it ever since with unstinted wonder and envy and admiration. It is, a some wag once said, a book that should not be read, only *re*-read.

Before a Girl

It was Dorothy Richardson (1873–1957) who first employed a stream of consciousness method consistently, seven years before the publication of *Ulysses*, in her third novel *Painted Roofs* (1915). The critic May Sinclair first applied the term 'stream of consciousness' when she reviewed the book in *The Egoist* (April 1918), although Richardson herself preferred the term 'interior monologue'. Here's a brief extract from Chapter 2, in which the central character is nervously preparing to embark on a teaching career:

> It was a fool's errand . . . To undertake to go to the German school and teach . . . to be going there . . . with nothing to give. The moment would come when there would be a class sitting round a table waiting for her to speak. She imagined one of the rooms at the old school, full of scornful girls . . . How was English taught? How did you begin? English grammar . . . in German? Her heart beat in her throat. She had never thought of that . . . the rules of English grammar? Parsing and analysis . . . Anglo-Saxon prefixes and suffixes . . . gerundial infinitive . . . It was too late to look anything up. Perhaps there would be a class to-morrow . . . The German lessons at school had been dreadfully good . . . Fraulein's grave face . . . her perfect knowledge of every rule . . . her clear explanations in English . . . her examples . . . All these things were there, in English grammar . . . And she had undertaken to teach them and could not even speak German.

Richardson's technique suggests the fragmented and contingent nature of thought, its flickering intermittency and (courtesy of the ellipses) something of the 'stream', the elision between thoughts. There is no reason to believe Joyce ever read *Painted Roofs*, but connecting Richardson and Joyce is a shared tendency to render human consciousness as fragmentary and incoherent. But neither Richardson nor Joyce was the first writer to explore ways of representing human thought in prose, and for an impressive earlier attempt we have to go back to what is routinely described the greatest novel of the 19th century.

In Book III, Chapter 13, of Tolstoy's *War and Peace* (1869) there is an episode in which Count Rostov, riding towards the battle front at Austerlitz and on the brink of falling asleep, notices in the distance a black knoll with a white patch on it and he asks himself drowsily whether it might be a glade in the wood lit up by the moon, or some unmelted snow, or some white houses:

> 'I expect it's snow . . . that spot . . . a spot *une tache*,' he thought. 'There now . . . it's not a *tache* . . . Natasha . . . sister, black eyes . . . Na . . . tasha . . . (Won`t she be surprised when I tell her how I've seen the Emperor?) Natasha . . . take my sabretache . . .'

A passing hussar warns him that he is heading into the adjacent bushes, but the dreamlike association of ideas continues as a childish drowsiness overwhelms him:

> But what was I thinking? I mustn`t forget. How shall I speak to the Emperor? No, that's not it that's tomorrow. Oh yes! Natasha . . . sabretache . . . saber them . . . Whom? The hussars . . . Ah, the hussars with mustaches. Along the Tverskaya Street rode the hussar with mustaches . . .

The great Joyce scholar and biographer Richard Ellmann quoted this passage in his Foreword to Adaline Glasheen's *A Census of Finnegans Wake* (1956), making the point that long before Joyce and the modernists other writers had found ways to represent the workings of the mind, in states of tension or repose, whether alert or asleep, or half asleep (as in this case). Tolstoy was among the first writers to explore the tendency for language to lose its purchase on the real world, to become permeable and contingent and to lapse into puns ('*tache*/Natasha'), as Joyce did, chronically, in *Finnegans Wake*.

The *Wake*, according to the novelist Tom McCarthy, resembles a constantly transmitting radio station, always audible in the background like (if I may muddy the metaphor) the wireless broadcasts in Jean Cocteau's film *Orphée*. It's an attractive idea and has an analogue appeal, but I see the *Wake* more as a de-commissioned nuclear power plant, leaking its contents into the earth beneath and sky above. The *Wake* is, for its many admir-ers, the *fons et origo* of true modernist writing, an infinitely rich and complex source of interest and significance. For others it's a spectacular dead end, marking the premature conclusion of the modernist tradition, or at least a pause in its progress. *Finnegans Wake* loomed over the 20th century, as did *Ulysses*, although that's a different kind of looming, and I get the impression that *Ulysses* today has the greater presence and, through writers like McBride, a greater influence on a younger generation. I recall discussing the *Wake* with McBride and her brisk judgement: 'There's no pleasure in it.' I agree, although she'd be the first to admit that there's much more to literature, just as there's much more to life, than mere pleasure. Martin Amis, interviewed at the Brooklyn Academy of Music by *New Yorker* fiction editor Deborah Treisman, made an amusing comparison:

> If you go to Nabokov's house, metaphorically speaking, you get his best chair, in front of his fire, with his best wine. If you go to James Joyce's house, you come into this big drafty edifice, and there's no one there. And then you find him tinkering around in some scullery. And he offers you two slabs of peat around a conger eel, and a glass of mead.

The slabs of peat and conger eel were taken from Clive James's satirical poem *Peregrine Prykke's Pilgrimage through the London Literary World* (1974), where the dish was attributed to one 'Seamus Feamus', an Irish poet. But they deserve regular re-cycling.

When it comes to the literary representation of human con-sciousness there isn't such a great distance between *War and Peace* and *Ulysses,* but there is a huge difference between *Ulysses* and *A Girl Is a Half-formed Thing.* While acknowledging the central importance of Joyce to her writing, Eimear McBride has insisted that her technique is 'stream of *pre*-conscious' – an attempt, and it seems to me an entirely original one, to represent thought at the point immediately *before* it becomes articulate speech, before it is ordered into rational utterance. The effect may in a hundred years' time appear as quaint as Molly Bloom's unpunctuated interior monologue – but I doubt it, not least because McBride's novel has already found its place in an expanding and durable canon of women's writing at a time when earlier (male) modernists are falling out of favour. She speaks to a new generation of readers who may be wholly unaware of her predecessors, and not especially interested.

'Not a mind, but a mind *thinking*' – that was the American poet Elizabeth Bishop's description of Gerard Manley Hopkins, an English poet she particularly admired, and this comes close to the effect McBride sets out to achieve. What we read on the page is not a description of the girl's thoughts but rather a direct representation of them, in all their scattergun energy and indeterminacy. In this Eimear McBride is clearly an 'episodicist', not a 'narrativist'. The problem with narrativism, according to the philosopher Galen Strawson, is that it may lead the artist to manipulate details of his or her life in an effort to work it up into a good story. This, he warns, can lead to 'falsification, confabulation, revisionism'. Episodic writing focuses almost exclusively on the here and now and does not attempt to shape actions and thoughts into theme or plot. *A Girl Is a Half-formed Thing* is the episodicist novel *par excellence* and as such can bear comparison with works by Woolf and Musil, Proust and Stendahl, Borges and Emily Dickinson. It is militantly fragmentary in both form and content.

The prose of *A Girl Is a Half-formed Thing* builds on a long tradition of fragmentation, and McBride's work could be seen as its apotheosis. In this she is heir to earlier modernist techniques which owe less to cinema (as many critics assume) than to an earlier visual spectacle, the significance of which has been largely overlooked. Both Joyce and Richardson and all the leading modernists of the 1920s were born in the 1870s and early

1880s, and therefore came of age before the advent of cinema as a popular entertainment in the late 1890s. They were, however, exposed as children to a now all but forgotten visual spectacle – the magic lantern.

Early in *Du côté de chez Swann* Marcel Proust (born 1871) describes his childhood *lanterne magique* which (in the Scott Moncrieff translation) 'substituted for the opaqueness of my walls an impalpable iridescence, supernatural phenomena of many colours, in which legends were depicted, as on a shifting and transitory window' ('*un vitrail vacillant et momentané*'). He recalls the projection on his bedroom wall of the medieval tale of Geneviève de Brabant and Golo, and his delight in the simple charm of the lantern's artifice:

> Riding at a jerky trot, Golo, his mind filled with an infamous design, issued from the little three-cornered forest which dyed dark-green the slope of a convenient hill, and advanced by leaps and bounds towards the castle of poor Geneviève de Brabant. This castle was cut off short by a curved line which was in fact the circumference of one of the transparent ovals in the slides which were pushed into position through a slot in the lantern.

That curved line marks the physical limit of the lantern's artifice, though not of its cultural function as a permeable membrane between our world and the world of myth. Proust next evokes the discomfort caused by this 'intrusion of mystery and beauty' into his private sanctum and 'the anaesthetic effect of custom being destroyed'. Golo's spectral misdeeds prompt 'a more than ordinarily scrupulous examination of my own conscience'. Proust sees the lantern projection as a disruption to the order of things that leads to an intense self-scrutiny, and in doing so anticipates the responses of a later generation of writers when confronted with cinema.

Writers born in the first decade of the 20th century, while likely in childhood to have seen magic lantern displays, were far more influenced by the overwhelmingly popular new medium of moving pictures, of cinema. In 1926 the schoolboy Louis MacNeice first encountered T. S. Eliot's poetry and later wrote:

> The cinema technique of quick cutting, of surprise juxtapositions, of spotting the everyday detail and making it significant, this would naturally intrigue the novelty-mad adolescent and should, like even the most experimental films, soon become easy to grasp.

Film had become a natural reference point for the MacNeice generation, a cultural 'given'. But his analogy is misleading because the techniques he regards as intrinsically filmic and that offer a key to Eliot's poetry are not derived from film, or at least not exclusively so – 'surprise juxtapositions' were a defining feature of magic lantern projections. MacNeice's view has since become a critical commonplace, and modernist literary prose is not infrequently described as the written equivalent of 'close-ups', 'tracking shots', 'pans', 'fades', 'dissolves', 'cuts' and so on. It is also often claimed that it is in the use of montage – the cinematic technique developed by Sergei Eisenstein – that the roots of modernist writing are to be found, but this is again to put the cart before the horse. The earliest film-makers (who necessarily grew up before cinema) were predisposed to adopt literary conventions in the construction of film narrative because they were all readers. Writers had long employed what later became cinematic techniques deployed by film pioneers such as D. W. Griffith. As the film critic Raymond Durgnat noted, Thomas Hardy in his novels anticipated a crucial cinematic strategy in his use of the anonymised observer ('A passer-by would have seen . . .').

Virginia Woolf (born 1882) spent the afternoon of Sunday, 14 March 1926 at a London Film Society screening of Robert Wiene's expressionist masterpiece *The Cabinet of Dr Caligari* (1920). We know what she made of this because she wrote a magazine piece entitled 'The Cinema' which appeared in the New York journal *Arts* in June. She describes a revelatory moment: '[A]t a performance of Dr Caligari the other day, a shadow shaped like a tadpole suddenly appeared at one corner of the screen. [. . .] For a moment it seemed as though thought could be conveyed by shape more effectively than by words.' Woolf's epiphany, prompted by a flaw in the print (or possibly in the projector), recalls Proust's memory (in the opening pages of *À la recherche du temps perdu*, a few lines after the dunked madeleine) of a magic lantern projection in his childhood nursery morphing around the irregular surfaces of a billowing curtain, the image violating its own pictorial boundary and the limitations of its intended meaning.

Earlier in the article Woolf describes her response to different kinds of film, starting with newsreel: '[A]t first sight, the art of the cinema seems simple, even stupid.' She then reflects on the mutability of banal events caught by the camera and captures something of the melancholy that permeates cinema: 'Further, all this happened ten years ago, we are told. We are beholding a world which has gone beneath the waves. Brides are emerging from the abbey – they are now mothers; ushers are ardent – they are now silent; mothers are tearful, guests are joyful; this has been won and that has been lost, and it is over and done with.'

'Ten years ago'? Woolf makes a point by implication, by suggesting but not employing the future perfect tense (i.e., all this *'will have happened ten years ago*, we shall in time come to realise'). In a spellbinding passage she reflects on the ephemeral nature of the image:

> We behold them as they are when we are not there. We see life as it is when we have no part in it. As we gaze we seem to be removed from the pettiness of actual existence. [. . .] From this point of vantage, as we watch the antics of our kind, we have time to feel pity and amusement, to generalize, to endow one man with the attributes of the race. Watching the boat sail and the wave break, we have time to open our minds wide to beauty and register on top of it the queer sensation – this beauty will continue, and this beauty will flourish whether we behold it or not.

It is the viewer, then, and not the spectacle that is spectral, as film has an objective existence independent of the spectator's gaze. The spectator is thus demoted, erased even, in an act that anticipates Roland Barthes' declaration of the death of the author. It is a modernist take on a perennial aesthetic consideration. The disruption of the *Caligari* screening may remind us of the line in Eliot's *Prufrock*:

> As if a magic lantern threw the nerves in patterns on a screen.

Magic lantern shows offered audiences a spectacle of the world in fragments and their immense popularity made them as influential as photography as a cultural mediator between 19th-century pictorial representations and the emergence of early cinema. One popular subject was based on the aristocratic itinerary of The Grand Tour, which served to shrink the world while at the same time expanding the viewer's horizons. In their heap of broken images magic lantern displays offer a visual correlative to *The Waste Land*'s deracinated fragments. In the section titled 'What the Thunder Said' we may be reminded of a sequence of rapid 'unpunctuated' dissolves between lantern slides of capital cities, an accelerated Grand Tour:

> Jerusalem Athens Alexandria
> Vienna London
> Unreal

At the end of the poem more unconnected fragments are jumbled together, as if slides have been randomly ordered before their projection:

> London Bridge is falling down falling down falling down
> *Poi s'ascose nel foco che gli affina*
> *Quando fiam uti chelidon* – O swallow swallow
> *Le Prince d'Aquitaine à la tour abolie*

Many magic lantern lectures offered the viewer a combination of songs, hymns, stories, recitations, religious stories, lectures and comic subjects. Likewise *The Waste Land*'s many thematic lists – of tarot cards, London districts, street names and buildings – are set against individual urban moments – sunsets, dooryards, sprinkled streets, novels, teacups and skirts that trail along the floor. Eliot is the lanternist, assembling and projecting the heterogeneous slides; in cinematic terms he is director, cameraman and cutter, assembling pre-existing fragments (the literary equivalent of stock library footage) into new combinations and juxtapositions, then introducing 'freshly shot' material to contextualise that footage. These fragments, once combined, *are* the ruins. It is not too fanciful to see the phonetic and topographical elision from 'Moorgate' to 'Margate' as the typographical equivalent of a dissolve between two lantern slides. Or, to be more precise, an aural dissolve between the phrases 'at Moorgate, and' and 'On Margate Sands'. This contrasts with the violent cut from Margate to Carthage, as if unrelated slides have been clumsily combined in a single projection. The discontinuities that characterise magic lantern projection – MacNeice's 'surprise juxtapositions' – predominate rather than the headlong seamless impact of film, trading as it does in an optical illusion, the persistence of vision.

Magic lantern performances rarely included any projected text but were often accompanied by the spoken word, usually delivered by the 'professor' or 'projectionist'. The emergence of film in the late 1890s saw the introduction and increasing sophistication of title cards, the explanatory texts appearing on screen briefly to identify characters, locations and plot points or to render dialogue – and what dialogue! 'Some excellent judges think that I resemble Satan' (from *The Penalty*, 1920); 'Give me something sentimental about a cat – or get out!' (*La bohème*, 1926). Title cards also offered prompts to the audience: ALL STORIES HAVE AN END (Hitchcock's *The Lodger, a Story of the London Fog*, 1927) and THAT NIGHT THE FIRST OF A STRANGE SERIES OF MURDERS OCCURRED (*The Cabinet of Dr Caligari*). The latter film shares a fragmentary, nightmarish and neurotic quality with Eliot's poetry of the 1920s. The titles of each of the five sections of *The Waste Land* can, without undue distortion, be read as film intertitles (or, of course, their magic lantern antecedents).

Such strategies appear in other modernist writing. The 'Aeolus' episode in *Ulysses* is broken up by headlines some of which are unambiguously cinematic, such as the 'establishing shot' of IN THE HEART OF THE HIBERNIAN METROPOLIS. There are documentary cues (HOW A GREAT DAILY ORGAN IS TURNED OUT), new characters are introduced (WILLIAM BRAYDEN, ESQUIRE, OF OAKLANDS, SANDYMOUNT), and so on. There's a remote echo of this in the five section headings of *A Girl Is a Half-formed Thing*, each prefaced by a roman numeral, like an order of service. In harking back to the fragmentary tropes of early modernist writing, McBride also, if unwittingly, builds on a pre-cinematic tradition that informed the sensibility of those writers who grew up before the age of the cinematograph.

Reading a collection of essays called *Where Have You Been?* by the Anglo-German poet and translator Michael Hofmann I was struck by his description of expressionist writing (in a piece about the poet Gottfried Benn), which seemed to me to apply to McBride: 'Literary Expressionism [. . .] can be seen as a simultaneous boosting of both style and content. Expressionism is gaudy, neo-primitive, volatile, provocative, antirational.' In literary Expressionism, Hofmann adds, the brain is eclipsed by the glands and the senses; it is momentary, 'it doesn't count days or verify destinations'. All of which can apply to the McBridean prose style. Certainly the girl's glands and their associated fluids seem on occasion to saturate the text – snot and mucus and tears all regularly trump the brain. Her pre-natal state floating in the womb and her final submersion in the waters of the lake are both anti-rational conditions, formless and beyond the familiar categories of experience. What happens in the novel and to the girl is volatile and provocative in both content and form, and there is (as it were) a reliable lack of the verifiable. So 'expressionism' is another label we might add to the critical terms we apply to the book.

We must never underestimate the extremely *literary* quality of these violent fragments. McBride can be a very traditional modernist in her thoughtful pillaging of the past, and her writing is rich in allusions to other authors, other books. She once offered me £50 if I could identify the line in the novel that's adapted from Mann's *Joseph and His Brothers*. I'm working on that. She also confirmed that the text contained 'lots of embedded lines but only for my own amusement and private homage to auld JJ. It doesn't matter a bit if no one ever sees.' It is likely to keep readers and academics of a certain tendency happily absorbed for years to come. Joyce would surely approve.

Academic reactions

The most lucid and penetrating consideration of *A Girl Is a Half-formed Thing* to date has been a lecture by the distinguished academic Jacqueline Rose entitled 'Modernism: The Unfinished Legacy', delivered on 26 June 2014 under the auspices of the British Association for Modernist Studies (BAMS). She has kindly allowed me to quote from this unpublished lecture, and particularly her thoughts on McBridean writing.

Before looking at Rose's lecture we need to be aware of a local kerfuffle prompted by the publication of a book in 2010 by the critic and academic Gabriel Josipovici (who seems to be a guiding light in the book you are now reading). In *What Ever Happened to Modernism?*, a study of Britain's failure to engage with the modernist tradition in writing, he made some casually disparaging remarks about some leading British writers:

> Reading Julian Barnes, like reading so many of the other English writers of his generation, Martin Amis, Ian McEwan, Blake Morrison, or a critic from an older generation who belongs with them, John Carey, leaves me feeling that I and the world have been made smaller and meaner . . . I wonder where it came from, this petty-bourgeois uptightness, this terror of not being in control, this schoolboy desire to boast and to shock.

I'd suggest that where it came from, at least in part, was the Pillars of Hercules, a pub in Soho which was the meeting place of many aspiring young writers in the early 1970s, including Amis, Barnes and McEwan. This was where Ian Hamilton, editor of *The New Review*, the best literary journal of the decade, held court, bought drinks and bounced cheques. A blokeish sodality prevailed and enduring loyalties were initiated among those jostling for the editor's attention. The writers Josipovici singles out shared values endorsed by their literary mentor and patron, although this does not really explain why a 'schoolboy desire to boast and to shock' informs their work (as Josipovici sees it), merely suggests its competitive origins.

But Josipovici had bigger fish to fry. He turned his attention to the critical praise surrounding Irène Némirovsky's posthumously published novel, *Suite Française*. Originally written in 1942, it was, Josipovici rightly observed, a 'run-of-the-mill middlebrow narrative'. What dismayed him was that so many serious reviewers had hailed the book as a modern classic when it was finally published:

> [T]he question is not why she should have written as she did, but what has happened to our culture that serious and intelligent and well-read reviewers, not to speak of prize-winning novelists and distinguished biographers, many of whom have studied the poems of Eliot or the novels of Virginia Woolf at university, should so betray their calling as to go into ecstasies over books like Némirovsky's while, in their lifetimes and now after their deaths, ignoring the work of novelists like Claude Simon, Georges Perec, Thomas Bernhard and Gert Hofmann.

I remember telling McBride that reading her novel had ruined me as a critic – that I could now no longer bear to wade through anything that was less than overwhelmingly good; that middlebrow heavyweight novels, no matter how artfully constructed and elegantly written, were no longer something I felt inclined to review, because life is too short to read merely adequate novels. I've more or less stuck to my guns, and over the past few years have reviewed only fictions that in some way seem to me to bring something new into the world, fictions that challenge the reader by investigating form and structure and language, by breaking new ground (novels such as *Munich Airport* by Greg Baxter, *Vanishing* by Gerard Woodward, *Spill Simmer Falter Wither* by Sara Baume, or, from the last century, the remarkable modernist writings of David Vogel, only recently translated into English from the original Hebrew). Following the success of *A Girl Is a Half-formed Thing* there now seems a slightly greater willingness on the part of editors of literary journals to publish reviews of off-trail novels from small independent publishers, and this is an encouraging sign.

But things could be better. In *What Ever Happened to Modernism?* Josipovici condemned the mediocrity of much contemporary writing and criticism. He confined his attack to a consideration of British writers – apart from Philip Roth and Toni Morrison no American authors are mentioned. It is British (or even English) cultural values that he has in his sights, and what better evidence is there of the dire state of literature than the near-decade it took for a superb modernist novel to find a publisher?

For Josipovici modernism is about art's response to the condition of being modern. This involves what he calls 'disenchantment', a condition that throws the serious artist into a state of crisis. Disenchantment has many causes but can be summed up as a loss of faith – not in a religious or political sense but rather a loss of faith in the very role of the artist. What, he asks, are artists for? Is their role to 're-enchant' the world, or is it to respond in some way to the state of disenchantment? What, in either case, gives them the authority to do so? Modernist writers and artists in the 1920s no longer had the confidence to suppose that they could grasp or record reality in prose or paint. The best they could do – all they could do, really – was to express their awareness of the fragility and contingency of any attempt to engage with the world. This Crisis of Representation wasn't confined to the written word – in Zurich in 1916 we see the origins of the anti-everything movement called Dada, and Marcel Duchamp's iconic *Fountain*, the signed urinal exhibited in 1917 which initiated a line of conceptual art that brings us inevitably to Tracey Emin's *My Bed* (1998), a study in disorganised abjection that shares certain features (but not originality) with *A Girl Is a Half-formed Thing*.

Following the Great War in Europe, the Wall Street Crash and the rise of Fascism and the loss of hope were all set against an existential loss of faith in the idea of a coherent human consciousness. The world could never be fully apprehended, fully known, fully understood by anyone, least of all by a writer or artist. So (and again), *what were artists for?* The writings of Joyce and Proust and Kafka and Woolf reflected and embodied this collapse of certainty: what could a writer write *about?* Could they bring enchantment back to a disenchanted world? Could they counter the collective disengagement from nature and from life that characterised the modern condition? If they could, what form would their writing and painting take? And why should anyone be interested? Josipovici counts himself among the disenchanted in a world where 'there is no place for natural, spontaneous creation'.

For Josipovici these are features of British culture, not Irish or American or European. This is where his thesis seems to me to become a tad parochial, focusing on our dim little island as a modernist backwater populated by middlebrow writers too timid or talentless to make a commitment to modernism, writers he describes witheringly as 'prep-school boys showing off'. But I'd go further – it's not just the usual cohort of attention-seeking schoolboys. Consider the following paragraph:

> Hi! My name is Nao and I am a time being. We are on our way to Budapest: Bastard and Chipo and Godknows and Sbho and Stina and me. East of the Tolly Club, after Deshapra Sashmal Road splits in

two, there is a small mosque. Two twists of smoke at a time of year too warm for cottage fires surprise us at first light. They appear more often now, both of them, and on every visit they seem more impatient with me and the world.

This paragraph is bolted together from the opening sentences of five of the shortlisted novels for the 2013 Man Booker Prize. I think this crudely reductive exercise proves that there's not much distinction in any of the writing, not much evidence of style, and not much to choose between the respective authors. The exotic names aside, this deodorised prose could have been written at any time since the middle of the last century, although it's only in relatively recent years that the present historic tense seems to have become the default setting for all novelists. Much modern fiction is like this: homogenised, style-free, relentlessly middlebrow and unambitious.

Which brings us, at last, back to Jacqueline Rose. She begins her lecture by suggesting the two forms that modernism might take today. On the one hand there's what she calls 'the Will Self–Gabriel Josipovici version', which assumes an 'intractable difficulty inside modernism' and involves 'a refusal to submit to the norms of representation'. This was certainly the case with modernist writers in the first part of the 20th century, and their refusal to accept representational norms alerts us, she says, to the crisis of *authority* explored by Josipovici. But most people, says Rose, and most writers, seem to carry on blissfully today as if none of this had ever happened, as if there were no crisis, no collapse of faith.

The second case for the difficulty of modernism she attributes to John Gray, for whom all things modern – not just literary modernism – are tainted by their association with the Enlightenment belief in the perfectibility of the world and of humanity. What seems like an optimistic embrace of progress and social melioration is, according to Gray, a malign belief that has led to no end of horrors historically, from Nazism to the events of

9/11. What unites the German National Socialists and the pilots who flew their hijacked aircraft into the Twin Towers was a shared aim to make a breach with the world and produce a new kind of human being, and human society – an aim that is unequivocally modern. Gray wants us to abandon such a utopian belief as a type of perversion that aims to subordinate the world to its own will.

In both the Self/Josipovici and Gray approaches, Rose argues, what is yearned for is 'a world that has shed the myth of perfection, of unity, of harmonious self-possession which is seen to have licensed some of the worst atrocities of modern times'. The danger comes from the adoption of any totalising belief, because a messy world collapsing under its own weight and contradictions is preferable to a cruel and unjust system that offers any imposed solution.

Rose makes it clear not only that modernism is a way of writing that reflects and articulates a disenchantment with the world, but that the question of modernist form and the question of historical memory are deeply aligned to each other and, what is more, that much of what constitutes modern memory (the legacy of slavery, the horrors of war, oppression and inequality) is simply unrepresentable. Modernism is, says Rose, 'a way of recording – although that is not quite the right word – a failure of historical memory in the formation of memory itself'. To put it another way, a driving question for modernism is to ask: how can the mind take the measure of history, when history will submit neither to the reason of the world nor to the mind that confronts it?

When Walter Benjamin said that we have pushed death from the centre of our experience, he was writing not specifically about war, but about the inability to countenance death, which he attributes to modernity. This takes on a new resonance in the context of the 20th-century violence which he did not live fully to see but on whose threshold his own life and death were set.

As Jacqueline Rose was preparing her lecture, she says, 'an

unexpected literary event brought the question of modernism's legacy crashing back into the public eye, way past the academy in which these debates are most often set'. She describes *A Girl Is a Half-formed Thing* admiringly as

> a book which I think more or less single-handedly dispatches the idea of trauma as un-representable, not by rejecting the idea that trauma is hard of speech and hearing, but by the way it stitches the question of what can be verbally transmitted through the generations into the fabric of the words (which would of course do as a definition of modernism).

As well as redefining the content of verbal transmission and creating a way in which trauma can be represented, Rose concisely defines the momentous impact of McBride's novel on literature:

> McBride therefore presents us with a question or rather provides her answer to the question – what can James Joyce be, or do, for us today? Along with everything else the book is telling us, one of the things it makes indisputably clear, *pace* Josipovici and Self, is that modernism is alive and well (although being alive and well is precisely what the novel throws into the deepest question).

This endorsement of the novel is of central importance in any consideration of its place in the world. But if modernism is alive and well, what about critical approaches to the subject?

Earlier critics such as William Empson and his Cambridge teacher I. A. Richards saw particular value in complexity and ambiguity, in conscious (and unconscious) poetic significance, and employed close textual analysis as an attempt to avoid the response of earlier generations who were content to find value in truth and beauty without bothering too much about how such abstractions were achieved. Close textual analysis has long since been superseded by critical theory, and the analysis of texts within their broader social and cultural setting. A thrilling aspect of Eimear McBride's novel is that it invites (or rather demands) close reading (what the French call *explication de texte*), and repays it. It also reactivates critical interest in earlier modernist writing. Rose quotes the passage from the 'Nausicaa' episode in *Ulysses* when Bloom is first aroused and then masturbates at the sight of Gerty McDowell playing on the beach:

> O sweety all your little girlwhite up I saw dirty bracegirdle made me do love sticky we two naughty Grace darling she him half past the bed met him pike hoses frillies for Raoul to perfume your wife black hair heave under embon señorita young eyes Mulvey plump years dreams return tail end Agendath swoony lovey showed me her next year in drawers return next in her next her next.

She reminds us that this passage is a compression of all the women who have featured in Bloom's day up to this point: McDowell, the actress Ann Bracegirdle, Molly, Martha Clifford and so on, a bravura performance by Joyce, 'writing that heaves under its own sensual weight, plumpness, embonpoint, girdles and swoons'. Bloom's sensual arousal is inextricable from the language that expresses it. She then refers to the last pages of *A Girl Is a Half-Formed Thing*, after the violent sexual assault in the woods. Understandably Rose did not choose to read the passage aloud, while admitting that the aftermath was nothing compared to the assault itself.

> I lie thisright place for me with my fingers ripped onthebody Mine is Lie in the ground faceWhere I Right for meyes. Think about your face. Something. Shush now. Right now. FullofslimeThere better now. And I am. Done with this done. Fill the air up. Smear the blood up is there any no no t reeeeelly. My work is. I've done my I should do. I've done the this time really well. And best of. It was the best of. How. Ready now. I'm screaming in the blackness. Scream until I'm done my body. Full of nothing. Full of dirt the. I am. My I can. There there breath that. Where is your face off somewhere. Where am I lay down this tool. I fall I felled. I banged my face head I think. Time for somewhere. Isgoinghome. (p.194)

This precedes by a few pages the final scene, the drowning, the embrace of oblivion, which Rose reads as 'another modernist return and tribute – how to write what the world might feel and look like as you drown?' It may be overly literal to see the novel as a series of flashbacks at the point of death by drowning, although that seems a perfectly legitimate structural ploy. Rose finally introduces the crucial element of agency – the girl is her own agent, and seeks to embrace violence, and especially sexual violence, as a component of her grief:

> For me, the genius of McBride's novel is that she can get all of this onto the same page or line or word, into the strangulated syntax of her prose. There is a point to be made here about the Catholicism which stifles and maims her – might this form of language be a way of sabotaging the Catholic confession while taking it at its word? [. . .] In terms of sexual politics, the novel can therefore be read as modernism's update, a type of demand that modernism make its reckoning with the sexual horror of the 21st century: not just a tribute, therefore, as McBride insists, but also, surely, a reproach.

Can any modern writing do justice to the sexual horror of the modern world? Rose answers the question by linking two girls:

> McBride has ushered Gerty McDowell along with Molly Bloom into the 21st century. This is not a man on a beach masturbating to the mental tune of a limping woman. At the opposite pole from trauma as unspeakable, *A Girl Is a Half-Formed Thing* is traumatised speech with no exit [. . .] Precisely because the novel is so thick with allusions to modernism, *A Girl Is a Half-Formed Thing* offers itself, I would suggest, as modernism's return of the repressed.

I dwell at length on Rose's lecture because it is a thoughtful consideration of the novel by a leading academic and because it expresses eloquently the excitement surrounding the book in the months after its publication – enough, in this case, to make a distinguished academic rethink her position. Rose rightly emphasises the sexual abuse that lies at the heart of the girl's narrative, but I feel she may underestimate the extent to which death, or more specifically dying, is a theme of equal weight. If 'the answer to everything is fuck' what's the question? And 'fuck' here has a powerful double meaning – as an act of sexual congress (however violent and exploitative) and as a nihilistic profanity. The girl rages against the dying of her brother's light, her sense of imminent loss feeding her sexual abjection. She adopts a complex set of behaviours to negotiate her rage, confusion and exploitation, seeking out forms of yearning abjection that amount to self-harm.

Jarlath Killlen offered some surprising thoughts on the language of *A Girl Is a Half-formed Thing*, and of corresponding genres:

> A neuro-linguistic approach would chime in well with recent developments in literary theory which have adopted evolutionary psychology as a way to interpret literary texts. So far, in my view, the results have not been promising, and I remain to be convinced. I suppose I am still persuaded by the view that novels are literary 'events' and need to be understood against other literary events.
>
> Linguistically, *Girl* is probably best understood in relation to a range of literary influences, not all of them necessarily intended by the author. The biggest influence is modernism, as far as I can see, the work of Joyce and Beckett. First-person Gothic narratives should also be taken into account. I'm not saying that I think relating the novel to the development of language is wrong, but that this would have to take a subordinate place to situating it in genre, tradition and literary history.

'Ireland's best-loved Irish writers'

Ireland provides no shortage of illustrious predecessors for the aspiring Irish writer of today – although the roster of talents is problematic and, when it comes to public awareness, emphatically male. This was outrageously the case in 1990 when the three-volume *Field Day Anthology of Irish Writing* immediately attracted critical flak for excluding most women writers from the canon. The fourth and fifth volumes (published in 2002) attempted to make up for this omission and are by any objective measure much more interesting than the original three volumes. A serious injustice was done and was belatedly corrected, but there's a long way to go yet.

Go to almost any Irish pub, especially outside Ireland, and the chances are you'll see on the wall a framed poster produced by the Republic's national broadcaster, Raidió Teilifís Éireann, and portraying 'Ireland's best-loved Irish writers'. They are, in no particular order, Jonathan Swift, Oscar Wilde, James Joyce, Brendan Behan, J. M. Synge, W. B. Yeats, George Bernard Shaw, Flann O'Brien, Oliver Goldsmith, Sean O'Casey and Patrick Kavanagh. The absence of Seamus Heaney is surprising, and that of Beckett simply astonishing, but that's not the worst of it.

To mark International Woman's Day on 8 March 2015 RTE produced another poster, this time featuring twelve women writers. *The Irish Times* invited dozens of Irish writers, critics and academics to nominate their favourite Irish woman writer, giving their reasons in a brief online essay. Readers were also invited to nominate their favourites. There were some fascinating contributions, and especially those nominating Irish Gaelic writers little known outside the country: Máire Mhac an tSaoi, Eiléan Ní Chuilleanáin, Eibhlín Dubh Ní Chonaill, Nuala Ní Dhomhnaill and Éilís Ní Dhuibhne. I don't know their work, but am intrigued. The series culminated on Saturday, 7 March, with a poster of twelve of the finest Irish women writers: Maria Edgeworth, Augusta Gregory, Somerville and Ross, Kate O'Brien, Elizabeth Bowen, Molly Keane, Mary Lavin, Maeve Brennan, Edna O'Brien, Jennifer Johnston, Eavan Boland and Anne Enright. (Should Eimear McBride have been included? I should say no, if only because she has yet to publish a second book so any such canonisation would appear premature.) Fine writers all, but I couldn't help feeling that what was really needed was a mixed-sex cohort, a step towards true parity of esteem.

Another problem – and I think it's a great one – is that all of these women are not so much writers as *novelists*. There's nothing of significance, it seems, written by any Irish woman from the past millennium other than novels. The hard-to-avoid implication is that novels are what women do best, bless 'em – making up stories.

'McBridean'

We've already encountered the term 'McBridean' but can you think of many – or indeed any – other female equivalents? Woolfean? Murdochian? Mantelic? Lessingish? None of these seems to be in circulation and this prompts the question: why are women writers so seldom thus eponymised?

The hierarchy of writing formulated by F. R. Leavis in *The Great Tradition* (1948) comprised Jane Austen, Joseph Conrad, George Eliot and Henry James, with a belated admission granted to D. H. Lawrence. (Leavis found no room for Joyce, and would only concede that Dickens had written one good novel, *Hard Times*.) This remains an institutionalised canon and is still widely taught in schools and universities. More recent critical approaches led to a greater concentration on genre writing – popular, often lowbrow, sometimes pulp. The 'purple prose' of romantic fiction – the style appropriated by Joyce in the 'Nausicaa' episode of *Ulysses* – was defined by the French feminist writer and critic Hélène Cixous as *l'ecriture feminine,* and is, she argues in *The Laugh of the Medusa* (1975), an attempt to reclaim language from patriarchal monopoly:

> Woman must write her self: must write about women and bring women to writing, from which they have been driven away as violently as from their bodies because their sexual pleasure has been repressed and denied expression.

In Cixous' view the genre is about a woman assuming control of her body (which the girl does) and taking command of her sexual pleasure (which in the girl's case is problematic, involving as it does abjection and violent debasement).

Literary modernism in the 1920s was dominated though

not monopolised by male writers – Eliot, Pound, Lewis, Ford, Lawrence, but we cannot overlook Virginia Woolf and Gertrude Stein as major (if very dissimilar) members of the modern movement. The fact is that *A Girl Is a Half-formed Thing* shocked everyone who read it, not just some hypothetical reactionaries who think a woman has no place at the high table. It shocked everyone because it's a shocking novel – harsh, volatile and distressing. I really cannot imagine anyone so reactionary as to be appalled by the fact that it was written by a woman, but by the fact that it was written at all. Confidently staking her claim in the modernist tradition, McBride seeks to recover the language and techniques of modernism from a male-dominated field.

I asked Jarlath Killeen about the relation of *A Girl Is a Half-formed Thing* to contemporary writing:

> I would place the reception of *Girl* in relation to its difference from a number of other very popular novels also narrated by young women, but very different young women than the narrator of *Girl*. If you look at some of the bestselling novels of the last five years – *Hunger Games*, *Twilight*, *Fifty Shades of Grey* – all of them have first-person female narrators, and all these female narrators are in the liminal period between adolescence and adulthood. Yet all these young women efface themselves and are usually the most uninteresting and forgettable characters in their own stories. While I wouldn't be interested in disparaging these novels, their enormous popularity does suggest something of a crisis in terms of female self-authorisation, a problem mentioned as well in Caitlin Moran's very personal account of feminism. While it may seem odd to suggest a connection between *Girl*, which is very clearly literary fiction, and the popular fiction novels I've mentioned, they are all drawing on the same contemporary cultural pressures and discourses. The difference between them is not simply that *Girl* is more 'literary' (a dangerous word to use anyway), but that its narrator is not content with becoming the least important character in her own story, and in fact the novel can be read as, *inter alia*, a successful protest against such subordination. For all her difficulty with language, the character makes herself intensely heard and felt by the reader.

I'd add an observation on the proliferation of anonymous narrators in recent novels. In March 2015 Sam Sacks in *The New Yorker* listed examples of novels published in the first few months of the year which together he describes as 'an epidemic of name-lessness'. This he links to the influence of W. G. Sebald, in whose novels unnamed, deracinated narrators meditate on histories of exile and loss. They are homeless observers, unmoored and soli-tary and because the narrator has no proper home, says Sacks, he can also have no proper name. Sebald dispenses almost entirely with conventions of plot and character and his spectral wander-ers exist in a marginal world, and this, Sacks rightly notes, is part of a broader fiction of displacement and exile underlying which there is a distrust of the act of writing itself, a loss of faith in the ability of language to address the condition of being hu-man. Which brings us back to Josipovici's disenchantment and the anonymous girl. She has no real home and spends much of her time between spaces she occupies temporarily, either out of doors or travelling to and fro. She is, in John Updike's phrase 'always just beginning'.

We are approaching the end of a book about beginnings. Eimear McBride has emphatically made her mark on literature and her future career will be one of great interest and, one sus-pects, of constant surprises. Who knows where her talent will take her?

Afterwords

Galley Beggar Press is today a thriving independent publisher with a commitment to publishing off-trail fiction for which there is clearly a market. There have been noteworthy debut novels from Andrew Lovett (*Everlasting Lane*), Jonathan Gibbs (*Randall*) and Paul Ewan (the man behind *How to be a Public Author* by Francis Plug). More recently, *Playthings* by Alex Pheby confirmed Galley Beggar's continuing support for non-commercial, experimental fiction. Since the partnership with Faber they have not considered other co-productions and are now happy to be operating as a leading independent publisher. Invited to outline the future of the press, Sam Jordison wrote to me:

> Future plans are really just to put out the best books we possibly can. We want to put out more – but not so many that we can't ensure quality and devote editorial time to them. We want to put out more short-story collections. And continue to believe in good writers and good readers. [. . .] Our long term strategy is to try to do more of the same. We don't want to take over the world. We just want to put good books into the world.

After leaving Galley Beggar Press Henry Layte set up a new publishing venture at the Book Hive, where he was was later joined by Rory Hill and Niki Medlik. The new company, called Propolis, was set up when Layte was contacted by Philippa Comber, who had written a fine memoir about her close friendship with W. G. Sebald in the 1980s. Sebald taught at UEA, and before his early death in a car crash in the city was Norwich's most celebrated writer.

The last words on the remarkable publishing history of a great modern novel go to Henry:

My reaction to its success was a little bit of frustration that it took most of the broadsheets so long to spot it, but utter joy that they did so in the end. I wasn't at all surprised, but of course nothing is guaranteed, so of course I was thrilled that the gamble paid off. But really, more than anything else, if I never publish anything again, or change career, or drop dead, I am so happy to have been part of that journey of watching someone – and something – become so successful, not for the sake of success itself, but because it's so deserved and it's hugely gratifying that, aside from anything else, we set out to say masterpieces are getting ignored because publishers think the public are stupid and don't want them, and we did.

McBride's 'Ivy Day in the Committee Room', a much-praised reworking and updating of Joyce's short story, was included in the 2014 anthology *Dubliners 100* published by Tramp Press, an independent firm founded in Dublin by Sarah Davis-Goff and Lisa Coen. It was reviewed in the *TLS* (4 June 2014) by Keith Hopper, who singled out McBride's contribution which, he says,

bristles with the linguistic energy of her superb debut, *A Girl Is a Half-formed Thing*. McBride's style – which is more Beckettian than Joycean – perfectly captures the male bravado of smoke-filled rooms, manically fuelled by delusion and drink. In a nice touch, the presiding spirit of Joyce's story, the noble Parnell, is counterpointed by the venal figure of Bertie Ahern, but the satirical point is carefully understated.

There have been a handful of other short pieces, notably 'After "The Private Life" by Henry James', published online by *Spolia Magazine*, and 'Me and the Devil', a short story commissioned by BBC Radio 4 as the third and final broadcast in a series called *New Irish Writing* and first transmitted on 27 March 2015, read by Damien Molony. McBride also reviews occasionally and makes regular, if carefully selected, public appearances, while continuing to work on her second novel, *The Lesser Bohemians*. But until the publication of that novel, discussion continues to centre on her debut. I asked the Goldsmiths Prize judge Tim

Parnell for his thoughts on the likely legacy of *A Girl Is a Half-formed Thing*:

> I'd love to think that it signalled a real change, but I fear it may well be a one off. On the positive side, the success of *A Girl* shows that there's a much bigger readership out there than anybody thought for formally difficult and challenging novels. Less positively, one suspects that *A Girl* might have sunk without trace had circumstances differed just a little and that fine books will languish without the extraordinary momentum that kept pushing it into public view. McBride has other books to write and the real test will be their reception. Something too may now be happening behind the scenes, as the McBride effect encourages publishers to take risks. I look forward to the day when we choose our shortlist from, say, 30 risk-taking and innovative submissions rather than the current handful that really fit the bill.

On 15 June 2015 – almost exactly two years since the author's first public appearance in a dingy suburban club – I found myself in a subterranean central London venue packed with literary types – agents, editors, publishers, writers and (thankfully in the majority) friends and fans. The event, promoted by Faber, was advertised as 'Work in Progress'. Alongside fellow Faber authors Viv Albertine, Harry Parker, Dan Richards and the star turn, Edna O'Brien, McBride was to read for the first time in public from *The Lesser Bohemians*, the book on which she has been working constantly since completing the novel that made her name, starting it in Cork almost a decade ago. It is scheduled for publication in September 2016.

'Whoever said you should never meet your heroes was a liar,' she said with a nervous laugh and a glance at O'Brien. The two had met and spent time together at the Yeats Festival in Sligo a few days earlier, where the senior author had signed Eimear's tattered paperback of *The County Girls*, the one she had read at the age of 14 and which had made such an impression on her. A few days later Toby Lichtig blogged about the event for the *TLS*:

McBride [. . .] read beautifully from a passage in which the novel's heroine, an eighteen-year-old drama student, newly living in London, unexpectedly runs into the thirty-eight-year-old man to whom she lost her virginity. The pair immediately begin to flirt, and one thing leads to another.

The syntax and wordplay will be immediately recognizable to readers of McBride's debut. Posturing banter and self-doubt combine in a cocktail of emotional febrility ('He is laughing and I almost am over my chasing brain'), before the pair head off in pursuit of crispy duck in Soho, the man striding ahead of her ('I'm lagging his gait'). Later, when she gets back to his place, guards, and clothes, are swiftly dropped, 'modesty flying everywhere'.

Toby's blog marked the first appearance of lines from the new novel in print. One that snagged my attention was a reference to the maddening 'Soviet three-queue system' in the old Foyle's bookshop, one of many specific locations – the Hungerford Bridge, Chinatown, a litany of familiar street names heading north through Bloomsbury via Mornington Crescent to Camden Town. It all seemed a far cry from the sparse rural settings of *A Girl Is a Half-formed Thing,* but immediately, emphatically McBridean in style.

This second novel is certain to prompt huge critical interest and comparisons will inevitably be made with her first. This is a traditional hurdle for all writers: their audience will complain if their next work is too different from, or too much the same as, what went before. Great artists sometimes fail because they are willing, indeed feel a compulsion, to take risks and to keep moving forward. Less accomplished artists tend not to fail because once they find out what they're good at they stick to it. Shakespeare had his share of duds while P. G. Wodehouse (and I'm a huge admirer) never did, because he stuck to what he did supremely well. We're back to A- and B-writers, although Wodehouse often strikes me as a B-writer in his commitment to the potential of language (he once described a certain type of young woman as 'the sand in civilisation's spinach'). What I suppose I'm saying is that the failures of a great writer are likely to be at least as interesting as the successes of lesser ones. On the strength of what we heard that evening it's clear that Eimear McBride is unafraid to take risks but is far from risking failure. Toby Lichtig wrote in his blog: 'If the excerpt we were treated to is anything to go by, we can expect a similarly compelling, linguistically dazzling, emotionally unruly literary bombshell.'

B-writers do not always take their readers with them. Think again of *Finnegans Wake* and what Ezra Pound called its 'circumambient peripherization'. At a literary festival in Cambridge McBride read the last pages of the novel and (in a break with tradition) continued by starting again on the first page, without a pause, producing the unfamiliar continuum:

> There's where. First. We pass through grass behush the bush to. Whish! A gull. Gulls. Far calls. Coming, far! End here. Us then. Finn, again! Take. Bussoftlhee, mememormee! Till thousendsthee. Lps. The keys to. Given! A way a lone a last a loved a long the river-run, past Eve and Adam's, from swerve of shore to bend of bay, brings us by a commodius vicus of recirculation back to Howth Castle and Environs.

I'd certainly like to hear her reading Joyce's mellifluous prose, avoiding the wearisome 'shoutmost shoviality' that characterises any recording I've ever heard and (it has to be said) saving me any future effort. I happen to think *Finnegans Wake* is a failure, but it's certainly not a mistake. As Joyce himself put it: 'A man of genius makes no mistakes; his errors are volitional and are the portals of discovery.'

Joyce has long been my favourite writer. While I have never managed to read his last book from cover to cover (but am always planning to do so), I admire his artistic integrity, his miraculous talent and his fabulous arrogance. When asked what he had done in the Great War, Joyce – who had spent much of the time in neutral Switzerland – replied: 'I wrote *Ulysses*. What did *you* do?'

Eimear McBride is not arrogant, but is certainly fearless. William Galinsky told me that 'she's interested in doing things she can't do, but is confident she can do, and is not scared or intimidated by the unknown', adding that she has more grit than confidence, and that this, he thought, was a particularly Irish aspect of her character. It's a nice distinction, and grit coupled with fearlessness is a formidable combination.

Her career has barely started. At her age Virginia Woolf had published only one book (*The Voyage Out*). Others followed.

Appendices

Appendix A: Select bibliography

This is necessarily provisional, and partial. I have included what are, at the time of writing, all of Eimear McBride's published works, including her reviews and other significant print and online appearances. Not included here are McBride's many print, online and radio interviews, or print, online and radio reviews of her work by other writers. The proliferation of coverage following the Goldsmiths Prize was so rapid and extensive that it was beyond my means to keep track of all the profiles, reviews, blurbs for other writers' books and festival appearances recorded on camera.

BOOKS AND PAMPHLETS BY EIMEAR MCBRIDE

1 *A Girl Is a Half-formed Thing*
   Published by Galley Beggar Press, Norwich, June 2013.
   Published by Faber and Faber, London, 2014.
   US edition published by Coffee House Press, Minneapolis, September 2014.
   Dutch edition: *Een meisje is maar half af*, translated by Gerda Baardman, published by Hollands Diep, February 2015.
   French edition: *Une fille est une chose à demi*, translated by Georgina Tacou, published by Buchet Chastel, August 2015; winner in September 2015 of the Prix Transfuge du meilleur roman anglophone (*Transfuge* is a cultural magazine with a particular interest in literature and cinema, founded in 2004 by Vincent Jaury and Gaëtan Husson).
   German edition: *Das Mädchen ein halbfertiges Ding*, translated by Miriam Mandelkow, published by Schoeffling + Co., August 2015.

   Extract in Spolia Magazine, Issue 3 (Casanova Issue, July 2013); http://www.spoliamag.com/downloads/issue-three/

An audiobook recording of the author reading the complete text of
A Girl Is a Half-formed Thing was issued by Faber & Faber in 2014.

2 'The Disorderly Notions of George Egerton'
Introduction to the online re-issue by Galley Beggar Press of
Wedlock by George Egerton (see Appendix B below).

3 'Through the Wall'
Short story in *The Long Gaze Back: An Anthology of Irish Women
Writers*, ed. Sinéad Gleeson (New Island, Dublin; September 2015)

4 'After "The Private Life" by Henry James'
Spolia Magazine October 2014; http://www.spoliamag.com/
excerpt-from-eimear-mcbrides-after-the-private-life/

5 'Me and the Devil'
Short prose fiction commissioned by BBC Radio 4 as the third
and final broadcast in a series called *New Irish Writing*, and first
transmitted on 27 March 2015. The reader was Damien Molony and
the producer Heather Larmour.

6 'Ivy Day in the Committee Room'
In *Dubliners 100*, ed. Thomas Morris (Tramp Press, Dublin, 2014).
Reviewed in the *TLS* by Keith Hopper.

CONTRIBUTIONS TO PERIODICALS

1 *Arimathea* by Frank McGuinness, *Guardian*, 9 November 2013:
review.

2 *Reasons She Goes to the Woods*, *Guardian*, 21 February 2014: review of
Deborah Kay Davies.

3 'Agota Kristof's Ghosts', *Times Literary Supplement*, 9 April 2014:
review of *The Notebook* and *The Illiterate* by Agota Kristof.

4 'My Hero: James Joyce': an account of a conversation with the
author, *Guardian*, 6 June 2014.

5 '1066 and All That', *New Statesman*, 3 September 2014: review of
The Wake by Paul Kingsnorth.

6 'The Wisdom of the Worlds', *Times Literary Supplement*, 1 October
2014: review of *History of the Rain* by Niall Williams.

7 'Woman on the Edge', *Times Literary Supplement*, 5 December 2014: review of *Marta Oulie by* Sigrid Undset.

8 'On *Dubliners*': *New Statesman*, June 2014

9 'In Praise of Edna O'Brien', *The Irish Times*, 7 March 2015.

Appendix B: 'The Disorderly Notions of George Egerton'

George Egerton was the pen name of Mary Chavelita Dunne Bright (1859–1945), widely held to be the most important of the 'New Woman' writers of the late nineteenth century. Born in Australia, she grew up in Dublin. Galley Beggar Press re-issued Egerton's essay *Wedlock* as an ebook to celebrate World Women's day in March 2013, and Eimear McBride's short introduction marked the author's first appearance in print. The GBP website included three memorable contemporary judgements of Egerton's work: 'Neurotic and repulsive' (*Blackwood's Edinburgh Magazine*), 'A deliberate outrage' (*Athenaeum*) and 'Crazy and offensive drivel' (*Saturday Review*).

Far from the outside world lies the inside of a woman. But farther when this story was written – it is to be hoped – than now. For all of literature men have crawled inside the skins of women and then recounted what they saw. They have described and accused and untangled and forgiven what they created. They have claimed those bodies for their own and in turn endowed them with all themselves. They have battled them and fated them until, wrote George Egerton, 'I realized that in literature, everything had been better done by man than woman could hope to emulate. There was only one small plot left to tell: the *terra incognita* of herself, as she knew herself to be, not as man had imagined her.'

And what must man have imagined of George Egerton – dragging from one end of the world to the other in all her obstinate Irishness (despite an itinerant upbringing she identified herself as 'intensely Irish'), writing her 'bitter' stories which bridled and spat at that most holy and catastrophic of constructs, 'Female purity', while shedding abusive husbands she did not want and acquiring clever lovers she did? Practising what she preached. Victorian man could not bear to imagine that, and a cartoon in *Punch* entitled 'Donna Quixote' was tilted her way. But on she rode, rejecting the title 'New Woman' and presuming – I am presuming – that Woman was already enough.

Much can be said about the style of *Wedlock*. Egerton is often described as a proto-modernist, something evident in the loose lock and release of perspective as the characters pass the baton back and forth throughout the tale. Taking hints from Ibsen (an acknowledged influence, and whose *A Doll's House* tramps around in similar territory to *Wedlock*), they also flit between the physical and the psychological, providing a rich and alarming account of themselves. The Irish Gothic tradition gets a nod in the thickish, Stoker-ish poolings of blood and there's an uneasy juxtaposition of near Greek Drama unfolding in all its Medea-in-law horror beneath a nit-picking bourgeois eye. The story also contains the unedifying sight of an author pleading her case for liberty and equality through the mouths of those she clearly feels are beneath her. There's the awful and awkward showcasing of her writer's ear in the old-fashioned reproduction of working-class speech; equally, her lazy generalisations about 'the poor' are fairly wearing. But then there are the women. Drunk and raging. Drunk and despairing. Struggling in the cages of their clothes through the cages of their lives. Women beset by loneliness and poverty. Women stripped of their children and every autonomy. Kicked and judged and loathed and owned. Dreaded, maddened, cheated, and vengeful. But worse again; in their vengeance, peaceful. Here are the insides of women inching out into the world like no one could imagine at all.

It has been said Egerton did not fulfil her promise as an artist and it's true that the last forty years of her life were lived far from the successes of her youth, but by daring in that time to write what could not then be imagined, George Egerton provided a sturdy pair of shoulders that many have hopped up on since.

Acknowledgements

My thanks are due above all to Eimear McBride, who generously agreed to be the subject of this monograph and also agreed (with understandable trepidation) to the use of some of our private email exchanges. Any initial reluctance was down to her uncertainty that the book and its author deserved merited close attention (although this was before *A Girl Is a Half-formed Thing* became a literary phenomenon). With many pressing calls on her time she has been patient, forbearing, generous, candid in her responses and unstintingly helpful throughout.

My sincere thanks also to Henry Layte of Propolis Press and the Book Hive, Norwich; to Sam Jordison and Eloise Miller of Galley Beggar Press; to Dr Jarlath Killeen of Trinity College Dublin and Fergal McBride for sharing their memories of their friend and sister; to Adam Mars-Jones for permission to quote his early review in full, to Dr Tim Parnell of Goldsmiths College, University of London, and to Professor Professor Jacqueline Rose of Birkbeck College for kind permission to quote from her unpublished lecture in Chapter 7 of *About a Girl*.

I am grateful to Jonathan Gibbs for permission to quote at length from his excellent blog on book design.

I also wish to thank all those who helped me in my researches and contributed in one way or another to this book. They are, alphabetically, as follows: Eric Karl Anderson, Tracy Bohan and Catrin Evans at the Wylie Agency, Craig Brown, Claudia Catt, Noah Charney, Vanessa Coode at the *London Review of Books*, Alan Crilly, Aoife Duffin, Polly Faber, Chris Fischbach of Coffee House Press, Kim Franklin and the Suffolk Writers' Group, William Galinsky, Jonathan Gibbs, Hannah Griffiths at Faber and Faber, Rory Hill, Joanna Hodgson, David Holzer, Jim and Vanessa Hopkins, Virginia Ironside, Professor Anne Janowitz, Dr Jarlath Killeen of Trinity College Dublin, Ramona Koval, Steph Knowles, Toby Lichtig, Fergal McBride, Elizabeth McCracken, Declan Meade and Thomas Morris of Stinging Fly Press, Niki Medlik, Jane Novak, JoAnna Novak, Donna Payne, Lucy Ryan, Alice Spalding and her colleagues at the Norfolk and Norwich Festival, D. J. Taylor, Jono Trench and Gill Persicke, Annie Tyler, Cathi Unsworth and Paul Willetts.

Parts of my interview with the author originally appeared in the May 2014 online edition of *The White Review* and are republished here with the editor's kind permission. For permission to quote from their respective publications I wish to thank the editors of the *Guardian*, the *London Review of Books* (www.lrb.co.uk) and the *Times Literary Supplement*.

My grateful thanks to my agent, Matthew Hamilton at Aitken Alexander; and also to the book's proofreader, Lesley Levene. My final and abiding thanks are to the three dedicatees of *About a Girl* which is, to adapt a simple phrase, 'for them'.

D.C.

London, January 2016